Energetic Medicine

6-minutes practice journal for vitality & emotional freedom

Qi Gong - moving meditation - breath work - mindfulness - affirmations

ancient knowledge - wisdoms - well-being

Jenna Robins BSc Hons
TCM Acupuncturist & Qi Gong Instructor

Terms and Conditions
LEGAL NOTICE

Contents.

In memory of Ian Robins (Dad) 1944 - 2019

Your loving energy is always with me

ACKNOWLEDGEMENTS

Thank you: To my parents for the love, adventures, and inspiration: Ian and Barbara Robins, two well-travelled free spirits. Teachers and colleagues: Dr Lingsoong, Annie Walker, Anoushka Deighton, Kelly Hanson, Mantak Chia, Grand Master Chen Zhenglei, Master Liming Ye, and a special thank you to Sifu Jamal Alek. I'm blessed to learn from such a gifted, humble Sifu.

Squiff creative media: andy@squiffweb.co.uk

Photography inside by Thomas Hague Shootmyproduct.co.Uk

To My Students and Patients.

It's a privilege to help your well-being flourish and practice grow.

"When one teaches, both learn."

Chinese proverb.

Six- Minute Moring Practice.

Each guided Qi Gong exercise and affirmations practice flows beautifully together to create a simple morning reboot. Your journal will help guide you through setting your daily intentions for your mind, body, spirit, and wellbeing. Through Qi Gong (the practice of moving meditation and breath work as one), we learn to focus our mind on the breath alone to help feel Qi energy flow through our very being, to let go by emptying the mind of negative thoughts patterns and habits, allowing us to shift us to a higher state of consciousness and awareness. Thus, enhancing the senses and improving our health. After 6-minutes of continual Qi Gong meditation, we write our positive affirmations, set our intentions, and remind ourselves what we are grateful for, cultivating our being. This helps improve the way we function and interact with our own thoughts, others, and the environment around us. 'Little and often' practice is life-changing and helps us achieve positive outcomes, to lift ourselves up through life's demands and challenging times. Or to simply see what positive changes you manifest through positive Qi flow energy practice. Taoists and Buddhist monks have started their day with meditation and self-cultivation for thousands of years; this is nothing new. However, in the west, such knowledge was not available to us for centuries, now we have the blessing of the ancient practice of Qi Gong.

We can quickly become lost in the rat race, fatigued and spiritually empty, then negative thoughts, patterns and habits take over us. We are all guilty of this, and I am no exception; I'm a spiritual human being like you; we all experience pain, negativity, and frustration in different ways at times in our lives. The key is to use these ancient skills to reset and uplift every morning, though experiencing the healing Qi Gong energy flow through you internal and externally. Energy medicine is within all of us. Activate Qi energy flow, experience it physically, consciously, emotional, and spiritually; Qi energy is chemistry. Whatever is happening in your life, reboot every morning with your practice and re-connect to your heart naturally. Use these ancient self-cultivating tools for your mind, body, spirit, health every day.

About Jenna Robins (BSc Hons)

Jenna has over 25 years of clinic experience as a holistic therapist, coach, acupuncturist, and columnist. She has worked in a myriad of settings, including complementary therapy clinics, NHS and private hospitals in the UK and hospitals in China. She spent years managing Neals Yard Remedies in London and Manchester while taking further studies. Later in life, Jenna trained to be a voluntary N.G.O. (non-government organiser) for Disaster Aid International, a charity organisation for humanitarian response and support to global communities. Jenna also has years of experience treating patients with PTSD, mental health issues, and chronic health conditions. During her acupuncture degree studies, she started practising Qi Gong and Tai Chi for her personal wellbeing and self-cultivation of mind and body. After ten years of practice, she took the next step to train to become a Qi Gong and Tai Qi Instructor. She teaches Qi Gong in her Wilmslow studio, and streams live classes. Jenna assists her Qi Gong Sifu (teacher) as part of her commitment to ongoing training to gain skills, knowledge, cultivation, and develop her practice.

Jenna Robins approach to wellness

A lifetime of helping patients has taught me that there is no one method to treat a person's mental and physical wellbeing. In everyday practice, I have never been a puritan: mixing different disciplines, integrating acupuncture, massage, herbal remedies, diet, and self-help techniques and referring patients to other health care professionals. Patients may also be taking conventional medication or in other treatment programmes; over the years, I have learnt to combine safe complementary methods that often result in effective outcomes for my patients. My six-minute practice follows the same philosophy.

When I first learnt Qi Gong and Tai Qi, I fell in love with them equally. Both are based around the concept of Qi (pronounced Chi), the energy that is our life force. Chen style is my preferred type of Qi Gong and Tai Chi. As Qi energy flows through us and around us, internally, this energy flows along acupuncture channels (also called meridians) that run throughout the body, keeping us healthy and providing us with the strength to live, grow and heal. When the flow of Qi is weak or stagnated, which can happen through periods of stress, negative emotions, physical exhaustion, or a life with no balance, we feel out of balance. Qi Gong and Tai Chi both work to free the movement of Qi energy flow, improving circulation, cognitive function, immunity, mental health, and fitness.

Tai Chi is a flowing sequence of movements aimed at working the entire body. Connecting you to your internal function and externally to your environment. Tai Chi is graceful and gentle, yet at the same time, postures command muscular strength with part soft and strong postures; as a martial art, both are physically demanding and build strength. Qi Gong also practised with Tai chi. It is less physically challenging and thus more manageable for all, irrespective of age or health issues and focuses more on the Yin internal practice of moving meditation. The aim is to stimulate the bodies energy centres, free the movement of Qi flow through the acupuncture channels calming the mind and connecting you to your higher conscious state of being.

As much as I love and practice both Qi Gong and Tai Chi, I have come to realise for my patients with complex health issues or hectic lifestyles; Qi Gong has proved to be much more achievable and effective than Tai Chi. Either because they did not have the physicality to conduct the movement or the time and patience to commit to Tai Chi practice. Qi Gong was simply more achievable for them. Over time, from the moving meditation methods of Qi Gong, I developed a short practical sequence that could easily fit into busy daily life. I added written affirmations and positive statements to strengthen a positive mental outlook, and hence I created my 6-minute Qi Gong and affirmation morning practice.

I enhanced the practice with Qi Gong knowledge for a greater understanding of this ancient art. The feedback and results from my patients were fantastic. The methods flowed beautifully together; people enjoyed the morning practice, felt empowered and achieved consistent positive life changes, including a reduction in pain, and anxiety, improving sleep, memory and mental health, elevated mood, physical energy, and wellbeing with a renewed sense of peace and happiness.

When life throws you lemons

For the last decade, my six-minute morning practice has been my cherished morning secret. Supporting me through life's challenging times. A welcome daily re-set that prepares me before stepping into the hecticness of the 21st century. At first, I could not believe how such a simple routine could improve my whole day. It clears my mind, improves my concentration, focus and productiveness giving me a deep sense of calm. Even when I find myself in a stressful environment or have difficult life situations, this mini morning practice has got me through, helping me remain calm and grounded in the face of adversity. Occasionally, I slip out of the habit of daily practice, but I always quickly return, as the difference I feel is profound.

You may be wondering if this practice can really help during life's challenging periods. For me, it's been a life raft during one of our most difficult years.

In 2019 we had our year of hell. My Mum's breast cancer returned; she went through distressing treatments again, and just as things started to look brighter, we suddenly lost Dad. It was a devastating shock. My immediate family live in France, so I travelled back and forth to support Mum as best I could. Whilst also struggling to keep running my busy clinics and teaching back in the UK. Organising Dad's funeral in another country was challenging, but with the loving support of my French-speaking nephew Patrick and sister-in-law Claire, we managed. Patrick conducted the whole funeral service beautifully. We had lovely support from good friends and neighbours in

Play Ben, with a full attended service, of friends, local community members and family members who made it over in the short notice, all to whom we were so grateful too. Dad was always a positive popular personality, and in the local village, he was known as the smiling, waving English man, which I discovered as everyone waved at me when I drove his car. Then months later, it was time to pack. My brother started on Dad's garage and workshop, and I packed up my parent's home. We were clearing possessions and giving away my parent's possessions. 'Letting go' of attachments with memories from the last fifty years was a hard task. Saying goodbye to family and friends, we moved Mum back to the UK to live with my partner and me. Huge changes for us all, especially difficult while struggling with bereavement and work. You really experience who is mindful and there for you during painful times.

On Brittany Ferries, as you come into port, the wake-up call music is the beautiful Celtic melody, of Troellenn, by Dremmwel. On our journey home, this music generated great memories of Dad and a flood of emotions and tears. It also triggered the realisation we had forgotten the French legal certificate for Dad ashes. Despite the panic, we knew Dad would have loved this, and we could hear him belly laughing at our disorganisation. I had to 'let go' of fear and giggle at the situation; as mum felt stricken with anxiety, I reassured her that I did not think the authorities would arrest us for accidentally smuggling Dad's ashes home. As a family, we had fun adventures at sea together, my parents were divers, and we had fun escapades on boats with other divers and later in life crossings to Brittany to visit family, but this was Dads last crossing with us. Riding the waves home on the boat is like a bereavement. The waves of emotional pain come and go but never leave you. To those who have loved and lost, I'm sure you know, when you lose someone you loved deeply, it feels like a deep empty void, the nothingness place, the coming and going of emotion, like the ebb and flow of the waves. Then the crest of the braker or the crashing storm. You just learn to sail through the rough days and give thanks for the love you had and still have with their spirit and energy. The love they gave you is embedded in your cells.

Months later, more sadness, the loss of Andy, my brother-in-law. Whose sudden death left Claire and my nephews in France bereaved and alone. As we planned when we could visit shortly after the global pandemic kicked in. Flights grounded and travel banned; we were unable to see our immediate close family.

Mum and I went down with covid early into the pandemic. A frightening time for most due to a lack of knowledge and heightened fear for my recently ill mother. I treated Mum and myself with acupuncture daily. Focusing on strengthening and clearing the lungs and improving immune health. We practised regular Qi Gong breath work to help reduce our symptoms and work the lungs. We both made a full recovery, and Barbara, my vulnerable seventy-four-year-old mum, came out in good health. Two weeks later, the UK went into full lockdown, with no return to work, no income for months and the hollowness of bereavement. The loss of loved ones, friends and patients during the pandemic was terrible. My heart goes out to everyone on the life journey of bereavement and to those who have experienced loss and bereavement in such cold, isolating times.

Throughout this year, I realised how important my morning practice had become. The welcome daily mental, spiritual and physical reboot lifted me up from my sadness or any stressful groove I found myself in. My practice moved my Qi force, improved my mood; I could feel the Qi energy run through me, energising my mind, body and spirit, lifting through the stress and darkest days of bereavement. My mini morning practice also motivated me to finally write my practice method into a user-friendly journal for publication. Writing this journal has been a cathartic experience, an enlightening therapy.

My six-minute daily practice is an effective commitment to self-cultivation and optimum health. I give thanks every day to my practice; it's a mini mind holiday, which over the last two years has been my sense of freedom during the lockdowns and global pandemic.
Good friends ask me today if I'm doing ok, or say, how have you not crashed? Of course, my grief gives me deeply sad, tough days and can leave you emotionally exhausted, but I have learnt from previous bereavements to let out the sadness and tears and lift my mind, body, and spirit energy through Qi Gong and my now treasured mini morning practice. I know how it can feel lonely and overwhelming for those on the journey of bereavement or going through other life challenges, riding the waves, and struggling through the dark days. But my morning practice, even on the toughest days, lifts me up, boosts my energy, mental and physical health, keeps me moving forward and grateful and reminds me that we are energy beings with the potential to heal ourselves through mindful energy practices.

Qi Gong and affirmations help you simply feel more emotional freedom, mental, physical and spiritual wellbeing with a renewed energy and positive outlook. To me, this practice is a precious treasure chest of self- empowering tools. Worth more than any diamond.

I hope you enjoy and feel the benefits of this mini morning practice as much as I, my students and my patients do. Remember, daily practice manifests powerful changes and feelings. It is key to feel the flow of healing Qi.

Blessings, Qi energy flow, and wellness to you all.

Jenna.

Chapter 1.

Qi Gong is an ancient practice for modern life. A brief introduction to Qi Gong.

How to use this book.

I created this book in sections. In chapters 1 and 2, you will learn a brief history of Qi Gong, theory and Qi energy. I suggest you read chapters 1 and 2 first to understand better how to empower your 6-minute practical Qi Gong daily practice.

The second section is chapters 3 and 4. This is the practical instruction guide to your Qi Gong exercises and your journal pages, which you complete every day, making a total valuable morning practice of 6 minutes.

Qi Gong in a nutshell.

Qi Gong meditation is a unique ancient practice for modern life. It empowers your self-healing, cultivation and wellbeing, increasing your more profound connection to self, the senses, the elements, and nature. Regular practice will Increase your self-awareness, your intuition, and Insight, powering up your vital force of Qi energy to gain a higher state of consciousness, helping improve your mental, emotional, physical, and spiritual wellbeing every day.

Qi Gong meditation.

The practice of Qi Gong (also written in western texts as Chi Gong or Chi Kung) involves a combination of specific postures, mind intention (mindfulness) and slow-flowing movements following your own unique calm breathing pattern. The word 'Qi' (pronounced Chi) has no direct translation into English. Qi is described as a vital force of expanding energy. This energy flows through every living thing. It gives us our strength, allows us to grow and keeps us healthy. The word 'Gong' translates to cultivate or master. Qi Gong is all about connecting to and controlling your subtle Qi energies, training the body's energy to circulate effectively to where it's needed, Improving all aspects of our health and mental wellbeing.

Chinese words can be difficult to comprehend to Western ears. However, once you translate the meanings, they are often enlightening. You will gain a deeper understanding of your Qi Gong practice and thus empower your daily life through the self-cultivation of your mind, body, spirit, and soul.

Qi Gong is rooted in Taoism.

The ancient Chinese system of Qi Gong, taught by Taoist master's to students through training and oral teachings and practice. Taoists believe the inner alchemy of the body is directly connected to the external alchemy of our environment. Humans have an intrinsic and important relationship with the universe, stars, planets, sky, mountains, rivers, forests, plant life, the ocean, and the earth. Taoists teach us that the connection of internal alchemy (mind, body, spirit, and soul) to the external alchemy of nature, all these elements need to be respected and connected. This harmonious relationship is embraced every day. Taoism also incorporates the concept of Yin and Yang, the balance of mind, body and spirit, and nature. When we are disconnecting from these elements in mind, body and spirit, we can manifest negative energy, disharmony, struggle, strife, and illness develops?

For centuries Taoists and Martial Master's developed this practice through meditation, the study of the body, nature, and medicine. The knowledge and wisdom of universal Qi energy and the vital force of inner alchemy was a closely guarded secret.

In 1972 Present Nixon visited hospitals in China. He saw first-hand the health benefits of acupuncture and Chinese Herbal Medicine. After Nixon's successful relations, China opened, and travel became easier. Masters and Sifus (teachers) migrated to the west and brought these healing methods with them. Later, Bill Moyer, the White House Press Secretary, further highlighted the benefits of Chinese Medicine, acupuncture, Qi Gong and Tai Chi in a documentary called, *Healing and the Mind* as the public started to experience the health benefits from Chinese medicine models and self-empowering meditation practices the knowledge spread and these healing methods spread globally.

One of the core beliefs in Chinese medicine is that the human's body has a network of channels or meridians, which run through the body. Subtle Qi energy flows through the channels, thus allowing the body to move, heal and grow. The free flow of Qi force has a twenty-four-hour clock which Qi travels through the body into different organs at different times of the day and night, maintaining the healthy functions of the bodies systems.

This Qi energy flow and rhythm is essential for our wellbeing and is replenished through food and the air we breathe. Qi can also become blocked, and stagnate through injury, emotional stress, poor diet, climate, or external living environment. The blockage or stagnation of Qi flow prevents energy from doing its job. As a result, we can suffer from pain, ill health, or emotional distress. At specific points on the channels, Qi is accessed through the application of acupuncture treatments and the practice of Qi Gong. Qi Gong helps the Qi flow correctly through the channels, which you can feel and experience with regular practice. You can then experience a reduction of symptoms and health improvements.

Everything is energy.
As we know, Qi in Chinese translates to 'a vital force of energy,' it will help your practice develop if you can grasp a basic understanding of the science of energy. This will also help fuse Chinese terms of Qi energy in relation to western science and English. The importance of energy medicine (EM) and our well-being is gaining acknowledgement and momentum as more evidence-based research about EM is published.

Quantum physics theory states that mass and energy are interchangeable; mass is a manifestation of energy. Therefore, everything, including humans, is energy stored in mass particle form. Science explains that according to the universal energy field, matter, psychological processes, thoughts, emotions, beliefs, and attitudes are composed of energy. In the human body, our cells, tissues, atoms, and systems are composed of energy; collectively, this energy is what science calls the human energy field. (D'Ambrogio, K 2021)

If you want to gain further insight into some fascinating theory's, research and evidence regarding EM, a remarkably interesting book worth reading is called 'Energy Medicine: The scientific Basis' by Professor James Oschman (2016). Quote: ' *Pulses of electricity, magnetism, sound, heat, vibration, and light that are transmitted to every part of the body via the circulatory system and extracellular fluids and thereby reach every cell in the body (see Figure 15.6). These signals may serve a variety of vital regulatory roles.*"(J Oschman 2016)

It could be argued that Qi is simply all the subtle energy that exists in humans, nature, and the universe. Qi Gong meditation is said to have the ability to help you connect with the body's energy, natures energy and the universal energy field through your experience in practice.

Even though research continues in the EM field and is a relatively new concept in western medicine, in western cultures, we are not educated to think of ourselves as energy beings; only more recently have we learnt how important energy practices and mindfulness is for our well-being.

The human body glimmers with energy, rhythmically emitting light through a process called photon emission. This light is 1000 times lower than the sensitivity to the naked eye, only recently researched by Western science (Kobayashi, M 2009). Through deep meditations, Taoists identified this energy a millennia ago. They learnt to harness energy through Qi Gong meditation and realised through specific spiralling movements; they could generate and control this body energy force. As you go through your practice journey, you will learn these spiral movements and begin to feel the same subtle energy flow that the ancient Taoists discovered. This will help you feel a sense of wellness and a higher cognitive state of awareness and intuition.

Sensations of Qi energy flow. Qi is energy and is everywhere. 'Qi' is felt as a sensation of tingling that surges running through your channels from your feet to the top of your head. Practitioners describe it as a pleasant electrical sensation. Spirals of Qi energy flow in the centre of the palms, the feet, the top of the head, and at the three 'Dantian' energy centres. Close your eyes and focus on these areas of the body. Allow yourself to feel a gentle sensation. The energy spirals move externally around the finger- tips, in the palms on the feet and at the Dantian centres. Through regular practice, this physical experience of Qi flow will develop. The first time you feel this, it is quite exhilarating. In the West, we are not as familiar as in the east with the concept of energy medicine and Qi; it is a new concept currently in great discussion by scientists, professors, and therapists. Yet energy medicine and Qi is an ancient concept of wellbeing in the east. It may take time to tune in and experience the sensations of Qi. Just relax, do not worry; if you cannot feel it immediately, be patient; this is not something you can force or rush. Stop searching for the feeling. Just practice, and it will happen when you are not expecting it! Go with the flow of your breath.

Self-Cultivation through mindful intension.

One part of Qi Gong practice is to cultivate one's mind by developing focus and concentration. During practice, your mind and thoughts are fully connected to practice. For example, as a beginner, your first learning is to use mind intention, to focus the mind solely on your breathing alone, allowing you to connect all movements to follow your natural breathing rhythm. Mind intention simply means to train the mind to focus solely on one or more specific tasks at the same time, thought, or body location as a focus acupuncture point while in moving breath meditation flow. This sounds simple, but it takes time to practice as a busy mind may scatter and float away with unwanted thoughts. Just learning to synchronise the movement to the breathing pattern takes patience and skill. If your mind floats away from your intention and focus, do not despair. The beauty of Qi Gong practice is you simply bring your mind and focus back to your breathing; when the movement flows again with the breath as one, you will slip back into a mediative state of mind. You can directly feel the internal energy change in of state of being; then, you can experience the sensation of Qi energy flowing through your body; this experience becomes more profound and your sensory perception stronger through regular practice.

When you have learnt to conquer one mind intention (to the breath and movement), you then continue to develop your mind to be able to focus on two places at the same time during practice. For example, the mindful focus and sole attention are on the breathing, movement with a focused visual on one or two acupuncture point locations. For example, this could be the centre of the palms. When you achieve this state of mind intention, your energy will shift into an altered state of higher consciousness. As you 'let go' of unwanted mind chatter, focus your mind intention, breath, and movement as one, you will fully experience the sensation of Qi energy flowing through the channels in the body and even around your body. You feel a deep connection to self, peace, and the universal energy, along with a feeling of oneness and euphoria. Every day is different in practice; if your mind wanders, bring your attention back to the breath and movement and keep repeating. Eventually, your mind will learn to empty, and you will feel the experience for yourself. Achieving this mediative state through practice helps you cope with life's stress and anxieties, equipping you with the tools to apply Qi Gong stationary postures standing or sitting. You can use these skills at work, in social settings or in bustling public spaces; no one would know you are practising Qi Gong meditation.

Health benefits and evidence. *Qi Gong and Tai Chi meditation has undergone rigorous random controlled trials (RCT's). Evidence has shown Qi Gong and Tai Chi both promote health and show significant positive health outcomes, improving physical health and cognitive function (Jahnke R et al. 2020). Trials have also shown that chronically ill patients practising guided meditations noted blood results with increased T-cells counts (William H et al. 1995). Therefore, this demonstrates the health benefits of Qi Gong and mindful meditation. Mindful meditation alone has shown to change physiological signals during mindfulness meditation (Ahani, A 2013)*

Qi Gong meditation can be either a stationary or in a moving form; moving with breath and meditation has shown to benefit all ages reducing anxiety, and depression, improving mood, cardiovascular health and in older citizens, it is recognised that the spiritual part of Qi Gong is a vital component of these moving activities contributing to successful ageing (Carol E et al. 2008).

However, larger-scale trails are needed. With the current evidence, we should not underestimate the overall health benefits of Qi Gong practice reported by people and health practitioners globally. The British Health Qi Gong Association continues to gather important data and evidence-based research reporting the health benefits of Qi Gong for all ages.

During the SARS (severe acute respiratory syndrome) outbreak in China in 2007 and the COVID 19 pandemic 2020, evidence shows that patients' have had an increased positive recovery due to the application of Acupuncture and Qi Gong breathing meditation practice (Peng J 2020).

Science-based evidence - the power of daily practice changing your chemistry.

When we feel distressed or suffer from prolonged stress, the body experiences cellular stress responses. Our body will release hormones, and brain activity will fire neurotransmitter signals to the nervous system, resulting in fight or flight responses which are all normal physiology responses. Such responses can trigger positives for the body, such as an increase in cell survival reaction. If the body cannot cope with these stress responses, it can eventually trigger cell death, resulting in heat shock, damaged proteins, oxidative stress, and DNA damage. Just these few actions alone demonstrate the importance of managing our prolonged stress for our mental and physical wellbeing and illness recovery. (Fulda, S et al. 2010)

Due to the stressful demands of life and the increasing popularity of eastern meditation practices in the west, there is a recognition for the importance of mindful meditation and demand for science-based research to understand and capture the physiological and psychological changes that take place when we practice meditation. This information is just a small glimpse into the positive chemical changes that can take place in the brain and body when we practice meditation such as Qi Gong.

Studies. Rigorous controlled trials (RCT's) observe and measure the positive effects that meditation can have on brain function and its networks by measuring participants brain activity (during meditation) with functional magnetic resonance imaging (fRMI) scanners. Other research methods measure chemical changes in the body and sample group outcome via quantitative and qualitative methods. For more science-based reading, please refer to the references and bibliography.

Breath work- deep, slow breathing changes your chemistry.

Slow, smooth, deep, controlled breathing is one element of Qi Gong meditation. The action of slow deep breathing makes us feel calmer, improving the way we think, feel, and perform, but what is happening inside our brain and body.

When we feel anxious or stressed, on top of all the chemical changes that take place, we tend to breathe shallow and rapidly; this action increases the carbon dioxide in the blood-boosting the noradrenalin levels. Noradrenalin is a hormone and a chemical messenger transmitting signals via the nervous system to the nerve endings. Noradrenalin levels can disrupt the brain neural networks, making it difficult to focus on one task. The saying goes, "I can't think straight or focus my thoughts". Slow controlled breaths have been shown to break this reactive chemical cycle by lowering the noradrenalin, allowing the breath to re-synchronising with the mind and refocus our thoughts. (Russo, M 2017) Science also acknowledges that through controlled deep breathing, we can significantly change the heart rate, lower blood pressure (Peng, J et al.), reduce pain, stress, and anxiety (Chow, Y 2007), by calming the autonomic nervous system. (Qin, Z et al.)

"A deep breath is the most precise pharmaceutical you could ever give yourself".

Neuroscientist Prof Ian Robertson.

Neuroplasticity- mindfulness (focused intention) the psychological and physiological effects.

Science has shown that when we meditate with mindful, focused intention, we enhance the activation of the prefrontal cortex, an area of the brain linked to positive emotions. Studies demonstrate that positive physiological changes take place in the brain through focused meditation. Other data provide evidence of the neuroplasticity effects, which is the ability of the neural network in the brain to change through growth and reorganisation. Thus, focused mindful intention has been shown to change the brains' physical structure. (Lazar et al., 2005) Other important systems such as the immune function improves, helping us fight off infection. (Davidson et al. 2003)

Conclusion.

Just these few elements of meditation and research demonstrate how you can empower your own health and chemistry through the daily attention to Qi Gong meditation practice, resetting every day, with mindful focused intension and the Qi Gong movement synchronised with the smooth deep rhythm of the breath work, you can change your chemistry, brake negative cycles and improving your mental physical and emotional performance. My patients now empower their health at home with my 6-minute daily practice of Qi Gong and affirmations as it resets and creates positive changes, the results speak for themselves, and my patient feedback has been positive.

The Yin Yang Symbol.

The Yin Yang symbol is thought to be at least 3,000 years old. It is a philosophy that represents the harmony found in the laws of science and nature. This balance of harmony relates to humans, animals, plants, and the elements and the universe. It represents every part of daily life, the balance we are all striving for. The two opposite forces are complementary to each other and interconnected in the natural world. Everything in life has yin yang. Yin represents stillness, cold, feminine, dark, passive, water, night, quiet, the moon, earth, sleep, nourishing and repairing. Yang represents masculine, light, heat, noise, the day, the sun, movement, and energy. As individuals, we are a mixture of both yin and yang to create the duality of balance. Yet this duality is constantly shifting and moving, as seen in our atoms. Our body naturally continually strives to reach a holistic equilibrium, to balance where possible.

Observe the Yin Yang symbol on every journal page, remember this symbol represents balance and harmony, set your intention to balance in the mind while you journal. Below are examples of yin yang meanings to help you understand the concept. Opposites yet complementary.
Duality and balance, chaos, and order. Yin Yang energies are opposites. They are fundamental to each other's function; there is always yin with yang and yang within yin.

Ying Yang Symbol

Yin	Yang
Internal	External
Feminine	Masculine
Moon	Sun
Cold	Hot
Water	Fire
Earth	Heaven
Dark	Light
Night	Day
Yin	**Yang**
Intuitive	Analytical
Rest	Activity
Calm	Excessive
Soft	Strong
Stillness	movement
Conservation	Transformation
Storage	Change
Inside	outside
Deficiency	Excess
Immunity	pathogens viruses
Nature	Cosmos
Microcosm	Macrocosm

Yin Yang channels.

The main acupuncture channels that connect to each other are represented as yin or yang. The general rule of thumb is that channels that run on the back or lateral sides of the arms, legs and torso body are 'yang' in energy. Channels that run on the inside of the arms, legs, torso, or front of the body are 'yin' in energy.

The acupuncture channels have organ names due to the fact that the channel in question anatomically runs through and connects to the organ and its function. Organs themselves are represented as yin or yang due to the function and action of the organ. There are many channels and extraordinary vessels; below are the main paired channels. You can feel your Qi energy in practice run along these main channels and at acupuncture points and dantian locations.

Yin		Yang. Paired Channels.
Heart	and	Small intestine
Liver	and	Gallbladder
Spleen	and	Stomach
Lungs	and	Large intestine
Kidneys	and	Bladder
Ren	and	DU

Modern life.

Modern life is all about running in the fast lane, way too much adrenaline and what we in Chinese medicine call 'excess yang Qi.' Living 'on the go,' over working, or overtraining to achieve the perfect body, rather than fitness balanced with mindful and emotional Yin based healing. Striving to achieve the 'best' career, more money, running businesses, busy homes and family life, late nights, stimulants to keep us awake, alcohol, drugs, and medications to escape from the stress, are very demanding on the mind, body, and soul. Prolonged stress levels with a lack of self-awareness and life pressures are unsustainable. We push on with our body and organs in a state of internal alarm, fight, or flight. Eventually, we crash. We know that prolonged stress impacts our immune function; prolonged stress lowers the immune capacity to fight off antigens. (McLeod, S 2010) The global COVID pandemic has highlighted how important it is to look after our health and immunity. We need to listen to our mind and body; as so many people, we ignore the early signs and symptoms of ill health. Qi gong will take you on a journey of self-realisation, growth, energy healing, and wellness.

Ego.

"A more modern conception that is certainly related to Freud's is to consider the ego as the self-consciousness system. The self-consciousness system is the narrating portion of human consciousness that reflects on one's thoughts, feelings and actions and inhibits or legitimizes them to oneself and to others. In this sense, ego is very similar to what is meant by the term identity. (…)" (Gregg Henriques, PhD 2021)

The ego is a mental construct that we need to navigate the world, regulate instincts, and mediate conflict of self and others. However, we need to have a great awareness of ego, to recognise our ego "the sense of separate self," Buddhist scholars often refer to this self as "the Illusion of separate self. "When governed by ego alone, without awareness, we allow our insecurities and therefore negative emotions to drive the way we think, feel, and interact with, our selves, people, and our world. Buddhist philosophy recognises the human ego as the 'false state' of being, teaching us to meditate mindfully, to strip away the insecurities and self-hatred, to obtain a balanced sense of self. Thus, elevating us to a higher state of awareness, living with more peace, humbleness and compassion.

Taoism and the Ego.

Taoism explains the ego is the energy of the focused, centred mind. The simplest explanation I have found that clarifies this issue is from two Daoist teachers from Wu Wei.com (www.wuwei.com 2021). When the ego centred mind focuses too much on one thing only, to the extreme, the ego is then out of balance and dominates your thinking, feeling, and action—for example, overthinking about one issue or emotion, being judgmental, controlling, striving to get 'one-up-man-ship,' being overly critical about the world, trying to achieve ultimate perfection. All these ego centric ways can lead to anxiety, frustration, and stress. When the ego-centred mind is out of balance, it simply dominates and rules, inevitably leading to delusions of grandeur.

Taoism the child like mind and the higher conscious mind.

Taoists teach us to realise that the ego is the focused childlike mind in physical reality. The mother mind is the higher consciousness; we call it the 'Shen' (spirit mind), the true heart or nature of self, which we connect to in Qi Gong practice. This is the non-physical aspect of the spirit mind. This higher state of mother (Shen) educates the child ego-mind. Taoists believe you should not fight the ego or try to destroy the ego-centric mind is part of who you are. We should acknowledge it through the practice of Qi Gong meditation, where we learn to control and work with the ego. The higher spirit mind working together with the ego focused mind brings balance. This balance of mindfulness is the true centre, the harmony and peace of mind, the place known as Wu Wei. In the centre of the Ying and Yang symbol, this place of being, of harmony, is represented. We teach our mind, discipline, self-cultivating the mind and spirit, functioning with more awareness of self, others, and our environment through our daily practice. Self-cultivation is to acknowledge this awareness, 'the truth,' not to allow your ego to ignore or hide from the truth. Daily Qi Gong meditation helps prevent the ego from overacting, thus bringing the ego centric mind back into balance.

That's why regular, little, and often practice is key to feeling free from the overactive ego. Practice helps us live from a place of awareness, compassion, truth, joy, and positivity. Teaching us when there is no other option but to sometimes 'let go.' Only you are the true master of your Qi Gong practice; by committing to your daily practice, you commit to your self-cultivation, enlightenment, and wellbeing. You will then function and interact in a more balanced way. Wu Wei.

Chapter 2.

Qi Gong theory, knowledge, and ancient secrets.

Things to learn before you start to practice.

Understanding basic knowledge, theory, and ancient spiritual secrets enhance your Qi Gong practice and journaling experience. In ancient times Daoist's and master's would only pass on knowledge to the chosen few they felt worthy; we are now lucky enough to have these ancient wisdoms.

The three treasures of Qi Gong.

The three treasures in Chinese medicine are related to the body. They are Shen, Qi, and Jing. The three treasures become energised and nourished through the practice of Qi Gong. Qi Gong exercises stimulate the Qi in the channels, connecting to the body's organs and functions.

The action of the treasures is vital for our total well-being as this affects the function of the individual's health. For your practice, it is important to grasp the meanings of Shen, Qi, and Jing.

The Shen: The spirit of the mind. Believed to reside in the heart and relates to the similar concept of the soul. When the Shen is at peace, we can find internal stillness and a sense of oneness.

Qi is all about movement. The vital force or Qi flows to transport and transform bodily blood fluids. Qi constantly circulates, moving through every organ and function on a 24-hour body clock cycle. It is the force that moves the blood to keep it flowing. Qi is in every organ system and cell in the body, running through all the acupuncture channels.

Jing is the "essence" of life. Our inherited constitution, the sperm and egg, the primordial DNA, our cells, atoms, and matter.

Acupuncture channels (meridians) transport Qi energy. There are twelve primary and eight extraordinary meridians in the body along which Qi flows. Each primary channel connects to specific organs. Six of these meridians are yin, and six are yang. All channels are, interconnected to each other and to other deeper channels in the body. This network of channels transports Qi energy to every system, organ, and cell. Along each channel at specific anatomical locations lie acupuncture points; this is where Qi energy is accessed and stimulated through the application of acupuncture, acupressure, and Qi Gong practice.

Qi flow and Qi stagnation. If you feel stressed or have injuries, Qi flow will stagnate along a meridian. This can lead to poor circulation and stagnated energy in the area resulting in pain, swelling, inflammation, tension, headaches, poor food absorption and gut health. Prolonged stagnation of Qi will result in illness as well as chronic health conditions. A good circulation of Qi is necessary for a healthy mind, body, and spirit. Through the practice of Qi Gong, specific movement and postures, the Qi in acupuncture channels is stimulated to flow. This can be physically felt and experienced; it feels like surges and runs of tingling energy flowing through the channels, and strong spiralling sensations can be felt at energy centres and acupuncture point locations.

Channels and acupuncture points. The acupuncture points lie along the 12 primary channels and eight extraordinary channels on the body. Each acupuncture point has a specific anatomical location and specific action. Stimulating these points creates the correct direction and flow of Qi, reducing disharmony or symptoms. Specific Qi Gong postures, movements, breath work and mind intention combined activates the free flow of Qi energy in the channels.

The 3 Dantian energy centres.

The three Dantian's energy centres are located at upper, middle, and lower locations from the head and torso. The Dantian's are described as your extra elixir energy fields. The Upper Dantian is located on the forehead and connects to your third eye and the glands in the brain, including the pineal gland. The middle Dantian located on the chest and heart connects to the thymus gland. The lower Dantian is located below the belly button; this is your powerhouse of stored Qi energy force. We focus on the lower Dantian, with breath at the beginning and end of every practice. Gathering all Qi energies externally and internally connecting Qi back to the lower Dantian, warming the 'Jing' essence of life. Please refer to the Dantian illustration

The Eyes: The 'Shen' The gateway to the spirit.

The eyes are a doorway to the health of your spirit; the Chinese medicine model states you can observe the health of your liver function and spirit through the eyes. The more you practice Qi Gong, the more lustre you will see in your eyes, clear and sparkling. If the eyes look dull or grey, this can be an indication that you are tired, emotionally low, overworked or have a poor diet or lifestyle. If your eyes are red, bloodshot, this indicates excess yang meaning, too much heat, toxins or pathogens that need treatment. During your year of journaling, observe your eyes, their radiance and health. Note any changes, and your eyes are a gateway and reflection of your wellbeing. As you develop in your daily practice, feeling calmer, happier, and healthier, see if your eyes start to reflect changes in appearance, aiding the internal health of the organs.

Shen, spirit. In Chinese medicine the mind referred to as the Shen. This is your consciousness and your mental health. The Shen is related to your vitality. It is said that the Shen has a spirit that resides in the heart, which is where it sleeps at night. If your spirit is disturbed, this can result in disturbed sleep, leading to insomnia. Qi Gong practice is a heartfelt practice; it will calm and soothe your spirit, calming the heart and lowering blood pressure, reducing anxieties and palpations calming the heart spirit aiding sleep. You will start to feel connected to your true nature your spirit in practice as anxieties melt away.

Wu Wei. Philosophy.

In relation to Qi Gong, the word 'Wu Wei' is a concept to express the meaning of effortless action. It relates to harmony, and free-flowing spontaneity, as a state of spirit and mind. To practice, Wu Wei is to 'let go of overthinking, unwanted churning and negative thoughts that do not serve you well. An important concept in Taoism and Confucianism. Try to add 'Wu Wei' into your life; try to let go of what thoughts do not serve you or your spirit. During your practice, on the out-breath, let go of unwanted thoughts send them down through the feet to the Earth. Think to yourself or start by saying out loud, breath out, 'I let go of negative thoughts to the earth,' repeat with every breath out through the nose, and as your hands float down to the earth until your thoughts become quiet with your mind solely focused of the breath. You are calming the mind with positive Qi energy and breath and learning to practice Wu Wei. It can take time to achieve this, but with regular practice, you will be able to use this skill in everyday life. Allowing you to change the way you tackle stressful situations or overthinking.

Practice tips.

Patience and focus are part of self-cultivation. During your Qi Gong practise as a beginner, you may find it difficult to focus. Your mind intention (focus on a particular area or mindful visualisation) can scatter and float away with other thoughts. Don't worry; just be aware of this, breathe deeply and bring your mind, focus and intention back to the practice and the breath alone. To help stop the mind from wandering in practice, set a timer for 5 minutes so you do not clock watch, close your eyes, and focus on the breath. Repeating daily practice will calm and train the mind to stay focused on practice alone.

Practice spaces. All you need is a small space you can stand and sit in with your arms stretched out. Find a place where you have no interruptions for 6 minutes. (For 5 minutes Qi Gong and 1 minute's journaling). In a busy house even, a bathroom is fine. If the environment is noisy, place relaxing music or sounds of nature in your headphones. With practice you will eventually be able to shut out all noise and focus on your breath alone and your movement following your breathing pattern. As you become more relaxed in your chosen space, you will let go, and your mind will become quiet. The most important thing is that you find a space with no interruption for the whole 6 minutes. This is your time with your practice and journal and yours alone. This is your morning treasure.

Foot positions.

The position you put your feet in is important in Qi Gong practice and will affect the outcome of your practice. To gather more yang external energy, point your feet slightly outwards. Imagine your feet are a clock. Put your left foot at ten to twelve and your right foot at ten past twelve. If the feet face forward at twelve o'clock, this will nourish your Yin internal energy. This will help stimulate the organs. Ideally, change the position of your feet daily. See if you feel any difference as your practice develops and make reflective notes. You may feel more comfortable with your hips and knees in one position than another; go with what feels comfortable for you.

Importance of saluting to practice.

At the start and end of your Qi Gong exercise practice, we salute. To salute, we place our hands upon the lower Dantian (lower abdomen, refer to photos). Close your eyes or gently gaze and bow forward; this helps set your mindful intention to practice alone and to let go of external distractions and give respect to yourself and your practice. This disciplines the mind to concentrate on practice and is another part of your daily self-cultivation.

Microcosmic orbit movement.

The microcosmic orbit is one of Qi Gongs most popular and well-known meditative practices. In the classical text, 'The Secret of the Golden Flower', the microcosmic orbit, accredited to the Taoist Lu Dongbin. (Referred to as the self-winding wheel of the law of the Tao (Dao), or the small heavenly circulation. This cosmic orbit movement stimulates channels and energy centres. All the joints are soft and open to allow energy to flow through. This exercise collects external yang Qi and stimulates internal energy.

To practice the microcosmic orbit movement, start with palms facing the sky; we gather subtle external energy with the fingers open. Through regular practice, you can feel this energy tingle and spiral around the fingers. Whilst conducting the exercise, as the movement follows your natural breathing pattern through the nose, take your mind to the breath alone, so the movement breath and mind are one; this is your aim. Don does not search with the mind for the feeling of Qi. Simple practice the oneness then will experience Qi circulate and flow. As your practice develops and with patience, eventually, you can fully experience the microcosmic orbit meditation. When you have the breath movement and mind synchronised, add a mind intension; Imagine golden roots from the feet connecting to the earth and at the same time visualise golden threads reaching up from the top of the head connecting to the sky, universe, and heavens. Qi will eventually circulate up the back and down the front, in the Dantian's and in the palms and feet, and the channels. (For the exercise, refer to chapter 3).

Qi Ball mass and pressure sensation.

One of the key elements of Qi Gong is, experiencing the 'ball of energy.' Circling and moving the hands following the breathing helps you learn to feel Qi as a physical sensation, like holding a ball of energy. You can experience a sensation of an expanding mass or force. It feels like a magnet pushing, pulling, and pulsing. We start by opening all the joints slightly, sitting into the hips. The hands and palms face each other about 3 inches apart, in front of the lower Dantian. Then make tiny circles with your hands, focusing on the centre of the palms, circle your hands clockwise then anti-clockwise. Keep your eyes open, and then try to close them, sensing and listening to what you feel. Just breathe naturally at this point. This circling action can build Qi, and as you practice, you may feel spirals of energy circling in the centre of the pam and or tingling in the hands. Then after a minute, breathe in through the nose and allow your hands to float out to shoulder width, breath out, float your hands back toward each other, palms 3 inches apart, then repeat. Keep your fingers open softly, about 80%, in a relaxed position, so Qi can flow to your fingertips. Your hands are not tense but not too relaxed and collapsed. Keep your mindful focus on the centre of your palms. With practice, you will begin to feel a mass of Qi force pushing your hands out or push your hands in; it feels like the force of strong magnets. During your morning practices, your Qi can flow strong, other days, it can be weaker, or you may not experience Qi sensation at all. This is completely normal as Qi force strength can become weak due to different factors, including how tired or stressed you are, a poor diet, the surroundings you are in, and how focused your breath movement and mind connection is. The more you practice, the more you cultivate the vital force of Qi flow, the more you sense and physically experience Qi energy.

Internal Qi energy mindful intention.

When in practice, and with your eyes closed, look for a tiny white light in the darkness of your mind's eye. It may take a while to find it, don't worry if it doesn't come immediately once you have found its focus on this light. By doing so, it will appear to expand; see if you can allow it to spiral and move. Keep concentrating on this light; it may evolve into a violet colour. You also may experience a sensation of pressure on the forehead; at the upper Dantian area, this is normal. Aim to keep your breathing relaxed in the belly (at the lower Dantian) rather than high up into the chest when you breathe out through the nose; breath down from the lower Dantain. Flow the rhythm of your breathing, focusing breathing down the legs to the bottom of the feet to the earth. Breathing in, visualise the breath is travelling up through the feet to the legs to the hands placed on the lower Dantian. Use this technique at the beginning of your practice, or Qi Gong stance, standing posture or sitting posture, to help feel Qi flow and focus the mind.

Qi energy release.

Holding the sun or moon exercise number 7. We can accumulate, trap and release Qi energy through specific movements. When stretching up and holding the sun or moon, we can block the Qi at the wrists by bending the wrists holding the sun above our heads in the full-body stretch. When the arms float down, the wrists stay blocked; when the arm is at 45 degrees, we open the wrists, so the hands face the earth, Qi will accumulate and rush to the fingertips. Repeat, build, release. You can experience a sensation of Qi firing out from the palms and fingers and circling around the fingertips externally.

Qi Gong stance.

In standing practice, we must sit into the hips like we are sitting on a stool and open all the joints softly. We open the back with our arms rounded in front of us, hands placed at the lower Dantian level, and fingers are open 80%. We refer to the joints as "gates," keeping all your gates open allows Qi to flow and circulate through the whole body via the channels. Initially, it feels unnatural to stand this way, as it can be difficult, in time, you will strengthen the muscles and mind. After one or two minutes of standing meditation, your leg muscles may shake, and your arms may become stiff and tense, your heart rhythm will increase, and you can become hotter. When this happens, take a deep breath in through the nose, let the tension go with the out-breath and try to override the mind telling you to give up. Stay in standing meditation a while longer to assess yourself. Time yourself so you can increase the length of standing meditation at each practice. This is part of training the mind to have discipline, strengthens and tones the muscles, increases fitness, and self-cultivates your mind, body and spirit. You will develop a long-standing meditation at every practice. Eventually you will increase to a full five minutes without tension and be strong enough to feel Qi flow and practice mindful meditation.

Tongue positions in practice.

The position of your tongue affects your Qi Gong practice.

There are three different tongue positions.

1. The tip of the tongue resting behind the top two front two teeth.

2. The tip resting against the top of the roof of the mouth.

Beginners practice number 1.

When you place the tip of the tongue in position one, the back jaw will relax and open (it is difficult to clench the jaw with this tongue placement), helping to relax facial muscles. The mouth will then start to produce more saliva to swallow (we call this excess yin). By swallowing the excess saliva, you will help to nourish a dry throat, reduce infection, and help relax the mind.

Tongue positions 2: Connects channels that meet in the mouth, connecting the Ren Mai and Du Mai up the back and down the front central line of the body, aiding the circulation of Qi and the microcosmic orbit meditation, also referred to as the small universe. (Chia, M 2019)

Correct posture and tension.

We know that electrical charges cannot travel well through bent and snapped wires. It is the same with regarding Qi flowing through channels and joints. Qi flows through open joints and open channels, so the correct posture to allow qi to travel is important. Remember, we are not so relaxed; we collapse into a poor posture or too tense that the joints are not open. We are strong yet soft. Refer to the body checklist before you start your practice, and remember to keep the gates open unless instructed otherwise.

Qi Gong hand positions.

1. During practice, while in moving meditation, standing, or sitting postures, keep your fingers open and stretched about 80% and your wrists in line with the forearms unless instructed otherwise.

2. In Qi Gong stance (standing meditation), place your hands in front of the lower Dantian to create a round ball with the arm stretched out and rounded.

3. In standing and sitting meditation, the fingers and thumbs face each other; this is an internal Yin practice.

4. Lotus palm. When the fingers are open, we place the little finger and thumb slightly forward, creating a cup in the palm, applied when pushing hands forward and to the side. The lotus palm position helps to activate the energy in the centre of the palms.

5. The little fish area. On your palm, in line with the little finger distal from the wrist crease, is a fleshy muscle called the hypothenar. We call this this 'little fish'. (The thumb muscle is the big fish)

The heart acupuncture channel runs through the little fish to the tip of the little finger. Observe the little fish area on the palms before and after you practice. You will see your little fish area becomes red and full of blood. Practice stimulates the heart channel improving circulation calming the heart and mind. If your palms are still cold or have extra blood flow, you have Qi stagnation and poor circulation; this will improve with practice.

Palms pushing forward and to the side with the breath to feel Qi spiral.

When pushing hands with the lotus hand position, focus on the centre of the palms. Visualise breathing in and out through the centre of the palms. Repeat and practise until you feel relaxed. Synchronise the movement to your breathing pattern, breath out, push out-breath in your arms, and hand come back into the starting position. Repeat, and in time you will feel the Qi energy circulate in the palms like a spiral.

The Inner smile.

During your practice and especially whilst pushing your hands forward. Open your eyes wide and smile to yourself internally. This action is to help stimulate the liver channel, which connects to the eyes. Daoist philosophers tell us to inner smile to our organs, thank them and send them love to aid harmony of organ and cell function, increasing the vitality of mind, body and spirit. (Mantak Chia 2008)

Eye positions - closed or gentle gaze.

When in practice, you can choose either to keep your eyes closed or open. Keeping your eyes closed allows you to feel and listen more closely. If you choose to keep your eyes open, then take your gaze downwards at 45 degrees. Gently focus on your peripheral vision.

Breathwork.

Learning to control your breath takes time and practice. The aim is to keep your breath is smooth, quiet, and natural. Do not hold or force your breath. Ideally, breathe in and out through the nose as this gives you a slow, controlled, deeper breath. The aim is to keep the chest relaxed without over-expanding the lungs keeping your breath down into the lower Dantian belly. Western therapies have taken this ancient Taoist breathing technique and renamed it 'Diaphragmatic Breathing.' The breath is the gateway to reach your higher consciousness and spiritual vitality.

The gate of all wonders.

During your meditation and with practice, you can connect to internal and external universal energies. This is a difficult concept to grasp; this means connecting to the intersection of the macro-universe and the micro-universe. The Macro model explains energy within nature and the gigantic universe; the micro is energy at a subatomic level. To help you grasp this concept, on a micro-level, it helps to understand that the human body is complex and made of many elements, but to simplify, the human body is made of organs and cells. Skin cells, muscles cells, bone cells, nerve cells. Cells made of proteins, molecules, and water. In the centre of cells are DNA and RNA. Molecules are a collection of atoms. Atoms are present in human cells at the micro-level and macro-level within nature and the cosmos. Within the laws of gravitational physics and quantum mechanics, the macro and micro universal models explain the way in which energy particles behave in both worlds. In ancient Chinese medicine, the vital force of energy referred to as 'Qi,' we acknowledge that Qi energy resides internally within humans, all living things, and externally in the elements and cosmos. The famous Daoist philosopher 'Lao Tzu' explained during meditation that you can experience 'the door' or the 'gate to all wonders" This is where the quantum duality of Yin and Yang energies merges harmoniously. This experience is a feeling of space in time and is also known as "The Middle Way." (Ursula, K) Advanced practitioners can experience being in this space and time continuum through daily practice. It's like a space between heaven and earth. It feels like you see fully with your eyes closed and feel a sense of leaving the physical form, yet fully present in the higher conscious connecting to outer universal energy particles. This takes years to practice; it is different for us all, do not search for this experience; just practice daily, and you will develop your senses and go deeper internally and externally as you journey through Qi Gong practice.

Acupuncture point locations Point to focus on during Qi Gong practice.

1. Bai Hui acupuncture point.

Bai Hui is a beautiful acupuncture point at the very top of the head where all the yang channels meet. This point benefits the brain and helps connect the mind, body, and spirit. It is the gateway to consciousness, travelling to' heaven's gate' and is the cosmic universal connection to the Tao, the source of pure divine light and energies. This is on the 'Du' or the 'governing' channel. This meridian originates in the lower abdomen emerging in the perineum. It then travels up the spine, over the head, down the face to the philtrum, the area under the nose. With regular practice and the correct posture, you can feel Qi energy like an electrical loop running and travelling up the Du channel along the spine to the top of the head, down the face to the lips down the front Ren channel.

2. Lao Gong - hand acupuncture point.

Lao Gong is the fire point of the pericardium meridian. This meridian originates in the chest, connects to the pericardium, travelling down the inner arm, through the palm to the middle finger. In practice, when pushing the hands forward and to the side, pulling the middle finger stimulates the pericardium meridian, calming the heart and the Shen (spirit). The centre of the palm collects more external Yang Qi. When you place your hands onto the hips and waist, you are then connecting the Lao Gong point in the palms to the girdle vessel. This channel circulates around the waist connecting to the internal organs in this area. Refer to Figure 1.

1. Yong Quan - Foot acupuncture point.

Long Quan is an acupuncture point in the kidney channel. Its name translates to 'the bubbling well.' This is the beginning of the kidney meridian, which starts at the sole of the foot, then travels to meet the spleen meridian at the ankle. This channel ascends the inside of the leg and connects to the kidney and the Du channel of the spine, ascending and ending at the roof of the mouth. When you are rooted during practice, the Qi spiralling and tingling at this footpoint can be a strong sensation. To feel calm and grounded, we connect to the earth (yin energy) with our breath and mind intention, imagine breathing out through the feet with golden roots growing out of the centre of the foot to the earth; this action is rooting. Refer to Figure 1.

2. Guan Yuan: abdominal acupuncture point.

Guan Yan is located at the lower Dantian, located three finger-widths below the navel (about 3.5 inches). Its name translates to the Gate of origin.' As it connects you to your original birth Yuan Qi. Traditionally women should place their hands on to the lower Dantian by placing the left hand over right, and men placing the right hand over left. Circling your hands over this point is both warming and soothing. The hand placement is not set in stone, but we practice this way in Chen style Qi Gong and Tai Chi to create more balance. Refer to Figure 2.

3. Ming Men: lower back area and acupuncture point.

Ming Men is located below the posterior ribs near the kidneys, Point Du 4.

This area nourishes us and helps to warm our constitution, hence the name Gate of fire and life.' It helps to balance the water and fire element, the bladder, kidneys, and adrenal function. If you practice Qi Gong in the evening, face your Min Men to the light of the moon to absorb more yin during meditation. In the daytime, to warm your body and help Qi flow, expose your Ming Men to the sun to absorb more yang energy in practice. We tap the Ming Men in the warmup to stimulate circulation and warm kidney essence, improving blood flow. Refer to Figure 1.

Figure 1 Hand, foot, and head acupuncture points.
Qi energy flow that can be at these acupuncture points in practice.

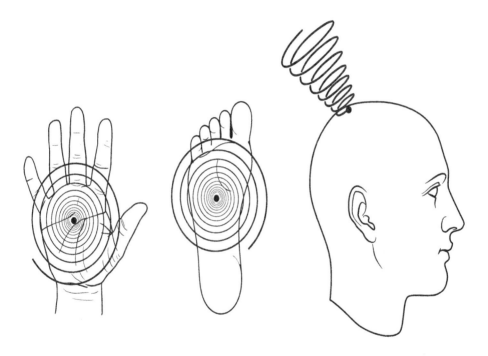

Hand Point	Foot Point	Head Point
Lao Gong	Yong Quan	Bai Hui (DU20)

Gathers Eternal Qi Rooting point Universal Qi and Cosmic Orbit.

Yang Energy Yin Energy Yin and Yang Energy

32

Figure 2 The three Dantian energy centres.

This diagram shows the following: The cosmic orbit circuit. Illustrating the connection of the Ren channel (at the front of the body) and the Du channel (at the back of the body) travelling like a circuit of energy. Extra acupuncture Acupoints locations.

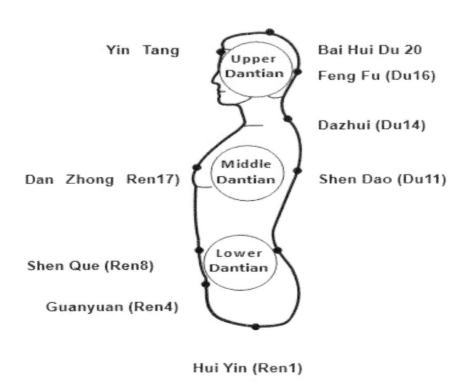

Muscles shaking in practice.

During your practice, especially during standing meditation, you may experience your arms and legs shaking. This happens because energy and blood flow into these areas. As your muscles become stronger and you can cope with the duration of standing posture, shaking will eventually lessen. Sometimes the rushing of Qi flow alone can make this happen. If you feel tension or pain, breathe in, stand up tall a little, then breathe down and sit back into your hips and joints posture like you are sitting on a stool. Try not to collapse completely; try to hold your posture longer each time you practice.

End of practice bouncing across the body.

At the end of your practice, relax all the joints and muscles by gently bouncing into the joints (Opening the joints) while kicking out the legs and feet across the body, sending negative energy to the earth. Finish by swinging your arms across your body, sending any stiffness, tension, or stagnated energy out and down to the earth.

Closing the pores after practice.

Qi Gong and breathwork warms your body and opens your pores. Closing the pores after practice is important. It helps prevent the invasion of external pathogens and cold damp or chills invading the body. We do this by patting down the outside of the body and pat up the inside of the arms, legs and chest. End your practice by dry massaging on your face, scalp, ears, and the back of your skull.

Extra self-help tools - acupressure and tapping techniques.

Once you have mastered your practice, you will want to expand your practice. Add the following techniques to your practice or to your day when you feel you need it. Pressing or tapping acupuncture points helps relieve tension, calms the mind, and stimulates the Qi at the acupuncture point. Refer to the acupressure and tapping demonstration photos.

Acupressure.

Acupressure is a gentler, surface treatment of acupuncture points. You can apply pressure using your fingers and thumbs to stimulate specific points on the channels. Use the pads to the tips of the thumbs and fingers in a back-and-forth motion or circulate on the points. Massage about 30 rotations and repeat bilaterally. Each side of the body has the same adjacent point. You can access more information about the actions of acupuncture points on the web.

Tapping.

As well as pressure, you can also use tapping to stimulate acupuncture points. To do so, place five fingers together like the beak of a bird to tap large areas. Use two fingers to tap points in smaller areas. Tap the acupuncture points about 30 times whilst focussing on your breath to bring calmness. Repeat three times for three rounds. Relax and repeat when required during the day. For example, tapping the centre of the chest is good to open a tight chest, stimulate the lung function, and help lift sadness.

Tapping 'Yin Tang' acupuncture Point.

Otherwise known as 'The hall of impression,' this extraordinary point calms the mind and spirit. Located on the forehead between the eyebrows (at the glabella), tap with two fingers at this point. Breath in and out slowly through the nose. Tap with the left hand, then repeat with the right hand. At the same time, state a positive affirmation aloud to yourself. Examples: "I can achieve my goals, I am calm and energised, I have clarity of mind, I have patience, I have compassion, I let go of my stress." This can help anchor and strengthen your affirmations.

Pounding (tapping) acupuncture point 'Yangling Quan' leg points.

Otherwise known as 'the meeting point of the sinews,' this acupuncture point adds to your practice by releasing muscular tension and blood flow to the tendons, gently pounding or tapping this acupuncture point which is located on the gallbladder channel below the knee (patella). It is on the outside of the leg just under the head of the fibular; the bony prominence can easily be located. With the inside of the hand in a fist shape, gently tap this area. Repeat this action 30 times on each side. On an emotional level, it helps reduce frustration and agitation. (Refer to demonstration 1: Pounding)

35

Demonstration 1. Pounding - tapping acupuncture point 'Yangling Quan.

Correct hands placement on your Dantain women place the left hand over the right connecting the thumbs into the 'tigers' mouth.'

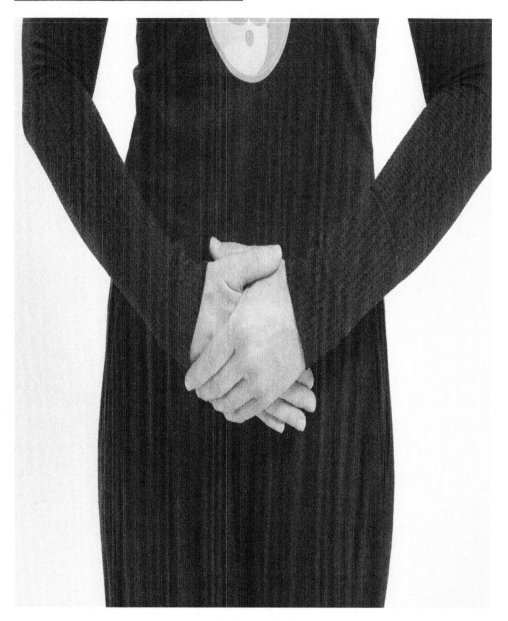

Men place your right hand over the left hooking the thumbs together in the 'tigers' mouth'.

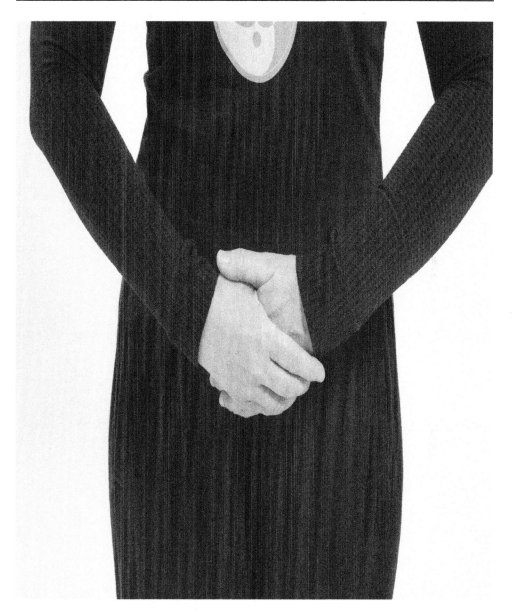

Tapping and Acupressure Demonstrations.

1. **Chest Lung Acupuncture points. For Lung health and lifting sadness.**

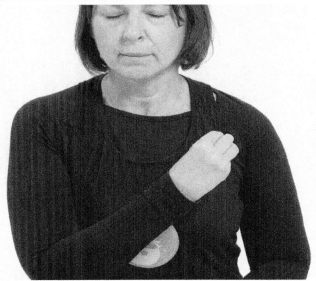

2. **Yin Tang acupuncture point, located between the eyebrows, calms the mind.**

3. **Acupuncture location 'Feng Chi' meaning head wind gate.**

Further study to increase your knowledge of acupuncture channels and points.

The Ren conception channel, the sea of yin and blood.

This channel runs from the perineum up the front midline of the body to the lower lip. It is a Yin channel important for fertility and balance. It also helps reduce anxiety, lessen palpitations, and calm the spirit. The lower and middle Dantian energy centres can be located on this channel. The lower dantian is located at 'Guanyuan' under the navel called the gate of Origin; this is the sea of Qi energy. The front channel connects to the backchannel called the 'Du' channel. They connect and run like a circuit from front to back; this is the cosmic orbit. In Qi Gong practise, this channel connects internally to our lower vital organs, our Jing or essence of life, and source of life force. This is one energy circuit, activated and connected when we practice the microcosmic orbit exercise.

'Ruzhong ' ren channel point.

Rhzhong acupuncture point is in the centre of your chest, directly between your nipples. Tap this area to unbind and open the chest. This point is useful for breathlessness, a tight chest, anxiety, and coughing.

'Ming Men' meaning gate of life on the DU channel.

This channel originates in the abdomen, runs through the perineum up the back along the spine to the top of the head, descending over to the face to the top lip, connecting to the front central Ren channel as explained above. The lower back (lumbar region) is referred to as the Ming men, meaning the 'gate of life or fire'. The Ming men' energy centre can be found on the lower back under lumber vertebra number 3. The 'gate of life and fire; area, spreads across the lower back. We tap this area in practice with the back of our hands to warm and circulate the kidney Qi.

'Dazhui' acupuncture point meaning the great vertebra.

Located at neck cervical vertebra number 7, this is the meeting point of the 6 Yang channels of the hands and feet. Travelling up to the top of the head to join 'Bai Hui', Dazhui experienced in practice when Qi energy circulates and runs to the top of the head.

Si Shen Chong meaning 'Heaven's gate'.

Four acupuncture points surround 'Bai Hui ' at the top of the head. During Qi Gong meditation, we can take our awareness to this 'heaven's gate' or the doorway to connect to the great universal Qi and beyond. When in practice with our focus on the breath and the top of the head, we are rooted to the earth through the feet at the same time. The saying goes, 'As above so below.' Like a tree connecting to two different worlds, the roots and the branches. When you are in your higher self, you can connect to the universal source of ancestral energy. Taoists describe this experience as the space between heaven and earth, in space and time. You can feel a shift in your mind and energy and feel physically lighter. It can feel like an out-of-body experience, but your spirit remains rooted and balanced in mind-body because you are in a physically rooted Qi gong posture. Refer to figure 1b.

'Dai Mai' meaning 'the belt channel.'

This belt channel flows horizontally around the waist above the hips dividing us into two halves. It binds to other vertical channels. In our warm-up exercises, we connect to this channel by placing our hands on to the hips and circling the waist, which will move Qi or energy in this belt channel. This is an extraordinary channel or ancestral channel because it is the energetic controller of our genetic ancestry. It is connecting to the Ren, therefore our fertility. This channel connects the upper and lower parts of the body, aiding the health and balance of vital organs.

'He Gu' meaning joining valley original source point 'Tigers Mouth.

This acupuncture point is located on the hand between the first and second metacarpal bones, in the triangle of flesh between the thumb and first finger. In Qi Gong practice, we refer to this area as 'The Tigers mouth.' We connect both hands into the tiger's mouth; then, we place our hands on the lower dantian. (Refer to the correct hand placement on the lower Dantain photo figure). Find the sore point in the middle of the triangle and massage with the thumb. You can tap this point with the fingers or add acupressure. Stimulating this point helps the defensive 'Wei Chi' (meaning your immunity) fight off pathogens, cold wind invasion from external environmental factors. This point is excellent to reduce headaches, aid immunity, clear sinuses and connect to the lung channel. (Do not stimulate this point in pregnancy.)

Diagram of 'Hu Gu' (Large intestine 4) acupuncture point.

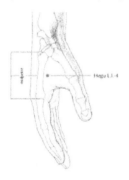

'Zhong Fu' middle palace.

This acupuncture point is located at the chest toward the armpit, In the depression below the collarbone (clavicle). Connect all your fingers and thumb together, then gently tap and massage this point to improve lung and immune health. In Chinese Medicine, the Lungs energetically can be affected by the emotion of sadness. (In the west, when we are sad, we call this heartache) However, when we are deeply sad or bereaved, people often state experiencing a hollow feeling or a heavyweight in the centre of the chest. Vibrating the lung channel through tapping this area can help lift the feeling of sadness and depression stimulate the lung channel while helping to alleviate coughing, wheezing, chills and fevers.

Auricular Acupressure.

The auricular points are all located on the ears. The ears, hands and feet are microsystems of the body's acupuncture channel system. Like channels, auricular points are also bilateral, and they correlate to body parts and systems. You can stimulate these points by massaging the ears at the end of your practice, or any time in the day to relive stress and create internal balance. At the end of Qi Gong practice, we massage with acupressure to the ears by pressing upwardly, inside of the ears, and then pressing down the outside of the ears.

Acupressure 'Feng Chi' Head Wind Gate.

(acupuncture point GB 20) Location is found at the back of the skull. About 1.5 inches (1.5cun) in the hollow on either side of the spine. These points lie on the gallbladder channel at the back of the skull base. Massage this area with two fingers or thumbs. Stimulation of this area helps clear headaches, dizziness, muscular tension, and tired eyes. Then massage with your fingers over the head (yang meridians), pushing back to the base of the skull.

The Yin Yang Symbol. Yin Yang represents the harmony found in the Laws of Science and Nature. Found in Humans, animals, plants, and our environmental elements and within the cosmos. Yin always resides within Yang, and Yang resides within Yin. They are never separate; one cannot function without the other; they are the ever-changing interconnecting force of duality as seen in the laws of the universe, science and nature.

Yin	Yang
Internal	External
Feminine	Masculine
Moon	Sun
Cold	Hot
Water	Fire
Earth	Heaven

Yin	Yang
Intuitive	Analytical
Passive	Active
Calm	Excessive
Soft	Strong
Yin	**Yang. Paired meridians.**
Heart &	Small intestine
Liver &	Gallbladder

Spleen and   Stomach

Lungs and   Large intestine

Kidneys and   Bladder

Mind Intention and Pathology. Mind intention can create pathological changes in the body's functions with positive or negative outcomes. Trials and studies had shown when cancer patients were asked to meditate for twenty minutes a day, visualising cells attacking their tumour in a cage; the group that meditated produced three times the number of T-cells (T-Lymphocytes) cells which are major adaptive components of the immunity they directly kill infected host cells. We can create change with our mind and brain and resulting in a change in chemistry. Think of the brain and mind as the body's hard drive. This shows the importance of a positive, focused, calm mind intension through meditation movement and breath evidence has shown many positive outcomes for mental and physical wellness.

Importance of Saluting to Practice.
At the start and end of your Chi Gong exercise practice, it is important to breathe and salute. This sets your mind intention into practice giving respect to self and respect to your practice. This is part of your self-cultivation.

The Inner Smile. When you push your hand forward, open your eyes wide and inner smile to yourself. This will stimulate the liver meridian and liver function and the Shen spirit in your heart and clear your mind. Through mind intension and smiling internal to your organs, thanking your organs, and sending them love will only benefit your organ function and help activate healing cells, increasing vitality and inner peace.

Chi Energy Release.
To feel Chi energy flow, we increase the circulation through practice breath and the correct positions. We can build a trap and release chi energy flow through specific movements. When stretching up and holding the Sun or Moon, we block the Chi at the wrists by bending the wrist finger up, then breathe out and open the wrist at 45 degrees; with fingers open, you can feel the accumulated Chi flow down the arms to the fingertips. Build and repeat and practice.

Little Fish Palm Area.
The muscle is called the hypothenar on your palm above the wrist crease located on the medial aspect (the little finger side). We call this area the 'little fish'. The heart channel runs down this

area through the little fish into a little finger. During exercise 3, the little fish, the heart channel, and acupuncture point heart seven is stimulated, calming the spirit, Shen, and mind.

In exercise 3, observe your little fish palm area. Is it becoming redder, pumped with blood? This is your aim.

Acupuncture Points and Chi Gong. Acupuncture points are located along the main 12 meridians at specific anatomical locations. Acupuncture points have specific actions sending signals to the brain, organs, systems, the nervous system, hormones, and cells. Chi Gong practice and mind intension also stimulate the meridians and acupuncture points, thus also affecting systems, organs, hormones, the nervous system, and cells. Both practice and facilitate the movement of chi energy in the body.

Chapter 3.

Qi Gong: Warm-up and meditation practice instructions.

<u>Check the end of practice tips and demonstration photos before you start.</u>

Find your uninterrupted space for practice.

Follow the mind and body preparation list.

Salute to practice.

Step out shoulder width and relax.

Set your timer to 6 minutes.

Start your warmup exercise for one minute, then go to your Qi gong meditation exercise. Connect your mind intention (focus) on breathing.

Keep going with your Qi Gong exercise until you hear the timer.

Write your affirmations, intentions, and grateful sentence.

<u>Warm-up sequence. 17 movements in total.</u>

Practice one warm-up sequence for one whole minute before you move on to your Qi Gong meditation exercise. Start at exercise number 1 and progress every day to the next foundation exercise in the sequence of order. Follow the instructions. Take in deep breaths to help you relax, then breathe naturally while you warm up.

<u>Start with the mind and body preparation.</u>

1. **Stand with your feet together.**
2. **Place your hands on your lower Dantian centre.** Women place the left hand over the right. Men place the right hand over the left. Refer to Figure 1a & 1b.
3. **Breathe through the nose.** Take two deep breaths to let go of tension. Then breathe smoothly down into your Dantian (belly). Do not force the breath or hold your breath. Relax your chest. Focus your mind intention to the centre of the palms.
4. **Head placement.** Keep your head up. Imagine a golden thread holding your head up from the top of your head; keep your chin slightly tucked in but do not strain your neck muscles.
5. **Tongue.** Place the tip of the tongue resting on the maxilla. This is the area on the roof of your mouth behind your two front teeth. Your jaw should be open and relaxed. Your mouth will

produce more saliva. Swallow the excess saliva; this is nourishing Yin. The tongue placement is important for mind and meridian connection.

6. Salute. Bow forward, giving respect to self and to your practice.

7. Step your left foot out to the side, no more than shoulder-width.

Sink into the right foot, bear your weight in the right foot, step out mindfully with the left foot. Shoulder width apart. Relax shoulders down, soften the joints of the knees, hips, lower back wrists.

8. Eyes closed for a minute, keep closed during practice or gaze down.

Gaze your eyes look 45 degrees down, head up. Focus on your peripheral vision (the sides) to relax the eyes.

9. Breathe through the nose.

Take two deep breaths to let go of tension down to the earth—smooth, relaxed, natural breathing.

Relax the chest down. Mind intention; focus on the centre of the palms.

Practice Tips - starting position – relax and let go of mind and body tension. Figure1 a .

Breath through the nose, focus the mind and breathing down to the Dantian and hands.

<u>**Figure 1b.**</u>

<u>**Connecting your mind intention (focus) on the 3 Dantian's areas and acupuncture points,**</u>

Like the roots and branches of a tree, anchor to the earth. Imagine golden roots growing out through the bottom of the feet connecting to the earth and send the higher conscious mind

Above, imagine golden threads at the top of the head reaching up to the stars and universe. As above so below, the place of balance in Yin Yang. The 3 Dantian's areas are located on the head, chest, and belly.

At the end of your practice - bouncing across the body – 2 demonstration photos.

Bouncing across the body moves Qi, which moves blood, thus improving circulation. Bouncing helps relax stiff muscles and joints after practice, especially after your Qi Gong stance postures (still standing or sitting postures). Bouncing also sends remaining stagnated Qi energy to the earth.

Close the Pause after practice.

We always pat the torso and then down the outside of the legs and arms and up the inside of the body, down the Yang and up the Yin. The action of Qi Gong moving meditation with breath and mind will open the pause. Patting the skin close to pause helps prevent chills and cold, damp environmental elements and pathogens from invading, thus supporting your 'Wei Chi' your immunity.

You are now ready to start your 6-minute practice: The warm-up Exercises.

Warm-up 1. Head Rotation.

- Breathe naturally.
- Hands-on the hips connecting to girdle meridian.
- Feet shoulder-width apart.
- Slowly rotate the head clockwise ten times and anticlockwise ten times. (Gently, do not strain)
- Gently look up and down five times each way.
- Lift Head-up gently and tuck the chin in. Slowly look over the left shoulder, then move to look over the right shoulder five times on each side.

Demonstration 3. (3 Demonstration photos)

Warm-up 2: Wrists, elbows, and shoulders rotations.

- Breathe naturally.
- Clasp hands together at chest height.
- Circle the wrists clockwise 20 times.
- Change direction 20 times.
- Separate the hands and circle the elbows; palms face each other and pull in towards the Lower Dantian. (Bending to soften the joint and knees), up and down action with the legs, rotate palms and elbows 20 times.
- Change direction.
- Push away, swim out away from the body out, and round repeat 20 times.
  Demonstration 2. (Two wrist rotation demonstration photos)

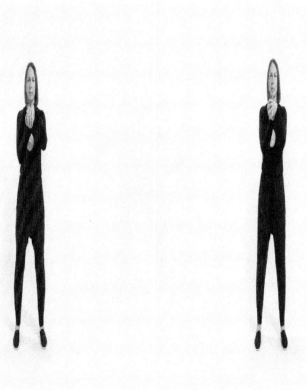

Warm-up 3: Wrists, elbows, shoulders, wave up and down the front of the body.

- Breathe naturally.
- Clasp hands and create a wave, a figure of eight shape, moving up and down slowly.
- At the same time, shift your weight from the centre of your left foot to the right foot.
- Reverse change direction of the hands.

Demonstration 3. (Four demonstration photos)

<u>Warm - up 4 : Circle elbows and shoulder rotations.</u>

- Breathe naturally.
- Rest your hands on the chest.
- Slow large circles rotate both elbows circle back eight times.
- Change direction circle elbows forward eight times.
- Change and alternate left elbow forward then right elbow forward eight times.
- Change and alternate, elbows circling back eight times.
- Relax, shake arms loose.

Demonstration 4. (Five demonstration photos)

Warm-up 5: Arms rotations.

- Breathe naturally.
- Place the right hand resting on the left shoulder.
- Circle the left arm 'back' 8 times.
- Turn your palm as you rotate the arm back; this helps the shoulder rotate and gently rotate—the waist with the movements.
- Change direction and rotate arm forward.
- Sink into the hips joints as you rotate the waist. All joints are open.
- Repeat with the opposite side.
-

Demonstration 5. (Five demonstration photos)

Rotating the arm backwards.

Rotating the arm forwards.

Change arms

Warm-up 6: Open the chest.

- Breathe naturally.
- Open the chest. Fist together in front of the chest, small stretch for 2.
- Open arms to out to the side, palms up, big stretch for 2.
- Repeat eight times.
-

Demonstration 6. (Five demonstration photos)

Warm - up 7 : Thumbs on the chest elbows out to the side rotate the waist looking behind.

- Breathe naturally.
- Elbows up, thumbs resting on the chest, rotate your waist to the left, two times, and the 2nd time look behind you. Gently stretch, but do not overstretch.
- Change and rotate to the right two times on the 2nd look behind you.
- Repeat six times on each side.

Demonstration 7 (Three demonstration photos).

<u>Warm-up 8: Pendulum swinging arms, swing from your centre, your Dantain.</u>

- Breathe naturally.
- Swing arms across the front and back of the body five times
- Tapping the lower back area (Ming men gate of fire)
- Keep the flow going.
- Swing the arms, moving the hands up to tap the arms, left hand tapping right arm right-hand taps left arm five times.
- Swing higher up to tap up over the shoulders, hands meeting the at the shoulder blades. Never force the stretch. Go within your own range.
- Change and reverse, move down to the arms.
- Slow down, relax the arms swing them like a pendulum across the body, use the central Dantian, focus on staying centred and rooted into the centre of your feet.
- Swing across the body five times.

Demonstration 8. (Six demonstration photos).

Warm-up 9: Circle the waist. Keep your head central and still.

- Breathe naturally.
- Hands placed on the hips. The head stays central, do not rotate the head.
- Slowly circle the hips clockwise ten times, then anti-clockwise ten times.
- Take the mind awareness to the centre of the feet. Feel your weight move from the outside of the feet from sides heals to toes.

Demonstration 9. (Three demonstration photos).

Warm-Up 10: Swimming arms, opening hips and knees.

- Breathe naturally.
- Scoop up the hands from the sides, hand and arms stretch forward, swimming action.
- Bend the knees and sit into the hips stand when swimming forward.
- Repeat fifteen times.

Demonstration 10. (Six demonstration photos).

Warm-up 11: Bow step knee to toe.

- Breathe naturally.
- Place your hands on the hips. Turn the right foot out to ten past the hour.
- Sink your weight into the right foot. Step forward to the left foot off the central line.
- Bend the left knee forward. (The left knee must not go past the left toes).
- Slow controlled movements make the thigh muscles work harder.
- The right leg stays straight behind. You can slightly sit into the right hip if more comfortable.
- To finish, lean your weight back into the back foot, then slide in the front foot.
- Stand up change sides.
- Repeat on the other side. Pump the knees twenty times each leg.

Demonstration 11. (Four demonstration photos).

Warm-Up 12: Forward stretching the hamstrings. Sitting pumping quads.

- Breathe naturally.
- Hand on hips
- Feet shoulder-width apart bend forward, straight back, head up in line with the spine.
- Bounce forward ten times.
- Hand on knees, come up into sitting potion and slowly bounce ten times.
- Change side and repeat.
- Feet together, bending forward ten times.
- Feet together hands placed on knees sitting up and down pumping thighs.
- Slowly ten times, working the thigh muscles.

Demonstration 12. (Five demonstration photos).

Warm-up 13: Inside leg stretching. Wide side bow step. Gentle to deeper stretching.

- Breathe naturally.
- Side leg stretches. Place your hands placed on your hips—wide side bow step. Step as far as comfortable, sit into your hips.
- Foot positions: The leg stretching to the side, place this foot forward, then bend the opposite knee, with the foot position placed at an angle in line with the knee.
- Lean and stretch the leg, place your weight into the thigh and the centre of the foot, support yourself with the hands placed on the thigh. Gently bounce and stretch ten times.
- Change sides and repeat.

Demonstration 13. (Two demonstration photos.).

Warm-up 14: Full body stretch, torso, arms, and hamstrings.

- Breathe naturally.
- The left foot steps forward, lift the toes up to place the heal on the ground and stretch the back of the leg. Hold the stretch. Clasp your hands together.
- In one movement, place the front foot flat, lift the back foot, heal up, the arms stretched up above over the head. Repeat up and down ten times.
- Change sides step forward with the right foot, repeat the same full stretch.

Demonstration 14. (Two demonstration photos).

90

Warm-up 15: Body stretch and balancing. Lift up on your toes, palms face the sky.

- Breathe naturally.
- Clasp the hands together, stretch arms above the head, palms facing the sky, head facing forward. (You can also keep the elbows bent and arms rounded, if more comfortable).
- Lift, stretch up. Lift the heals 1-inch, stretch, breath, balance, hold. While balancing, breath in and out three times.
- On the 3rd breath, stretch up further, lift further on the toes stretch.
- On the out-breath, separate hands, float arms down, sink down onto the whole foot, 'gently' tap the heals.
- Repeat five times.
-

Demonstration 15. (Six demonstration photos).

Warm-Up 16: Stretch up one palm to the sky one palm to earth.

- Breathe naturally.
- Sit into your hips and root down into the soles of your feet.
- Stretch the left arm and palm up to the sky above the head, fingers facing towards the face.
- The right palm faces the earth, finger facing towards the lower Dantain.
- Stretch up further, then release, open the elbow joint, relax the shoulders down.
- Breath out, float the hand down to the lower Dantian.
- Breath in and change sides.
- Repeat three times on each side.

Demonstration 16. (Two demonstration photos).

Warm-up 17: Foot, ankle, and knee rotations.

- Breathe naturally.
- Place your hands on your hips, connecting to the waist channel.
- The left toe steps out to the side or slightly behind. Circle the knee, ankle, and toes clockwise for ten, then change to anti-clockwise ten times.
- Change sides (foot) and repeat.

Demonstration 17. (One demonstration photo).

Qi Gong: Moving Meditation Practice Notes.

Breathe the Correct Way. The movement always follows the natural breath, whether it is short or long. As your breath becomes relaxed, the chest becomes relaxed, not over-expanding, the breath becomes deeper, smoother, and slower. Keep your movement synchronised with the breath, in and out, as it becomes relaxed as one. Then your mind intention can synchronise, Qi energy will start to flow.

Mind Intension. If your mind 'scatters' and floats away, re-focus, always bring your mind intention back to the breath to calm the thoughts, repeat every time you float away. Oneness is the goal of mind cultivation and Qi energy.

Qi Gong exercise instructions. Start day one with exercise number 1, day two exercise number 2, and continue each day until you complete all exercises and postures.
After your warmup, set your timer for 5 minutes so your breath, movement and mind are your sole focus in practice.

Expand your Qi Gong practice.
When you have mastered all your warm-ups and Qi Gong exercises, you will have the tools for a one-hour practice session, adding to your daily practice. Just follow the numbers in sequence order. Warming up first, then Qi Gong practice. Start with 15 minutes and develop on to an hour at your leisure.

Patience is Cultivation. Do not rush or strain movements. Slow the breath, do not hold the breath. Practice will teach you how to relax and control a smooth breath. Daily practice will improve your movement range, develop breath control, postures and awaken the senses to feel Qi energy flow. As my Sifu Jamal reminds me, do not search for the feeling of Chi, simply practice, and Qi will start to flow.

I encourage you to increase your Qi Gong practise, but please remember; little and often is effective, and daily practice is key to feeling healthy. To feel free, and feel Qi. The more you practice, the better you feel, and the more you experience.

Qi Gong. Moving meditation: 14 Exercises.

Preparation of body and mind before practice starts. Go through your body checklist.

At the end of your meditation.

1. Bounce across the body five times; this relaxes the connective tissue and releases negative energy to the earth, releasing stiffness and stagnation.

2. Pat down the body to close the pause. Pat Downward on the outside and pat up the Inside. Refer to the demonstration below. Meditation opens the pares; patting is important as this action helps prevent chills, supports your immunity, and prevents cold winds and pathogens from invading the body.

Starting practice, prepare, relax, and salute to your practice; step out.

Starting demonstration photos. Breath, relax and root yourself. (Four demonstration photos).

Salute to practice.

Step out with the left foot.

Qi Gong exercise 1: Rooting, open arms to the side.

(Round the elbows, open the fingers, pointing down to the earth. Qi flows down the arms through to the fingers.)

Body check 1st.

- *Hands placed onto your Lower Dantian.*
- *Breathe through the nose let go of tension.*
- *Salute to practice.*
- *Sink your weight into your right foot.*
- *Step out with the left foot, slowly and controlled, place your toes to the left, roll the left foot down.*
- *Feet are shoulder width.*
- *Centre yourself, soften the joints, sink into the hips, bend the knees.*
- *Keep the head up chin in. (Open the back Du channel)*
- *Tongue: Place the tip of the tongue behind the two front teeth. (Relaxing the jaw)*
- *Close your eyes or relaxed gaze down 45 degrees.*

(5 minutes: Set your timer to five minutes to focus solely on your practice).

1st Position: Place your hands onto your Lower Dantian.

Practice: Breath slowly and smoothly, in and out through the nose.

Relax, let go of tension. Breathe down smoothly, relax the chest.

1st mind intension to the centre of the feet, rooting to the earth. Imagine breathing in and out through the centre of the feet.

2nd mind intention to the centre of the palm on the Dantian. Imagine breathing in and out through the palms to the Dantian.

3rd Advanced mind intention try to imagine connecting all the points, breathe in through the feet, up to the Dantian palms and back down to the earth through the feet.

2nd Position: Separate the hands to the side of the body.

Open the fingers 80% pointing to the earth. Open the armpits, open the elbow joints.

Shoulders relaxed down. Let the Qi flow down through the fingers to the earth.

102

Mind intention: focus on keeping all your joints and gates open, tail bone down. Breath down to the lower Dantian and hands. Relax. Hold for 3- 4 minutes.

If you become stiff, hold the posture, breath in stand-up, breath out, sit back into your joints.

Let go of tension repeat.

Mind intention: Focus on breathing down into the lower Dantian and to the centre of the feet. (Keep the chest relaxed).

Five minutes completed.
- *Hand back to the lower Dantian.*
- *Left foot, steps in slowly controlled.*
- *Salute to practice.*
- *Pat down the outside of the body and up the inside.*
- *Bounce across the body to finish and relax.*

Exercise 1: Demonstrating rooting. (Three demonstration photos).

Exercice 2 : Micro cosmic orbit.

(Collecting External Universal Qi Energy. Nourishing Internal Yin Energy. Connecting all Meridians Activating Hands, Feet, and the Three Dantian Energy Centres.)

Body check 1st.

- *Hands-on the lower Dantian.*
- *Breathe through the nose let go of tension.*
- *Salute to practice.*
- *Sink your weight into your right foot.*
- *Step out with the left foot, slowly and controlled, place your toes to the left, roll the left foot down.*
- *Feet shoulder width*
- *Centre yourself, relax the joints, sink into the hips, soften the knees.*
- *Head up chin in. (Open the Du channel)*
- *Tongue: Place the tip of the tongue behind the two front teeth. (Relaxing the jaw)*
- *Close your eyes or relax your gaze.*

(5 minutes: set your timer to focus and time your practice).

Practice: Step out to the left, place the toes down, gently roll the foot down, root to the centre of the feet. Relax, soften all the joints, "open the gates. Separate your hands. Sink down into the hips. Breath in; your arms and palms float out to the sides, travelling up towards the sky, the legs straighten, synchronising with the arms pushing the legs straight (do not lock the knees). The palms meet above the head, fingers are open and face each other.

Breathing out smoothly, movement following the breath, the arms and hands float down the front of the body. At the same time, sit gently back into the hips as the arms float down. The hands finish by facing the earth to complete a circle. (The cosmic orbit) Breathe in and repeat the circle action.

Repeat: Continuously flow by synchronising the movement to the natural smooth breathing pattern. Close your eyes focus on your breath. Imagine gathering external energy around you, bringing it to your internal energy.

Five minutes completed.

- *Left foot, steps in slowly controlled.*
- *Hands on to the lower Dantian.*
- *Salute to practice.*
- *Pat down the body outside up the inside.*
- *Bounce across a few times.*

Demonstrating exercise 2 : Micro cosmic orbit (Seven demonstration photo).

Sitting micro cosmic orbit practice. (Three demonstration photos).

113

Exercise 3: Arms float forward palms up.

(Opening the heart and pericardium channel)

- **Body check 1ˢᵗ.**
- *Hands-on the lower Dantian.*
- *Breathe through the nose let go of tension.*
- *Salute to practice.*
- *Sink your weight into your right foot.*
- *Step out with the left foot slowly and controlled, place your toes to the left, roll the left foot down.*
- *Feet shoulder width*
- *Centre yourself, relax the joints, sink into the hips, soften the knees.*
- *Head up, chin in. (Open the Du channel)*
- *Tongue: place the tip of the tongue behind the two front teeth. (Relaxing the jaw)*
- *Close your eyes or relax your gaze.*

(5 minutes set your timer to focus and time practice)

Practice: Breathing in, arms float up and forward, palms facing up, tilt the inside (little finger) of the palm up. Breathing out, turn the palms over, the arms and hands float down following the out-breath. The palms end facing towards the earth at the side of the body. Breathing in, turn the palms over to the sky and float the arms up. Movement follows the breath.

Keep the hips open. Feel rooted into the feet. Lower back open with tail bone down. When the hands float up palms facing up, lead with the inside of the wrist, tilt the wrist up by the little finger; this action stimulates the heart and pericardium channel and the 'little fish" area of the palm. **Repeat.**

Mind intension: Focus on the breath, the centre of the palms and relaxing the middle Dantain keeping the chest relaxed down, send your breath to the lower Dantian down the legs to the centre of the feet. Breathing in reverse the mind intention.

5 minutes completed.

- *Left foot, steps in slowly controlled.*
- *Hands-on the lower Dantian.*
- *Salute to practice.*
- *Pat down the body outside up the inside.*
- *Bounce across a few times.*

Demonstrating exercise 3: Arm flat forward (Five demonstration photos).

Exercise 4: Holding the wall.
(Stimulating Yin Yang channels – Open and Close. Tension and Energy Release)

Body check 1st.

- *Hands-on the lower Dantian.*
- *Breathe through the nose let go of tension.*
- *Salute to practice.*
- *Sink your weight into your right foot.*
- *Step out with the left foot slowly and controlled, place your toes to the left, roll the left foot down.*
- *Feet shoulder width.*
- *Centre yourself, relax the joints, sink into the hips, soften the knees.*
- *Head up chin in. (Open the Du channel)*
- *Tongue: Place the tip of the tongue behind the two front teeth. (Relaxing the jaw.)*
- *Close your eyes or relax your gaze.*

(5 minutes set your timer for practice).

Practice. Separate the hands. With arms at the side of the body, open the elbows and open the fingers, hold the posture, breath out and let go of tension.

The fingers may tingle, Qi is moving down. Open the joints, bend the knees, gently sit into the hips and the centre of the feet. Start by breathing in; the arms float forward following the breath, Breath out, the arms float back, stand up as if you are holding a wall behind you, finger and hands stretched open, hold the wall, squeeze the buttocks and the thighs (quads). Relax the shoulders down. Breath out, relax, let go of all muscular tension, sit down into the hip's arms float forward.

Repeat. Synchronise the movement to follow the breathing as one.
Mind intention: focus on the floating relaxed movement and then standing tension of muscles and the centre of the palm, relax, feel the energy release. Close your eyes. This helps bring awareness to your balance in the centre of the feet and your sensitivity to Qi flow.

5 minutes completed. *Left foot, steps in slowly controlled.*

- *Hands-on the lower Dantian*
- *Salute to practice.*
- *Pat down the body outside up the inside.*
- *Bounce across a few times.*

Demonstration exercise 4: Holding the wall (Six Demonstration photos).

Exercices 5 : Side stretching.
(Opening the Pericardium Channel).

Body check 1st.
- *Hands-on the lower Dantian.*
- *Breathe through the nose let go of tension.*
- *Salute to practice.*
- *Sink your weight into your right foot.*
- *Step out with the left foot slowly and controlled, place your toes to the left, roll the left foot down.*
- *Feet shoulder width.*
- *Centre yourself, soften the joints, sink into the hips, soften the knees.*
- *Head up chin in. (Open the Du channel)*
- *Tongue, place the tip of the tongue behind the two front teeth. (Relaxing the jaw)*
- *Close your eyes or relax your gaze.*

(5 minutes: set your timer to focus and time practice).

Practice: Separate the hands, fingers open. Breath in, arms float out to the sides, stretch the middle finger, sit the shoulders down. Stand up, straight legs, do not fully lock the knees, palms face the earth, keep the elbow joints open. Stretch out with the middle finger, fingers open.
Breath out, float the arms back down, sinking and sitting down, tail bone down, relax shoulders and elbows. Hands meet at the lower Dantain. Breath in, arms float out, stand up, fingers open.

Repeat. Synchronise movement to the breathing as one.
Mind intention: Focus on the breath alone, and then develop onto the mind focusing on the centre of the palms. **Advanced mind intention.** Connect mind intension to all three 3 points. Breathing in through the feet, Dantian, and hands. Breath in through the feet to the Dantian hands and out through the Dantian back down the legs to the feet. Imagine breathing in through the feet, to the lower Dantian, and hands and then reverse the mind intension with the out-breath.

Five minutes completed.
The left foot steps in slowly controlled.
Hands-on the lower Dantian

Salute to practice.

Pat down the body outside up the inside.

Bounce across a few times.

Demonstrating exercise 5: Side stretch (Four demonstration photos).

Exercise 6. Float hands up and down the front Ren.

(Opening the Yin channels. The Ren conception channel and other yin channels).

Body check 1st.

- *Hands-on the lower Dantian.*
- *Breathe through the nose let go of tension.*
- *Salute to practice.*
- *Sink your weight into your right foot.*
- *Step out with the left foot slowly and controlled, place your toes to the left, roll the left foot down.*
  Feet shoulder width.
- *Centre yourself, come off the joints, sink into the hips, soften the knees.*
- *Head up chin in. (Open the Du channel)*
- *Tongue, place the tip of the tongue behind the two front teeth. (Relaxing the jaw)*
- *Close your eyes or relax your gaze.*

(5 minutes: set your timer to focus and time practice).

Practice: Separate the hands to the side, open all gates and joints, fingers open.

Hands in front of the lower Dantian turn the palm to the sky.

Breathe in; palms float up the front of the body (the Ren channel) to the chin, elbows float out to the side, stand up at the same time. (Do not lock the knees)

Breathe out, turn the palms over to face the earth (under the chin) push down to earth as you breathe down to your lower Dantain. Sink down into the hips, open the joints and root.

Repeat: Sync the movement to the breathing as one.

Mind intention: Focus the mind on the breath, the centre of the feet, palms and the lower dantian. Imagine a golden thread at the front of the body travelling up to the chin and back down to the lower Dantian. **Advanced mind intention**. Add this focus to your first mind intention, imagine the golden thread (channel) travelling from the lower dantian up the front central line of the body to the face, to the top of the head, then breathing down, imagine the golden thread travels down the back of the head and spine to the tail bone. It loops under the body like a circuit, travelling back up the front and activating the Ren and the Du channel. Keep the lumber open; you can eventually feel Qi travel up the front and down the back.

5 minutes completed.

- *The left footsteps in slowly controlled.*
- *Hands-on the lower Dantian*
- *Salute to practice.*
- *Pat down the body outside up the inside.*
- *Bounce across a few times.*

Demonstrating exercise 6: Hand floating up and down the front (Four demonstration photos).

133

Exercise 7. Hands holding the sun or the moon.

Body check 1st.

- *Hands-on the lower Dantian.*
- *Breathe through the nose let go of tension.*
- *Salute to practice.*
- *Sink your weight into your right foot.*
- *Step out with the left foot slowly controlled, place your toes to the left, roll the left foot down.*
- *Feet shoulder width*
- *Centre yourself, soften the joints, sink down into the hips, soften the knees.*
- *Head up chin in. (Open the Du channel)*
- *Tongue, place the tip of the tongue behind the two front teeth. (Relaxing the jaw)*
- *Close your eyes or relax your gaze.*

(5 minutes: set your timer to focus and time practice).

Practice: Separate the palms, hold to the side of the body, open the fingers. Let the Qi flow. Palms hold the Qi at the lower Dantain. The fingers are open, float the palms to the front, elbows follow up out at the sides; hands turn at the chin, keep going, the head follows the hands. Stretch up above the head, look at the back of the hands holding the Sun or the Moon. Breathing out, open the arms, relax the shoulders, the arms float down, open your joints sinking into the hips on the way down. When the arms are at 45 degrees, open the wrist so the palms face the earth; you can feel the Qi rush to the fingertips. Keep the flow of the movement to the breath; the hands float down to meet at the lower Dantian. Repeat.

Repeat: Breath in smoothly, the palms face the sky travelling up the front Ren channel again, reach for the sky. Repeat the sequence.

Mind intention: Focus the mind on one long smooth breath in and out. Do not hold or force the breath. Synchronise the movement to the long smooth breath. Breath.

Advanced mind intention. Imagine holding a golden ball in the palms like the sun; yang Qi or imagine holding the moon, white glowing light of yin Qi. Practice in the morning sunshine or evening moonlight. When you open the writs at 45 degrees, close the eyes and sense into the yang Qi or yin Qi travelling down the inside and outside of the arms to the fingers.

5 minutes completed.

- *The left footsteps in slowly controlled.*
- *Hands-on the lower Dantian.*
- *Salute to practice.*
- *Pat down the body outside up the inside.*
- *Bounce across a few times.*

Demonstrating exercise 7: Holding the sun or the moon. (Eight demonstration photos).

Exercise 8. Push hands forward wide eyes with an inner smile.

(Stimulates the liver channel and all the yin yang channels).

Body check 1st.

- *Hands-on the lower Dantian.*
- *Breathe through the nose let go of tension.*
- *Salute to practice.*
- *Sink your weight into your right foot.*
- *Step out with the left foot slowly controlled, place your toes to the left, roll the left foot down.*
- *Feet shoulder width.*
- *Centre yourself, soften the joints, sink into the hips, soften the knees.*
- *Head up chin in. (Open the Du channel)*
- *Tongue, place the tip of the tongue behind the two front teeth. (Relaxing the jaw)*
- *Close your eyes or relax your gaze.*

(5 minutes: set your timer to focus and time practice).

Practice: Separate the hands, open the armpits, relax shoulders down, open the gates and joints. Breathe in; palms float up the front of the body, the elbows are out to the sides level with the shoulders. Turn the hands to face forward; fingers are open stretched 80%. Squeeze the elbows together at the back, sit the shoulders down.
Breathe out, push hands and arms slowly forward.
Eye open wide, gaze across the fingers, inner smile to self. (The advanced move is to lean slightly forward, gripping the floor with the toes and the heels down still rooted). Breathe out, relax the arms down to the sides, sit down into the hips, then bend the elbows like a piston. Breathe in, elbows squeeze behind, turn hands face forward.
Breathe out push slowly forward. When pushing forward, push the thumb and the little finger slightly forward to create a cup in the palm. Repeat Sinking the movement to four breaths in and out. Advanced breathing is two long smooth breaths in and out.

Repeat: Mind intension: imagine breathing in and out through the centre of the palm. Practice with the eyes open and the eyes closed.

140

5 minutes completed.

- *The left footsteps in slowly controlled.*
- *Hands-on the lower Dantian.*
- *Salute to practice.*
- *Pat down the body outside up the inside.*
- *Bounce across a few times.*

Demonstrating exercise 8: Pushing hands forward. (Eight demonstration photos).

Exercise 9. Pushing hands to the sides. Lean forward toes grip the floor. Stay rooted.

Body check 1st.

- *Hands-on the lower Dantian.*
- *Breathe through the nose let go of tension.*
- *Salute to practice.*
- *Sink your weight into your right foot.*
- *Step out with the left foot slowly and controlled, place your toes to the left, roll the left foot down.*
- *Feet shoulder width.*
- *Centre yourself, soften the joints, sink into the hips, soften the knees.*
- *Head up chin in. (Open the Du channel)*
- *Tongue, place the tip of the tongue behind the two front teeth. (Relaxing the jaw)*
- *Close your eyes or relax your gaze.*

(5 minutes set your timer to focus and time practice).

Practice: Separate the hands, open the armpits, relax the shoulders down, open the gates, i.e., joints. Breathe in; the palms float up the front, elbows out to the side, level with the shoulders. Turn the hands to face forward; fingers are open 80%. Squeeze the elbows together at the back, sit the shoulders down. Turn the hands to face the side of the body, push slowly to the sides. Keep the wrists bent, finger pointing to the sky. Breathe out, relax down, sink into the hips, arms float down. Repeat.

Repeat: With slow controlled breath and movements.

Mind intension: Focus the mind to the centre of the palms, imaging breathing in and out through the palms. When pushing to the side, tilt the little finger and the thumb slightly forward to create a cup in the palm. This stimulates the point in the centre of the palms. With practice, a spiral of Qi energy circulates in the palms, keeping the breath and movement as one.

Five minutes completed.

- *The left footsteps in slowly controlled.*
- *Hands-on the lower data in*
- *Salute to practice.*

- *Pat down the body outside up the inside.*
- *Bounce across a few times.*

Demonstrating exercise 9: pushing hands to the side (Six demonstration photos).

Exercise 10. Open to the earth sky and universe.

Body check 1st.

- *Hands-on the lower Dantian.*
- *Breathe through the nose let go of tension.*
- *Salute to practice.*
- *Sink your weight into your right foot.*
- *Step out with the left foot slowly and controlled, place your toes to the left, roll the left foot down.*
- *Feet shoulder width.*
- *Centre yourself, soften the joints, sink into the hips, soften the knees.*
- *Head up chin in. Open the Du channel)*
- *Tongue tip at the roof of the mouth. (Connection of channels)*
- *Close your eyes or relax your gaze.*

(5 minutes: set your timer to focus and time practice).

Practice: Separate the hands, open the armpits, relax shoulders down, open the gates, i.e., joints. Breathe out; the head drops down to face the earth, palm turn open to the side. Root into your feet, straight back, tail bone down, hands separate open to the earth. Breathe in; the hands come together, fingers facing to earth, pull the elbow up the hands follow float up the centre line and separating at the face, open the arms and hands to the sky and the universe, fingers open, look to the heaven's breath out. Breathe in, arm and hands close, so they meet floating down the ren the front channel, head following the hands back down to the earth, drop the head the to earth. Repeat.

Repeat: synchronising the movement to the breath.
If you become tired, relax at the bottom, open your arms to the earth, and start again.

Mind intension: Focus on the smooth, controlled breath. Movement following the breath. Imagine opening the yin to the earth and yang to the sky. Keep rooted.

Five minutes completed.

- *The left footsteps in slowly controlled.*
- *Salute to practice.*

152

- *Pat down the body outside up the inside.*
- *Bounce across a few times.*

Demonstrating exercise 10 open to the earth and the sky. (Eight demonstration photos).

Exercise 11. Draw a heart.

Body check 1st.

- *Hands-on the lower Dantian.*
- *Breathe through the nose let go of tension.*
- *Salute to practice.*
- *Sink your weight into your right foot.*
- *Step out with the left foot slowly controlled, place your toes to the left, roll the left foot down.*
- *Feet shoulder width.*
- *Centre yourself, soften the joints, sink into the hips, soften the knees.*
- *Head up chin in. (Open the Du channel)*
- *Tongue, place the tip of the tongue behind the two front teeth. (Relaxing the jaw)*
- *Close your eyes or relax your gaze.*

(5 minutes: set your timer to focus and time practice).

Practice: Separate the hands, open the armpits, relax the shoulders down, open the gates, joints. Breathe in, breathe out, drop the head down as the hands open to the earth. Sit in the centre of your feet, tail bone down, straight back. Breathe in, the back of the hands come together, arms float forward straight in front, level with the shoulders. Breath out, draw a heart, hands come together, then sit down into the hips. When sitting, bring the palm together under the chin like a flower. Breathe in, stand up, turn the palms to point down, elbows out to the side. Breathe out; hands float down to the earth down the front central line. Breathe in, repeat the arms float out in front, draw a heart repeat the movement.

Mind intension: Synchronising the movement to breathing and posture. For added discipline and strength, hold the sitting position for 20 seconds rooted, sit down lower each time.

Five minutes completed.

- *The left footsteps in slowly controlled.*
- *Salute to practice.*
- *Pat down the body outside up the inside.*
- *Bounce across a few times.*

Demonstrating exercise 11: Drawing a heart. (Fifteen demonstration photos).

161

Exercise 12. Qi Gong stance Dantian meditation.

Body check 1st.

- *Hands-on the lower Dantian.*
- *Breathe through the nose let go of tension.*
- *Salute to practice.*
- *Sink your weight into your right foot.*
- *Step out with the left foot slowly and controlled, place your toes to the left, roll the left foot down.*
- *Feet shoulder width.*
- *Centre yourself, soften the joints, sink into the hips, soften the knees.*
- *Head up chin in. (Open the Du channel)*
- *Tongue, place the tip of the tongue behind the two front teeth. (Relacing the jaw)*
- *Close your eyes or relax your gaze.*

(5 minutes: set your timer to focus and time practice).

Practice: Separate the hands, open the armpits, relax the shoulders down, open the gates and joints. Let the Qi energy flow to the fingers. Breathe in, hands and arms hold a circle at the lower Dantain. Sit into your joint, keep all the gates open, straight back, tailbone down, chin in. Breathe in and out through the nose. Finger open, thumbs up, hold breath down into your Dantian. Feet position toes pointed outward; stance collect Yang external Qi. Feet pointing forward nourishes Yin Qi. Relax your eyes, gaze, or close your eyes. Head up. Thumbs up for awareness behind you. If your arms or legs tire in holding position or you become stiff. Breathe in on the out-breath, bounce across a few times and go straight back into Qi Gong stance. Mind intention is to stay in position when the mind wants to give up. Build up your mental and physical strength in Qi Gong stance. The mind is weak and will want to say stop. Breathe, relax, let go of tension and hold.

Five minutes completed.

- *The left footsteps in slowly controlled.*
- *Salute to practice.*
- *Pat down the body outside up the inside.*
- *Bounce across a few times.*

Demonstrating exercise 12: Qi Gong standing and sitting meditation postures.

(Three demonstration photos).

Sitting meditation posture: Eyes closed: Mind intension to the breath and lower Dantain. Internal Yin meditation.

Standing and sitting meditation posture: Eyes with a relaxed gaze, focusing on the peripheral vision. Develop internal meditation with the eyes gently open with some external awareness.

Exercise 13. Circling palm Qi energy: Building the Qi energy ball, hands float in and out.

Standing or sitting.

Standing is preferable as all energy gates are open once you master standing, then progress to sitting.

Body check 1st.

- *Hands-on the lower Dantian.*
- *Breathe through the nose and let go of tension.*
- *Salute to practice.*
- *Sink your weight into your right foot.*
- *Step out with the left foot slowly controlled, place your toes to the left, roll the left foot down*
- *Feet shoulder width.*
- *Centre yourself, soften the joints, sink into the hips, soften the knees.*
- *Head up chin in. Open the Du channel)*
- *Tongue, place the tip of the tongue behind the two front teeth. (Connection of channels)*
- *Close your eyes or relaxed gaze.*

(5 minutes: set your timer to focus and time practice).

Practice: Separate the hands, open the armpits; like you have an egg under the armpits, hands are down at the side of the body, fingers open. Allow the Qi to flow. Relax your shoulders down, open the gates, and joints to allow Qi to flow through every joint.

Breathe in; on the out-breath, sink down into your hips and stance, let go of tension. Sit into the centre of your feet, rooting tail bone down, chin in.

Move your hands and palms to the lower Dantian, place the palms facing each other 2 inches apart, your fingers stay open.

Move the hands make tiny circles clockwise, close your eyes.

Change direction, keep circling.

Close your eyes keep going.

Repeat for 2 minutes.

With your awareness of your breath and posture, all gates are open, keep breathing smoothly, relax the chest.

Floating hands out shoulder width:

Breathe in; the hands float out to shoulder width only.

Breath out, float hands back together 2 inches apart.

Repeat for 30 seconds; what do you feel?

Repeat circling the palms building the Qi and floating the hands out and into the correct breathing direction.

Repeat for 5 minutes: Practice both movements, palms circling and then floating hands out and in.

Mind intention: Focus on the centre of the palms and the movement following the breath with the hands floating out and in to synchronise the movement breath and mind as one.

Close your eyes. Sense into your practice; you will feel more Qi sensation from regular practice. Simply feel sense and be aware. Stay rooted.

Five minutes completed.

- *The left footsteps in slowly controlled.*
- *Salute to practice.*
- *Pat down the body outside up the inside.*
- *Bounce across a few times.*

Demonstrating exercise 13: Building the Qi: Palms circling, floating out and in the with breath. (Five demonstration photos standing and sitting practice).

Qi spiralling sensation in the centre of the palms. 'Lao Gong,' acupuncture point located in the palm connecting to the pericardium channel.

178

Exercise 14. Warming the Dantian energy source.

Body check 1st.
- *Hands-on the lower Dantian.*
- *Breathe through the nose let go of tension.*
- *Salute to practice.*
- *Sink your weight into your right foot.*
- *Step out with the left foot slowly controlled, place your toes to the left, roll the left foot down.*
- *Feet shoulder width.*
- *Centre yourself, soften the joints, sink into the hips, soften the knees.*
- *Head up chin in. (Open the Du channel)*
- *Tongue, place the tip of the tongue behind the two front teeth (Relaxing the jaw)*
- *Close your eyes or relax your gaze.*

(5 minutes: set your timer to focus and time practice).

Practice: Separate the hands, open the armpits, place the hands at the sides, finger open let the Qi flow down. Place your palms on the lower Dantian. Women left hand over right and men right hand over the left. Step out to the left, shoulder width. Sink into your feet and root yourself. Relax Women: start rotating anti-clockwise, small circles, getting larger over the whole abdomen. Change hands over and reverse direction getting slowly smaller.
Men: Place your right hand over the left, start with small clockwise circles, getting larger over the whole abdomen. Change hands over and reverse the direction. Repeat.
Relax let go of tension synchronise the movement to the breath. Breathing out the hands' circle down breathing in the hands circle up the abdomen.
Mind intension: Follow the breathing and imagine the lower Dantian getting warmer, building energy and into the palms. Close your eyes for more internal focus to develop your senses.

Five minutes completed.
- *The left footsteps in slowly controlled.*
- *Salute to practice.*
- *Pat down the body outside up the inside.*
- *Bounce across a few times.*

<u>Stepping Out and warming the lower Dantain:</u> Sink down into the right foot, seek the ground with the left toe, gently place the toe on the ground and then root into both feet. Open the gates, open the lumbar, tail bone is down and chin in head up. (Four demonstration photos)

<u>Sitting posture warming the Dantain.</u>

Chapter 4

Journaling: Qi Gong and affirmations. The importance of daily journaling.

Daily journaling will focus your Qi Gong practice and give you the incentive and motivation to start your day with 6-minutes of self-empowering energy medicine. Journaling gives you the space and time to reflect on your practice experience, tracking your thoughts, feelings, physical and spiritual experience of vital Qi energy flow. The more you practice, the more you experience a higher state of consciousness. The two integrated models of Qi Gong meditation and writing affirmations complement each other beautifully, a balanced Yin Yang practice of harmony. Both models will fast track you to vitality. Writing notes and journaling is part of your self-cultivation. Reflection increases awareness, growth, knowledge, wisdom and peace.

How to write Affirmations.

When writing affirmations, we write them in the present tense stating what we desire right now. For example, we write an affirmation as if the feeling or event has already happened. Write the affirmation with confidence. This will help create new neural pathways to positive thinking, helping to override negative thought patterns, which do not serve you well. Journaling affirmations promotes healthy cognitive function impacting healthy behaviours creating positive change. (Harris, P 2008) As Isaac Newton acknowledged in the laws of attraction, the universe mirrors what we think, so to manifest positive change and emotions, your affirmations need to be positive, simple and clear. Remember to acknowledge what you are grateful for every day; this also lifts the Qi and positivity.

Affirmation Examples.

Do NOT use 'doing words', for example, "I am 'going' to feel confident today." Instead, state, "I am confident today."

I can take a break today.
I can commit to my practice.
I can feel lighter today.
I can be kind to myself and others.

I can forgive and move forward.

I can achieve what I put my mind to.

I can laugh at myself.

I have strength to be calm.

I have Insight when to know when to listen with intent.

I have family and friends that love me.

I have compassion.

I have adventure in my soul.

I have joy and purpose.

I am willing to learn.

I am focused.

I am open to innovative ideas.

I am open to change.

I am patient and confident.

I am committed to my self-healing.

I am grateful to be alive.

I am grateful for my vitality and health.

I am grateful for my partner, friends and family.

I let go of childhood fears.

I let go of negative thoughts.

I let go of negative environments.

I let go of tension to the earth.

I let go of fear and anxiety.

I let go of overthinking.

Daily Journaling. Little and often daily practice is what makes the difference to achieve all the internal and external benefits of Chi Gong affirmations and Manifestations.

DAILY PRACTICE.

6-minute morning practice is key to feel free and feel Qi

Date................................

1. Complete a 1-minute warm-up exercise. Warm-up number.................
2. Complete 4-minutes of Qi Gong exercise practice. Exercise number ....

3. Read your daily wisdom.

4. Write your affirmation.

6. Notes. Write reflections and experiences for daily practice.

Wisdom. *There is as much internal space inside you as there is in the whole universe.*

Positive Affirmations.

Write in 'present tense' positive statements, use one emotion, add a goal, keep it brief and simple. Do not use 'doing' words.

I can.. I have..

I am .... I let go of ....

Today I am grateful for...

....
.

Practice reflection notes.

DAILY PRACTICE & JOURNALING

6-minute morning practice is key to feel free and feel Qi

Date..................................

1. Complete a 1-minute warm-up exercise. Warm-up number.................

2. Complete 4-minutes of Qi Gong exercise practice. Exercise number ....

3. Read your daily wisdom

4. Read a knowledge theory paragraph.

5. Write your affirmations.

6. Notes. Reflection and experience of your daily practice.

Wisdom. *The more we take care of our internal environment, the less we are at the mercy of the external environment. Annie Walker.*

Positive Affirmations.

Write in 'present tense' positive statements, use one emotion, add a goal, keep it brief and simple. Do not use 'doing' words.

I can.. I have...

I am.. I let go of ....
Today I am grateful for...

....

Practice reflection notes.

DAILY PRACTICE AND JOURNALING.

6-minute morning practice is key to feel free and feel Qi

Date..................................

1. Complete a 1-minute warm-up exercise. Warm-up number.................

2. Complete 4-minutes of Qi Gong exercise practice. Exercise number ....

3. Read your daily wisdom.

4. Read a knowledge theory paragraph.

5. Write your affirmation.

6. Notes. Reflection and experience of daily practice.

Wisdom. *A question to a Sifu. What is forgiveness, Sifu? Sifu answer's; It is a fragrance that flowers give when they are crushed.*

Positive Affirmations.

Write in 'present tense' positive statements, use one emotion, add a goal, keep it brief and simple. Do not use 'doing' words.

I can.. I have...

I am.. I let go of ....

Today I am grateful for...
....

Practice reflection notes.

185

DAILY PRACTICE.
6-minute morning practice is key to feel free and feel Qi
Date.................................
1. Complete a 1-minute warm-up exercise. Warm-up number..................
2. Complete 4-minutes of Qi Gong exercise practice. Exercise number ....
3. Read your daily wisdom
4. Read a knowledge theory paragraph.
5. Write your affirmations.
6. Notes. Reflection and experience of your daily practice.

Wisdom. *Most of us in our hearts know the 'true 'Way' the 'Tao' way. Listen to your heart. Jenna Robins.*

Positive Affirmations.
Write in 'present tense' positive statements, use one emotion, add a goal, keep it brief and simple. Do not use 'doing' words.

I can..I have...

I am .... I let go of ....

Today I am grateful for..

....

Practice reflection notes.

DAILY PRACTICE.
6-minute morning practice is key to feel free and feel Qi
Date.................................
1. Complete a 1-minute warm-up exercise. Warm-up number..................
2. Complete 4-minutes of Qi Gong exercise practice. Exercise number ....
3. Read your daily wisdom.
4. Read a knowledge theory paragraph.
5. Write your affirmation.
6. Notes. Reflection and experience of your daily practice.

Wisdom. *In every walk with nature, one receives far more than one seeks. John Muir.*

Positive Affirmations.
Write in 'present tense' positive statements, use one emotion, add a goal, keep it brief and simple. Do not use 'doing' words.

I can...I have................... ....

I am .... I let go of ....

Today I am grateful for..
....
Practice reflection notes.

186

DAILY PRACTICE & JOURNALING
6-minute morning practice is key to feel free and feel Qi
Date.................................
1. Complete a 1-minute warm-up exercise. Warm-up number.................
2. Complete 4-minutes of Qi Gong exercise practice. Exercise number ....
3. Read your daily wisdom
4. Read a knowledge theory paragraph.
5. Write your affirmations.
6. Notes. Reflection and experience of your daily practice.

Wisdom. *The only person you need to be better than is the person you were yesterday. Bruce Lee*

Positive Affirmations.
Write in 'present tense' positive statements, use one emotion, add a goal, keep it brief and simple. Do not use 'doing' words.

I can... I have..

I am... I let go of ....
Today I am grateful for...
....

Practice reflection notes.

DAILY PRACTICE & JOURNALING
6-minute morning practice is key to feel free and feel Qi
Date.................................
1. Complete a 1-minute warm-up exercise. Warm-up number.................
2. Complete 4-minutes of Qi Gong exercise practice. Exercise number ....
3. Read your daily wisdom
4. Read a knowledge theory paragraph.
5. Write your affirmations.
6. Notes. Reflection and experience of your daily practice.

Wisdom. *As we become what we think and thus feel. Be mindful of your thoughts today.*

Positive Affirmations.
Write in 'present tense' positive statements, use one emotion, add a goal, keep it brief and simple. Do not use 'doing' words.

I can... I have..

I am... I let go of ....
Today I am grateful for...
....

Practice reflection notes.

DAILY PRACTICE & JOURNALING
6-minute morning practice is key to feel free and feel Qi
Date...................................
1. Complete a 1-minute warm-up exercise. Warm-up number..................
2. Complete 4-minutes of Qi Gong exercise practice. Exercise number ....
3. Read your daily wisdom
4. Read a knowledge theory paragraph.
5. Write your affirmations.
6. Notes. Reflection and experience of your daily practice.

Wisdom. *Wherever life plants you, you can grow and blossom with grace.*

Positive Affirmations.
Write in 'present tense' positive statements, use one emotion, add a goal, keep it brief and simple. Do not use 'doing' words.

I can... I have..

I am.. I let go of ....
Today I am grateful for...
....

Practice reflection notes.

DAILY PRACTICE & JOURNALING
6-minute morning practice is key to feel free and feel Qi
Date...................................
1. Complete a 1-minute warm-up exercise. Warm-up number..................
2. Complete 4-minutes of Qi Gong exercise practice. Exercise number ....
3. Read your daily wisdom
4. Read a knowledge theory paragraph.
5. Write your affirmations.
6. Notes. Reflection and experience of your daily practice.

Wisdom. *You're always one decision away from a different life.*

Positive Affirmations.
Write in 'present tense' positive statements, use one emotion, add a goal, keep it brief and simple. Do not use 'doing' words.

I can... I have..

I am.. I let go of ....
Today I am grateful for...
....

Practice reflection notes.

DAILY PRACTICE & JOURNALING
6-minute morning practice is key to feel free and feel Qi
Date.................................
1. Complete a 1-minute warm-up exercise. Warm-up number.................
2. Complete 4-minutes of Qi Gong exercise practice. Exercise number ....
3. Read your daily wisdom
4. Read a knowledge theory paragraph.
5. Write your affirmations.
6. Notes. Reflection and experience of your daily practice.

Wisdom. *Open your arms to change, but don't let go of your values. Dalai Lama*

Positive Affirmations.
Write in 'present tense' positive statements, use one emotion, add a goal, keep it brief and simple. Do not use 'doing' words.

I can... I have...

I am... I let go of ....
Today I am grateful for...
....

Practice reflection notes.

DAILY PRACTICE & JOURNALING
6-minute morning practice is key to feel free and feel Qi
Date.................................
1. Complete a 1-minute warm-up exercise. Warm-up number.................
2. Complete 4-minutes of Qi Gong exercise practice. Exercise number ....
3. Read your daily wisdom
4. Read a knowledge theory paragraph.
5. Write your affirmations.
6. Notes. Reflection and experience of your daily practice.

Wisdom. *It's not what we have but who we have.*

Positive Affirmations.
Write in 'present tense' positive statements, use one emotion, add a goal, keep it brief and simple. Do not use 'doing' words.

I can... I have...

I am... I let go of ....
Today I am grateful for...
....

Practice reflection notes.

DAILY PRACTICE & JOURNALING
6-minute morning practice is key to feel free and feel Qi
Date...................................
1. Complete a 1-minute warm-up exercise. Warm-up number..................
2. Complete 4-minutes of Qi Gong exercise practice. Exercise number ....
3. Read your daily wisdom
4. Read a knowledge theory paragraph.
5. Write your affirmations.
6. Notes. Reflection and experience of your daily practice.

Wisdom. *The best teachers are those who show you where to look but don't tell you what to see. A.K.Trenfor.*

Positive Affirmations.
Write in 'present tense' positive statements, use one emotion, add a goal, keep it brief and simple. Do not use 'doing' words.

I can.. I have...

I am.. I let go of ....
Today I am grateful for...
....

Practice reflection notes.

DAILY PRACTICE & JOURNALING
6-minute morning practice is key to feel free and feel Qi
Date...................................
1. Complete a 1-minute warm-up exercise. Warm-up number..................
2. Complete 4-minutes of Qi Gong exercise practice. Exercise number ....
3. Read your daily wisdom
4. Read a knowledge theory paragraph.
5. Write your affirmations.
6. Notes. Reflection and experience of your daily practice.

Wisdom. *Trust what you feel, not what you hear.*

Positive Affirmations.
Write in 'present tense' positive statements, use one emotion, add a goal, keep it brief and simple. Do not use 'doing' words.

I can.. I have...

I am.. I let go of ....
Today I am grateful for...
....

Practice reflection notes.

190

DAILY PRACTICE & JOURNALING

6-minute morning practice is key to feel free and feel Qi
Date..................................
1. Complete a 1-minute warm-up exercise. Warm-up number.................
2. Complete 4-minutes of Qi Gong exercise practice. Exercise number ....
3. Read your daily wisdom
4. Read a knowledge theory paragraph.
5. Write your affirmations.
6. Notes. Reflection and experience of your daily practice.

Wisdom. *Cultivation of self is key to self-control. If you don't cultivate your mind, body and spirit, you may not control your thoughts or reactive actions. Jenna Robins.*

Positive Affirmations.
Write in 'present tense' positive statements, use one emotion, add a goal, keep it brief and simple. Do not use 'doing' words.

I can.. I have...

I am.. I let go of ....
Today I am grateful for...
....

Practice reflection notes.

DAILY PRACTICE & JOURNALING

6-minute morning practice is key to feel free and feel Qi
Date..................................
1. Complete a 1-minute warm-up exercise. Warm-up number.................
2. Complete 4-minutes of Qi Gong exercise practice. Exercise number ....
3. Read your daily wisdom
4. Read a knowledge theory paragraph.
5. Write your affirmations.
6. Notes. Reflection and experience of your daily practice.

Wisdom. *When quick to judge, we need judging; when quick to temper, we need tempering; when boasting good deeds, we need modesty; when challenged, we need grace.*

Positive Affirmations.
Write in 'present tense' positive statements, use one emotion, add a goal, keep it brief and simple. Do not use 'doing' words.

I can.. I have...

I am.. I let go of ....
Today I am grateful for...
....

Practice reflection notes.

DAILY PRACTICE & JOURNALING
6-minute morning practice is key to feel free and feel Qi
Date..................................
1. Complete a 1-minute warm-up exercise. Warm-up number..................
2. Complete 4-minutes of Qi Gong exercise practice. Exercise number ....
3. Read your daily wisdom
4. Read a knowledge theory paragraph.
5. Write your affirmations.
6. Notes. Reflection and experience of your daily practice.

Wisdom. *You will never be punished for making people die of laughter—Chinese Proverb.*

Positive Affirmations.
Write in 'present tense' positive statements, use one emotion, add a goal, keep it brief and simple. Do not use 'doing' words.

I can... I have..

I am.. I let go of ....
Today I am grateful for...
....

Practice reflection notes.

DAILY PRACTICE & JOURNALING
6-minute morning practice is key to feel free and feel Qi
Date..................................
1. Complete a 1-minute warm-up exercise. Warm-up number..................
2. Complete 4-minutes of Qi Gong exercise practice. Exercise number ....
3. Read your daily wisdom
4. Read a knowledge theory paragraph.
5. Write your affirmations.
6. Notes. Reflection and experience of your daily practice.

Wisdom. *Kindness in words creates confidence. Kindness in thinking creates profoundness. Kindness in giving creates love. Lao Tzu.*

Positive Affirmations.
Write in 'present tense' positive statements, use one emotion, add a goal, keep it brief and simple. Do not use 'doing' words.

I can... I have..

I am.. I let go of ....
Today I am grateful for...
....

Practice reflection notes.

192

DAILY PRACTICE & JOURNALING
6-minute morning practice is key to feel free and feel Qi
Date................................
1. Complete a 1-minute warm-up exercise. Warm-up number.................
2. Complete 4-minutes of Qi Gong exercise practice. Exercise number ....
3. Read your daily wisdom
4. Read a knowledge theory paragraph.
5. Write your affirmations.
6. Notes. Reflection and experience of your daily practice.

Wisdom. *Love all, trust a few, everything is real, but not everyone is true.*

Positive Affirmations.
Write in 'present tense' positive statements, use one emotion, add a goal, keep it brief and simple. Do not use 'doing' words.

I can.. I have..

I am.. I let go of ....
Today I am grateful for..
....

Practice reflection notes.

DAILY PRACTICE & JOURNALING
6-minute morning practice is key to feel free and feel Qi
Date................................
1. Complete a 1-minute warm-up exercise. Warm-up number.................
2. Complete 4-minutes of Qi Gong exercise practice. Exercise number ....
3. Read your daily wisdom
4. Read a knowledge theory paragraph.
5. Write your affirmations.
6. Notes. Reflection and experience of your daily practice.

Wisdom. *The spirit "the Shen" knows what to do to heal itself self; the challenge is to silence the mind and inner stillness to be able to listen to it. Jenna Robins*

Positive Affirmations.
Write in 'present tense' positive statements, use one emotion, add a goal, keep it brief and simple. Do not use 'doing' words.

I can.. I have..

I am.. I let go of ....
Today I am grateful for..
....

Practice reflection notes.

193

DAILY PRACTICE & JOURNALING
6-minute morning practice is key to feel free and feel Qi
Date.................................
1. Complete a 1-minute warm-up exercise. Warm-up number..................
2. Complete 4-minutes of Qi Gong exercise practice. Exercise number ....
3. Read your daily wisdom
4. Read a knowledge theory paragraph.
5. Write your affirmations.
6. Notes. Reflection and experience of your daily practice.

Wisdom. *Not all storms disrupt your life; some storms come to clear your life of clutter. Jenna Robins.*

Positive Affirmations.
Write in 'present tense' positive statements, use one emotion, add a goal, keep it brief and simple. Do not use 'doing' words.

I can.. I have..

I am.. I let go of ....
Today I am grateful for...
....

Practice reflection notes.

DAILY PRACTICE & JOURNALING
6-minute morning practice is key to feel free and feel Qi
Date.................................
1. Complete a 1-minute warm-up exercise. Warm-up number..................
2. Complete 4-minutes of Qi Gong exercise practice. Exercise number ....
3. Read your daily wisdom
4. Read a knowledge theory paragraph.
5. Write your affirmations.
6. Notes. Reflection and experience of your daily practice.

Wisdom. *The person that follows the crowd will usually go no further than the crowd. The person who walks alone is likely to find themselves in places no one has been before. Albert Einstein.*

Positive Affirmations.
Write in 'present tense' positive statements, use one emotion, add a goal, keep it brief and simple. Do not use 'doing' words.

I can.. I have..

I am.. I let go of ....
Today I am grateful for...
....

Practice reflection notes.

DAILY PRACTICE & JOURNALING
6-minute morning practice is key to feel free and feel Qi
Date.................................
1. Complete a 1-minute warm-up exercise. Warm-up number.................
2. Complete 4-minutes of Qi Gong exercise practice. Exercise number ....
3. Read your daily wisdom
4. Read a knowledge theory paragraph.
5. Write your affirmations.
6. Notes. Reflection and experience of your daily practice.

Wisdom. *Everything we hear is an opinion, not a fact. Everything we see is a perspective, not the truth.*

Positive Affirmations.
Write in 'present tense' positive statements, use one emotion, add a goal, keep it brief and simple. Do not use 'doing' words.

I can.. I have..

I am.. I let go of ....
Today I am grateful for...
....

Practice reflection notes.

DAILY PRACTICE & JOURNALING
6-minute morning practice is key to feel free and feel Qi
Date.................................
1. Complete a 1-minute warm-up exercise. Warm-up number.................
2. Complete 4-minutes of Qi Gong exercise practice. Exercise number ....
3. Read your daily wisdom
4. Read a knowledge theory paragraph.
5. Write your affirmations.
6. Notes. Reflection and experience of your daily practice.

Wisdom. *If the words do not add up, it's usually because the truth was not included in the equation.*

Positive Affirmations.
Write in 'present tense' positive statements, use one emotion, add a goal, keep it brief and simple. Do not use 'doing' words.

I can.. I have..

I am.. I let go of ....
Today I am grateful for...
....

Practice reflection notes.

DAILY PRACTICE & JOURNALING
6-minute morning practice is key to feel free and feel Qi
Date.................................
1. Complete a 1-minute warm-up exercise. Warm-up number..................
2. Complete 4-minutes of Qi Gong exercise practice. Exercise number ....
3. Read your daily wisdom
4. Read a knowledge theory paragraph.
5. Write your affirmations.
6. Notes. Reflection and experience of your daily practice.

Wisdom. *The human body is the microcosm of the universe.*

Positive Affirmations.
Write in 'present tense' positive statements, use one emotion, add a goal, keep it brief and simple. Do not use 'doing' words.

I can... I have...

I am... I let go of ....
Today I am grateful for...
....

Practice reflection notes.

DAILY PRACTICE & JOURNALING
6-minute morning practice is key to feel free and feel Qi
Date.................................
1. Complete a 1-minute warm-up exercise. Warm-up number..................
2. Complete 4-minutes of Qi Gong exercise practice. Exercise number ....
3. Read your daily wisdom
4. Read a knowledge theory paragraph.
5. Write your affirmations.
6. Notes. Reflection and experience of your daily practice.

Wisdom. *If you search everywhere yet cannot find what you are seeking, it is because what you seek is already in your possession. Lao Tzu.*

Positive Affirmations.
Write in 'present tense' positive statements, use one emotion, add a goal, keep it brief and simple. Do not use 'doing' words.

I can... I have...

I am... I let go of ....
Today I am grateful for...
....

Practice reflection notes.

DAILY PRACTICE & JOURNALING
6-minute morning practice is key to feel free and feel Qi
Date.................................
1. Complete a 1-minute warm-up exercise. Warm-up number..................
2. Complete 4-minutes of Qi Gong exercise practice. Exercise number ....
3. Read your daily wisdom
4. Read a knowledge theory paragraph.
5. Write your affirmations.
6. Notes. Reflection and experience of your daily practice.

Wisdom. *If you are always allowed to stop training when you feel discomfort, you will find it easy to give yourself permission to quit. Jet Lee.*

Positive Affirmations.
Write in 'present tense' positive statements, use one emotion, add a goal, keep it brief and simple. Do not use 'doing' words.

I can... I have...

I am... I let go of ....
Today I am grateful for...
....

Practice reflection notes.

DAILY PRACTICE & JOURNALING
6-minute morning practice is key to feel free and feel Qi
Date.................................
1. Complete a 1-minute warm-up exercise. Warm-up number..................
2. Complete 4-minutes of Qi Gong exercise practice. Exercise number ....
3. Read your daily wisdom
4. Read a knowledge theory paragraph.
5. Write your affirmations.
6. Notes. Reflection and experience of your daily practice.

Wisdom. *Doing what you like is freedom; liking what you do is happiness.*

Positive Affirmations.
Write in 'present tense' positive statements, use one emotion, add a goal, keep it brief and simple. Do not use 'doing' words.

I can... I have...

I am... I let go of ....
Today I am grateful for...
....

Practice reflection notes.

DAILY PRACTICE & JOURNALING
6-minute morning practice is key to feel free and feel Qi
Date.................................
1. Complete a 1-minute warm-up exercise. Warm-up number.................
2. Complete 4-minutes of Qi Gong exercise practice. Exercise number ....
3. Read your daily wisdom
4. Read a knowledge theory paragraph.
5. Write your affirmations.
6. Notes. Reflection and experience of your daily practice.

Wisdom. *If love is the treasure, laughter is the key.*

Positive Affirmations.
Write in 'present tense' positive statements, use one emotion, add a goal, keep it brief and simple. Do not use 'doing' words.

I can.. I have...

I am.. I let go of ....
Today I am grateful for...
....

Practice reflection notes.

DAILY PRACTICE & JOURNALING
6-minute morning practice is key to feel free and feel Qi
Date.................................
1. Complete a 1-minute warm-up exercise. Warm-up number.................
2. Complete 4-minutes of Qi Gong exercise practice. Exercise number ....
3. Read your daily wisdom
4. Read a knowledge theory paragraph.
5. Write your affirmations.
6. Notes. Reflection and experience of your daily practice.

Wisdom. *Stop trying to leave, and you will arrive, stop seeking, and you will see. Stop running away, and you will be found. Lao Tzu.*

Positive Affirmations.
Write in 'present tense' positive statements, use one emotion, add a goal, keep it brief and simple. Do not use 'doing' words.

I can.. I have...

I am.. I let go of ....
Today I am grateful for...
....

Practice reflection notes.

DAILY PRACTICE & JOURNALING
6-minute morning practice is key to feel free and feel Qi
Date.................................
1. Complete a 1-minute warm-up exercise. Warm-up number.................
2. Complete 4-minutes of Qi Gong exercise practice. Exercise number ....
3. Read your daily wisdom
4. Read a knowledge theory paragraph.
5. Write your affirmations.
6. Notes. Reflection and experience of your daily practice.

Wisdom. *Life is too short to spend it at war with yourself.*

Positive Affirmations.
Write in 'present tense' positive statements, use one emotion, add a goal, keep it brief and simple. Do not use 'doing' words.

I can.. I have..

I am.. I let go of ....
Today I am grateful for..
....

Practice reflection notes.

DAILY PRACTICE & JOURNALING
6-minute morning practice is key to feel free and feel Qi
Date.................................
1. Complete a 1-minute warm-up exercise. Warm-up number.................
2. Complete 4-minutes of Qi Gong exercise practice. Exercise number ....
3. Read your daily wisdom
4. Read a knowledge theory paragraph.
5. Write your affirmations.
6. Notes. Reflection and experience of your daily practice.

Wisdom. *This is the essence of Qigong, a total absorption of the senses and spirit. With this absorption comes rebalance. Garri Garripoli.*

Positive Affirmations.
Write in 'present tense' positive statements, use one emotion, add a goal, keep it brief and simple. Do not use 'doing' words.

I can.. I have..

I am.. I let go of ....
Today I am grateful for..
....

Practice reflection notes.

199

DAILY PRACTICE & JOURNALING
6-minute morning practice is key to feel free and feel Qi
Date................................
1. Complete a 1-minute warm-up exercise. Warm-up number.................
2. Complete 4-minutes of Qi Gong exercise practice. Exercise number ....
3. Read your daily wisdom
4. Read a knowledge theory paragraph.
5. Write your affirmations.
6. Notes. Reflection and experience of your daily practice.

Wisdom. *Act without expectation. Lao Tzu.*

Positive Affirmations.
Write in 'present tense' positive statements, use one emotion, add a goal, keep it brief and simple. Do not use 'doing' words.

I can.. I have...

I am.. I let go of ....
Today I am grateful for...
....

Practice reflection notes.

DAILY PRACTICE & JOURNALING
6-minute morning practice is key to feel free and feel Qi
Date................................
1. Complete a 1-minute warm-up exercise. Warm-up number.................
2. Complete 4-minutes of Qi Gong exercise practice. Exercise number ....
3. Read your daily wisdom
4. Read a knowledge theory paragraph.
5. Write your affirmations.
6. Notes. Reflection and experience of your daily practice.

Wisdom. *Ignorance is the night of the mind but a night without a moon or stars.*

Positive Affirmations.
Write in 'present tense' positive statements, use one emotion, add a goal, keep it brief and simple. Do not use 'doing' words.

I can.. I have...

I am.. I let go of ....
Today I am grateful for...
....

Practice reflection notes.

DAILY PRACTICE & JOURNALING
6-minute morning practice is key to feel free and feel Qi
Date...................................
1. Complete a 1-minute warm-up exercise. Warm-up number..................
2. Complete 4-minutes of Qi Gong exercise practice. Exercise number ....
3. Read your daily wisdom
4. Read a knowledge theory paragraph.
5. Write your affirmations.
6. Notes. Reflection and experience of your daily practice.

Wisdom. *Qi Gong is a way of being. Being soft yet strong. Qi Gong is a way of breathing, breathing deeply yet calm. Qi Gong is a way of standing, alert yet relaxed. Nigel Mills.*

Positive Affirmations.
Write in 'present tense' positive statements, use one emotion, add a goal, keep it brief and simple. Do not use 'doing' words.

I can.. I have..

I am... I let go of ....
Today I am grateful for...
....

Practice reflection notes.

DAILY PRACTICE & JOURNALING
6-minute morning practice is key to feel free and feel Qi
Date...................................
1. Complete a 1-minute warm-up exercise. Warm-up number..................
2. Complete 4-minutes of Qi Gong exercise practice. Exercise number ....
3. Read your daily wisdom
4. Read a knowledge theory paragraph.
5. Write your affirmations.
6. Notes. Reflection and experience of your daily practice.

Wisdom. *Many say change is painful, but it is the resistance to change that is painful. Buddha.*

Positive Affirmations.
Write in 'present tense' positive statements, use one emotion, add a goal, keep it brief and simple. Do not use 'doing' words.

I can.. I have..

I am... I let go of ....
Today I am grateful for...
....

Practice reflection notes.

DAILY PRACTICE & JOURNALING
6-minute morning practice is key to feel free and feel Qi
Date..................................
1. Complete a 1-minute warm-up exercise. Warm-up number..................
2. Complete 4-minutes of Qi Gong exercise practice. Exercise number ....
3. Read your daily wisdom
4. Read a knowledge theory paragraph.
5. Write your affirmations.
6. Notes. Reflection and experience of your daily practice.

Wisdom. *Attachment is the very opposite of love. Love says I want you to be happy. Attachment says I want you to make me happy. Tenzin Palmo.*

Positive Affirmations.
Write in 'present tense' positive statements, use one emotion, add a goal, keep it brief and simple. Do not use 'doing' words.

I can.. I have..

I am.. I let go of ....
Today I am grateful for..
....

Practice reflection notes.

DAILY PRACTICE & JOURNALING
6-minute morning practice is key to feel free and feel Qi
Date..................................
1. Complete a 1-minute warm-up exercise. Warm-up number..................
2. Complete 4-minutes of Qi Gong exercise practice. Exercise number ....
3. Read your daily wisdom
4. Read a knowledge theory paragraph.
5. Write your affirmations.
6. Notes. Reflection and experience of your daily practice.

Wisdom. *Light the lantern of your mind and keep it bright every single day. Sifu Yan Lei.*

Positive Affirmations.
Write in 'present tense' positive statements, use one emotion, add a goal, keep it brief and simple. Do not use 'doing' words.

I can.. I have..

I am.. I let go of ....
Today I am grateful for..
....

Practice reflection notes.

DAILY PRACTICE & JOURNALING

6-minute morning practice is key to feel free and feel Qi

Date.................................

1. Complete a 1-minute warm-up exercise. Warm-up number.................

2. Complete 4-minutes of Qi Gong exercise practice. Exercise number ....

3. Read your daily wisdom

4. Read a knowledge theory paragraph.

5. Write your affirmations.

6. Notes. Reflection and experience of your daily practice.

Wisdom. *You live most of your life inside your head so make sure it's a nice place to be. Buddha.*

Positive Affirmations.

Write in 'present tense' positive statements, use one emotion, add a goal, keep it brief and simple. Do not use 'doing' words.

I can... I have...

I am.. I let go of ....

Today I am grateful for...

....

Practice reflection notes.

DAILY PRACTICE & JOURNALING

6-minute morning practice is key to feel free and feel Qi

Date.................................

1. Complete a 1-minute warm-up exercise. Warm-up number.................

2. Complete 4-minutes of Qi Gong exercise practice. Exercise number ....

3. Read your daily wisdom

4. Read a knowledge theory paragraph.

5. Write your affirmations.

6. Notes. Reflection and experience of your daily practice.

Wisdom. *Your outer life reflects the quality of your Qi. When you glow inside, the whole world shines. Master Robert Peng.*

Positive Affirmations.

Write in 'present tense' positive statements, use one emotion, add a goal, keep it brief and simple. Do not use 'doing' words.

I can... I have...

I am.. I let go of ....

Today I am grateful for...

....

Practice reflection notes.

DAILY PRACTICE & JOURNALING
6-minute morning practice is key to feel free and feel Qi
Date...................................
1. Complete a 1-minute warm-up exercise. Warm-up number..................
2. Complete 4-minutes of Qi Gong exercise practice. Exercise number ....
3. Read your daily wisdom
4. Read a knowledge theory paragraph.
5. Write your affirmations.
6. Notes. Reflection and experience of your daily practice.

Wisdom. *If you want to awaken all of humanity, then awaken all of yourself. If you want to eliminate the suffering in the world, then eliminate all that is dark and negative in yourself. Lao Tzu*

Positive Affirmations.
Write in 'present tense' positive statements, use one emotion, add a goal, keep it brief and simple. Do not use 'doing' words.

I can... I have...

I am... I let go of ....
Today I am grateful for...
....

Practice reflection notes.

DAILY PRACTICE & JOURNALING
6-minute morning practice is key to feel free and feel Qi
Date...................................
1. Complete a 1-minute warm-up exercise. Warm-up number..................
2. Complete 4-minutes of Qi Gong exercise practice. Exercise number ....
3. Read your daily wisdom
4. Read a knowledge theory paragraph.
5. Write your affirmations.
6. Notes. Reflection and experience of your daily practice.

Wisdom. *Calmness gives you an advantage over your opponent; with it, you have much better instincts. Sifu Lui Ming Fai.*

Positive Affirmations.
Write in 'present tense' positive statements, use one emotion, add a goal, keep it brief and simple. Do not use 'doing' words.

I can... I have...

I am... I let go of ....
Today I am grateful for...
....

Practice reflection notes.

204

DAILY PRACTICE & JOURNALING
6-minute morning practice is key to feel free and feel Qi
Date...............................
1. Complete a 1-minute warm-up exercise. Warm-up number.................
2. Complete 4-minutes of Qi Gong exercise practice. Exercise number ....
3. Read your daily wisdom
4. Read a knowledge theory paragraph.
5. Write your affirmations.
6. Notes. Reflection and experience of your daily practice.

Wisdom. *The meaning of life is to be lived, and it is not to be traded and conceptualised and squeezed into a pattern of system. Bruce Lee.*

Positive Affirmations.
Write in 'present tense' positive statements, use one emotion, add a goal, keep it brief and simple. Do not use 'doing' words.

I can.. I have...

I am.. I let go of ....
Today I am grateful for..
....

Practice reflection notes.

DAILY PRACTICE & JOURNALING
6-minute morning practice is key to feel free and feel Qi
Date...............................
1. Complete a 1-minute warm-up exercise. Warm-up number.................
2. Complete 4-minutes of Qi Gong exercise practice. Exercise number ....
3. Read your daily wisdom
4. Read a knowledge theory paragraph.
5. Write your affirmations.
6. Notes. Reflection and experience of your daily practice.

Wisdom. *In challenging times and the winds of change, a fresh breeze can carry you towards your true destiny. Jenna Robins.*

Positive Affirmations.
Write in 'present tense' positive statements, use one emotion, add a goal, keep it brief and simple. Do not use 'doing' words.

I can.. I have...

I am.. I let go of ....
Today I am grateful for..
....

Practice reflection notes.

DAILY PRACTICE & JOURNALING
6-minute morning practice is key to feel free and feel Qi
Date..................................
1. Complete a 1-minute warm-up exercise. Warm-up number..................
2. Complete 4-minutes of Qi Gong exercise practice. Exercise number ....
3. Read your daily wisdom
4. Read a knowledge theory paragraph.
5. Write your affirmations.
6. Notes. Reflection and experience of your daily practice.

Wisdom. *Distance from people is required if they create constant chaos. Your allegiance is to your peace of mind and heart, not to their opinion of you.*

Positive Affirmations.
Write in 'present tense' positive statements, use one emotion, add a goal, keep it brief and simple. Do not use 'doing' words.

I can... I have..

I am... I let go of ....
Today I am grateful for...
....

Practice reflection notes.

DAILY PRACTICE & JOURNALING
6-minute morning practice is key to feel free and feel Qi
Date..................................
1. Complete a 1-minute warm-up exercise. Warm-up number..................
2. Complete 4-minutes of Qi Gong exercise practice. Exercise number ....
3. Read your daily wisdom
4. Read a knowledge theory paragraph.
5. Write your affirmations.
6. Notes. Reflection and experience of your daily practice.

Wisdom. *The heart loves kindness; you will always feel good when you reach out and lift someone up.*

Positive Affirmations.
Write in 'present tense' positive statements, use one emotion, add a goal, keep it brief and simple. Do not use 'doing' words.

I can... I have..

I am... I let go of ....
Today I am grateful for...
....

Practice reflection notes.

DAILY PRACTICE & JOURNALING
6-minute morning practice is key to feel free and feel Qi
Date...............................
1. Complete a 1-minute warm-up exercise. Warm-up number.................
2. Complete 4-minutes of Qi Gong exercise practice. Exercise number ....
3. Read your daily wisdom
4. Read a knowledge theory paragraph.
5. Write your affirmations.
6. Notes. Reflection and experience of your daily practice.

Wisdom. *Qi Gong gives us a deeper connection to self and mother earth. Let us work together to repair, protect, and respect her. She is our only home in the Universe. Jenna Robins.*

Positive Affirmations.
Write in 'present tense' positive statements, use one emotion, add a goal, keep it brief and simple. Do not use 'doing' words.

I can... I have..

I am... I let go of ....
Today I am grateful for...
....

Practice reflection notes.

DAILY PRACTICE & JOURNALING
6-minute morning practice is key to feel free and feel Qi
Date...............................
1. Complete a 1-minute warm-up exercise. Warm-up number.................
2. Complete 4-minutes of Qi Gong exercise practice. Exercise number ....
3. Read your daily wisdom
4. Read a knowledge theory paragraph.
5. Write your affirmations.
6. Notes. Reflection and experience of your daily practice.

Wisdom. *Think abundantly with excitement. Qi energy follows Intention. Jenna Robins.*

Positive Affirmations.
Write in 'present tense' positive statements, use one emotion, add a goal, keep it brief and simple. Do not use 'doing' words.

I can... I have..

I am... I let go of ....
Today I am grateful for...
....

Practice reflection notes.

DAILY PRACTICE & JOURNALING
6-minute morning practice is key to feel free and feel Qi
Date.................................
1. Complete a 1-minute warm-up exercise. Warm-up number..................
2. Complete 4-minutes of Qi Gong exercise practice. Exercise number ....
3. Read your daily wisdom
4. Read a knowledge theory paragraph.
5. Write your affirmations.
6. Notes. Reflection and experience of your daily practice.

Wisdom. *If you want to grow, you feed your soul and spirit; you feed them with energy. This energy is Chi. Mantak Chia.*

Positive Affirmations.
Write in 'present tense' positive statements, use one emotion, add a goal, keep it brief and simple. Do not use 'doing' words.

I can.. I have..

I am.. I let go of ....
Today I am grateful for..
....

Practice reflection notes.

DAILY PRACTICE & JOURNALING
6-minute morning practice is key to feel free and feel Qi
Date.................................
1. Complete a 1-minute warm-up exercise. Warm-up number..................
2. Complete 4-minutes of Qi Gong exercise practice. Exercise number ....
3. Read your daily wisdom
4. Read a knowledge theory paragraph.
5. Write your affirmations.
6. Notes. Reflection and experience of your daily practice.

Wisdom. *Life is ironic. It takes sadness to know happiness, noise to appreciate silence, and absence to value presence.*

Positive Affirmations.
Write in 'present tense' positive statements, use one emotion, add a goal, keep it brief and simple. Do not use 'doing' words.

I can.. I have..

I am.. I let go of ....
Today I am grateful for..
....

Practice reflection notes.

DAILY PRACTICE & JOURNALING

6-minute morning practice is key to feel free and feel Qi

Date...............................

1. Complete a 1-minute warm-up exercise. Warm-up number.................

2. Complete 4-minutes of Qi Gong exercise practice. Exercise number ....

3. Read your daily wisdom

4. Read a knowledge theory paragraph.

5. Write your affirmations.

6. Notes. Reflection and experience of your daily practice.

Wisdom. *That feeling we call 'intuition is your soul; listen to it, you can trust it. Mantak Chia.*

Positive Affirmations.

Write in 'present tense' positive statements, use one emotion, add a goal, keep it brief and simple. Do not use 'doing' words.

I can... I have..

I am.. I let go of ....

Today I am grateful for...

....

Practice reflection notes.

DAILY PRACTICE & JOURNALING

6-minute morning practice is key to feel free and feel Qi

Date...............................

1. Complete a 1-minute warm-up exercise. Warm-up number.................

2. Complete 4-minutes of Qi Gong exercise practice. Exercise number ....

3. Read your daily wisdom

4. Read a knowledge theory paragraph.

5. Write your affirmations.

6. Notes. Reflection and experience of your daily practice.

Wisdom. *If light is in your heart, you will find your way home. Search for the light inside. Kwan Yin.*

Positive Affirmations.

Write in 'present tense' positive statements, use one emotion, add a goal, keep it brief and simple. Do not use 'doing' words.

I can... I have..

I am.. I let go of ....

Today I am grateful for...

....

Practice reflection notes.

DAILY PRACTICE & JOURNALING
6-minute morning practice is key to feel free and feel Qi
Date.................................
1. Complete a 1-minute warm-up exercise. Warm-up number..................
2. Complete 4-minutes of Qi Gong exercise practice. Exercise number ....
3. Read your daily wisdom
4. Read a knowledge theory paragraph.
5. Write your affirmations.
6. Notes. Reflection and experience of your daily practice.

Wisdom. *Just as true humour is laughter at oneself, true humanity is knowledge of oneself. Alan Watts.*

Positive Affirmations.
Write in 'present tense' positive statements, use one emotion, add a goal, keep it brief and simple. Do not use 'doing' words.

I can... I have...

I am... I let go of ....
Today I am grateful for...
....

Practice reflection notes.

DAILY PRACTICE & JOURNALING
6-minute morning practice is key to feel free and feel Qi
Date.................................
1. Complete a 1-minute warm-up exercise. Warm-up number..................
2. Complete 4-minutes of Qi Gong exercise practice. Exercise number ....
3. Read your daily wisdom
4. Read a knowledge theory paragraph.
5. Write your affirmations.
6. Notes. Reflection and experience of your daily practice.

Wisdom. *If you cannot trust yourself, you cannot even trust your mistrust of yourself; without this underlying trust in the whole system of nature, you are emotionally paralysed.*

Positive Affirmations.
Write in 'present tense' positive statements, use one emotion, add a goal, keep it brief and simple. Do not use 'doing' words.

I can... I have...

I am... I let go of ....
Today I am grateful for...
....

Practice reflection notes.

DAILY PRACTICE & JOURNALING
6-minute morning practice is key to feel free and feel Qi
Date..................................
1. Complete a 1-minute warm-up exercise. Warm-up number..................
2. Complete 4-minutes of Qi Gong exercise practice. Exercise number ....
3. Read your daily wisdom
4. Read a knowledge theory paragraph.
5. Write your affirmations.
6. Notes. Reflection and experience of your daily practice.

Wisdom. *There is a price to be paid for every increase in consciousness. We cannot be more sensitive to please without being more sensitive to pain. Alan Watts.*

Positive Affirmations.
Write in 'present tense' positive statements, use one emotion, add a goal, keep it brief and simple. Do not use 'doing' words.

I can.. I have...

I am.. I let go of ....
Today I am grateful for...
....

Practice reflection notes.

DAILY PRACTICE & JOURNALING
6-minute morning practice is key to feel free and feel Qi
Date..................................
1. Complete a 1-minute warm-up exercise. Warm-up number..................
2. Complete 4-minutes of Qi Gong exercise practice. Exercise number ....
3. Read your daily wisdom
4. Read a knowledge theory paragraph.
5. Write your affirmations.
6. Notes. Reflection and experience of your daily practice.

Wisdom. *A flower unfolds to the best of its ability according to the condition it grows in, and so do you. Unfold to the best of your ability. Kuan Yin.*

Positive Affirmations.
Write in 'present tense' positive statements, use one emotion, add a goal, keep it brief and simple. Do not use 'doing' words.

I can.. I have...

I am.. I let go of ....
Today I am grateful for...
....

Practice reflection notes.

DAILY PRACTICE & JOURNALING

6-minute morning practice is key to feel free and feel Qi

Date.................................

1. Complete a 1-minute warm-up exercise. Warm-up number.................

2. Complete 4-minutes of Qi Gong exercise practice. Exercise number ....

3. Read your daily wisdom

4. Read a knowledge theory paragraph.

5. Write your affirmations.

6. Notes. Reflection and experience of your daily practice.

Wisdom. *If you care about what others think, then you will always be their prisoner. Lao Tzu*

Positive Affirmations.

Write in 'present tense' positive statements, use one emotion, add a goal, keep it brief and simple. Do not use 'doing' words.

I can.. I have..

I am.. I let go of ....
Today I am grateful for...
....

Practice reflection notes.

DAILY PRACTICE & JOURNALING

6-minute morning practice is key to feel free and feel Qi

Date.................................

1. Complete a 1-minute warm-up exercise. Warm-up number.................

2. Complete 4-minutes of Qi Gong exercise practice. Exercise number ....

3. Read your daily wisdom

4. Read a knowledge theory paragraph.

5. Write your affirmations.

6. Notes. Reflection and experience of your daily practice.

Wisdom. *If our orientation is toward perfection or success, we will never learn about unconditional friendship with ourselves, nor will we find compassion. Pema Chodron.*

Positive Affirmations.

Write in 'present tense' positive statements, use one emotion, add a goal, keep it brief and simple. Do not use 'doing' words.

I can.. I have..

I am.. I let go of ....
Today I am grateful for...
....

Practice reflection notes.

212

DAILY PRACTICE & JOURNALING
6-minute morning practice is key to feel free and feel Qi
Date.................................
1. Complete a 1-minute warm-up exercise. Warm-up number.................
2. Complete 4-minutes of Qi Gong exercise practice. Exercise number ....
3. Read your daily wisdom
4. Read a knowledge theory paragraph.
5. Write your affirmations.
6. Notes. Reflection and experience of your daily practice.

Wisdom. *If human beings can take a fresh look at themselves, as well as the universe, and change their rigid mentalities, humankind will make a leap forward. Li Hongzhi.*

Positive Affirmations.
Write in 'present tense' positive statements, use one emotion, add a goal, keep it brief and simple. Do not use 'doing' words.

I can... I have...

I am... I let go of ....
Today I am grateful for...
....

Practice reflection notes.

DAILY PRACTICE & JOURNALING
6-minute morning practice is key to feel free and feel Qi
Date.................................
1. Complete a 1-minute warm-up exercise. Warm-up number.................
2. Complete 4-minutes of Qi Gong exercise practice. Exercise number ....
3. Read your daily wisdom
4. Read a knowledge theory paragraph.
5. Write your affirmations.
6. Notes. Reflection and experience of your daily practice.

Wisdom. *Do not under any circumstances depend on a partial feeling. Allan Watts.*

Positive Affirmations.
Write in 'present tense' positive statements, use one emotion, add a goal, keep it brief and simple. Do not use 'doing' words.

I can... I have...

I am... I let go of ....
Today I am grateful for...
....

Practice reflection notes.

DAILY PRACTICE & JOURNALING
6-minute morning practice is key to feel free and feel Qi
Date.................................
1. Complete a 1-minute warm-up exercise. Warm-up number.................
2. Complete 4-minutes of Qi Gong exercise practice. Exercise number ....
3. Read your daily wisdom
4. Read a knowledge theory paragraph.
5. Write your affirmations.
6. Notes. Reflection and experience of your daily practice.

Wisdom. *The fragrance always stays in the hand that gives the rose—Chinese Proverb.*

Positive Affirmations.
Write in 'present tense' positive statements, use one emotion, add a goal, keep it brief and simple. Do not use 'doing' words.

I can... I have..

I am... I let go of ....
Today I am grateful for...
....

Practice reflection notes.

DAILY PRACTICE & JOURNALING
6-minute morning practice is key to feel free and feel Qi
Date.................................
1. Complete a 1-minute warm-up exercise. Warm-up number.................
2. Complete 4-minutes of Qi Gong exercise practice. Exercise number ....
3. Read your daily wisdom
4. Read a knowledge theory paragraph.
5. Write your affirmations.
6. Notes. Reflection and experience of your daily practice.

Wisdom. *One who smiles rather than rages is always the stronger.*

Positive Affirmations.
Write in 'present tense' positive statements, use one emotion, add a goal, keep it brief and simple. Do not use 'doing' words.

I can... I have..

I am... I let go of ....
Today I am grateful for...
....

Practice reflection notes.

DAILY PRACTICE & JOURNALING
6-minute morning practice is key to feel free and feel Qi
Date.................................
1. Complete a 1-minute warm-up exercise. Warm-up number.................
2. Complete 4-minutes of Qi Gong exercise practice. Exercise number ....
3. Read your daily wisdom
4. Read a knowledge theory paragraph.
5. Write your affirmations.
6. Notes. Reflection and experience of your daily practice.

Wisdom. *Every feeling is a field of energy. A pleasant feeling is an energy which can nourish. Irritation is a feeling which can destroy. Under the light of awareness, the energy of irritation can be transformed into energy that nourishes. Thich Nhat Hanh.*

Positive Affirmations.
Write in 'present tense' positive statements, use one emotion, add a goal, keep it brief and simple. Do not use 'doing' words.

I can... I have...

I am.. I let go of ....
Today I am grateful for..
....

Practice reflection notes.

DAILY PRACTICE & JOURNALING
6-minute morning practice is key to feel free and feel Qi
Date.................................
1. Complete a 1-minute warm-up exercise. Warm-up number.................
2. Complete 4-minutes of Qi Gong exercise practice. Exercise number ....
3. Read your daily wisdom
4. Read a knowledge theory paragraph.
5. Write your affirmations.
6. Notes. Reflection and experience of your daily practice.

Wisdom. *When another person makes you suffer, it is because he or she suffers deeply within, and their suffering is spilling over. Thich Nhat Hanh.*

Positive Affirmations.
Write in 'present tense' positive statements, use one emotion, add a goal, keep it brief and simple. Do not use 'doing' words.

I can... I have...

I am.. I let go of ....
Today I am grateful for..
....

Practice reflection notes.

DAILY PRACTICE & JOURNALING
6-minute morning practice is key to feel free and feel Qi
Date.................................
1. Complete a 1-minute warm-up exercise. Warm-up number.................
2. Complete 4-minutes of Qi Gong exercise practice. Exercise number ....
3. Read your daily wisdom
4. Read a knowledge theory paragraph.
5. Write your affirmations.
6. Notes. Reflection and experience of your daily practice.

Wisdom. *Health is the greatest possession; contentment is the greatest treasure. Confidence is the greatest friend. Lao Tzu.*

Positive Affirmations.
Write in 'present tense' positive statements, use one emotion, add a goal, keep it brief and simple. Do not use 'doing' words.

I can... I have..

I am... I let go of ....
Today I am grateful for..
....

Practice reflection notes.

DAILY PRACTICE & JOURNALING
6-minute morning practice is key to feel free and feel Qi
Date.................................
1. Complete a 1-minute warm-up exercise. Warm-up number.................
2. Complete 4-minutes of Qi Gong exercise practice. Exercise number ....
3. Read your daily wisdom
4. Read a knowledge theory paragraph.
5. Write your affirmations.
6. Notes. Reflection and experience of your daily practice.

Wisdom. *When I let go of what I am, I became what I might be. Laozi*

Positive Affirmations.
Write in 'present tense' positive statements, use one emotion, add a goal, keep it brief and simple. Do not use 'doing' words.

I can... I have..

I am... I let go of ....
Today I am grateful for..
....

Practice reflection notes.

DAILY PRACTICE & JOURNALING
6-minute morning practice is key to feel free and feel Qi
Date.................................
1. Complete a 1-minute warm-up exercise. Warm-up number.................
2. Complete 4-minutes of Qi Gong exercise practice. Exercise number ....
3. Read your daily wisdom
4. Read a knowledge theory paragraph.
5. Write your affirmations.
6. Notes. Reflection and experience of your daily practice.

Wisdom. *Qi Gong is a strategy for freedom from our cage of isolation. Garri Garripoli.*

Positive Affirmations.
Write in 'present tense' positive statements, use one emotion, add a goal, keep it brief and simple. Do not use 'doing' words.

I can.. I have...

I am.. I let go of ....
Today I am grateful for...
....

Practice reflection notes.

DAILY PRACTICE & JOURNALING
6-minute morning practice is key to feel free and feel Qi
Date.................................
1. Complete a 1-minute warm-up exercise. Warm-up number.................
2. Complete 4-minutes of Qi Gong exercise practice. Exercise number ....
3. Read your daily wisdom
4. Read a knowledge theory paragraph.
5. Write your affirmations.
6. Notes. Reflection and experience of your daily practice.

Wisdom. *Don't seek, don't search, don't ask, don't knock, don't demand, relax. If you relax, it comes. If you relax, it's there; if you relax, you start to vibrate with it. Osho.*

Positive Affirmations.
Write in 'present tense' positive statements, use one emotion, add a goal, keep it brief and simple. Do not use 'doing' words.

I can.. I have...

I am.. I let go of ....
Today I am grateful for...
....

Practice reflection notes.

DAILY PRACTICE & JOURNALING
6-minute morning practice is key to feel free and feel Qi
Date................................
1. Complete a 1-minute warm-up exercise. Warm-up number..................
2. Complete 4-minutes of Qi Gong exercise practice. Exercise number ....
3. Read your daily wisdom
4. Read a knowledge theory paragraph.
5. Write your affirmations.
6. Notes. Reflection and experience of your daily practice.

Wisdom. *The silence of peace is a true friend who never betrays.*

Positive Affirmations.
Write in 'present tense' positive statements, use one emotion, add a goal, keep it brief and simple. Do not use 'doing' words.

I can.. I have..

I am.. I let go of ....
Today I am grateful for..
....

Practice reflection notes.

DAILY PRACTICE & JOURNALING
6-minute morning practice is key to feel free and feel Qi
Date................................
1. Complete a 1-minute warm-up exercise. Warm-up number..................
2. Complete 4-minutes of Qi Gong exercise practice. Exercise number ....
3. Read your daily wisdom
4. Read a knowledge theory paragraph.
5. Write your affirmations.
6. Notes. Reflection and experience of your daily practice.

Wisdom. *The roots of all goodness lie in the soil of appreciation. Dalai Lama.*

Positive Affirmations.
Write in 'present tense' positive statements, use one emotion, add a goal, keep it brief and simple. Do not use 'doing' words.

I can.. I have..

I am.. I let go of ....
Today I am grateful for..
....

Practice reflection notes.

DAILY PRACTICE & JOURNALING
6-minute morning practice is key to feel free and feel Qi
Date.................................
1. Complete a 1-minute warm-up exercise. Warm-up number.................
2. Complete 4-minutes of Qi Gong exercise practice. Exercise number ....
3. Read your daily wisdom
4. Read a knowledge theory paragraph.
5. Write your affirmations.
6. Notes. Reflection and experience of your daily practice.

Wisdom. *Action your ideas so that you will not only accomplish something but so that you can make room for new ideas to flow.*

Positive Affirmations.
Write in 'present tense' positive statements, use one emotion, add a goal, keep it brief and simple. Do not use 'doing' words.

I can... I have...

I am.. I let go of ....
Today I am grateful for...
....

Practice reflection notes.

DAILY PRACTICE & JOURNALING
6-minute morning practice is key to feel free and feel Qi
Date.................................
1. Complete a 1-minute warm-up exercise. Warm-up number.................
2. Complete 4-minutes of Qi Gong exercise practice. Exercise number ....
3. Read your daily wisdom
4. Read a knowledge theory paragraph.
5. Write your affirmations.
6. Notes. Reflection and experience of your daily practice.

Wisdom. *Butterflies remind us that it's never too late to transform ourselves.*

Positive Affirmations.
Write in 'present tense' positive statements, use one emotion, add a goal, keep it brief and simple. Do not use 'doing' words.

I can... I have...

I am.. I let go of ....
Today I am grateful for...
....

Practice reflection notes.

DAILY PRACTICE & JOURNALING
6-minute morning practice is key to feel free and feel Qi
Date.................................
1. Complete a 1-minute warm-up exercise. Warm-up number..................
2. Complete 4-minutes of Qi Gong exercise practice. Exercise number ....
3. Read your daily wisdom
4. Read a knowledge theory paragraph.
5. Write your affirmations.
6. Notes. Reflection and experience of your daily practice.

Wisdom. *Anger will never disappear so long as thoughts of resentment are cherished in the mind. Anger will disappear just as soon as thoughts of resentment are forgotten.*

Positive Affirmations.
Write in 'present tense' positive statements, use one emotion, add a goal, keep it brief and simple. Do not use 'doing' words.

I can.. I have...

I am.. I let go of ....
Today I am grateful for...
....

Practice reflection notes.

DAILY PRACTICE & JOURNALING
6-minute morning practice is key to feel free and feel Qi
Date.................................
1. Complete a 1-minute warm-up exercise. Warm-up number..................
2. Complete 4-minutes of Qi Gong exercise practice. Exercise number ....
3. Read your daily wisdom
4. Read a knowledge theory paragraph.
5. Write your affirmations.
6. Notes. Reflection and experience of your daily practice.

Wisdom. *Ego enjoys the prize; soul enjoys the journey. Ego is me; soul is we.*

Positive Affirmations.
Write in 'present tense' positive statements, use one emotion, add a goal, keep it brief and simple. Do not use 'doing' words.

I can.. I have...

I am.. I let go of ....
Today I am grateful for...
....

Practice reflection notes.

DAILY PRACTICE & JOURNALING
6-minute morning practice is key to feel free and feel Qi
Date..................................
1. Complete a 1-minute warm-up exercise. Warm-up number..................
2. Complete 4-minutes of Qi Gong exercise practice. Exercise number ....
3. Read your daily wisdom
4. Read a knowledge theory paragraph.
5. Write your affirmations.
6. Notes. Reflection and experience of your daily practice.

Wisdom. *Stress is not what happens to us; it's our response to what happens. Re-pence is something we can change. Maureen Killoran*

Positive Affirmations.
Write in 'present tense' positive statements, use one emotion, add a goal, keep it brief and simple. Do not use 'doing' words.

I can.. I have..

I am.. I let go of ....
Today I am grateful for..
....

Practice reflection notes.

DAILY PRACTICE & JOURNALING
6-minute morning practice is key to feel free and feel Qi
Date..................................
1. Complete a 1-minute warm-up exercise. Warm-up number..................
2. Complete 4-minutes of Qi Gong exercise practice. Exercise number ....
3. Read your daily wisdom
4. Read a knowledge theory paragraph.
5. Write your affirmations.
6. Notes. Reflection and experience of your daily practice.

Wisdom. *Every day we are born again; what we do today is what matters today.*

Positive Affirmations.
Write in 'present tense' positive statements, use one emotion, add a goal, keep it brief and simple. Do not use 'doing' words.

I can.. I have..

I am.. I let go of ....
Today I am grateful for..
....

Practice reflection notes.

DAILY PRACTICE & JOURNALING
6-minute morning practice is key to feel free and feel Qi
Date.................................
1. Complete a 1-minute warm-up exercise. Warm-up number.................
2. Complete 4-minutes of Qi Gong exercise practice. Exercise number ....
3. Read your daily wisdom
4. Read a knowledge theory paragraph.
5. Write your affirmations.
6. Notes. Reflection and experience of your daily practice.

Wisdom. *Never respond to rudeness. Try not to take it personally, be silent and simply leave them with their energy.*

Positive Affirmations.
Write in 'present tense' positive statements, use one emotion, add a goal, keep it brief and simple. Do not use 'doing' words.

I can.. I have...

I am... I let go of ....
Today I am grateful for..
....

Practice reflection notes.

DAILY PRACTICE & JOURNALING
6-minute morning practice is key to feel free and feel Qi
Date.................................
1. Complete a 1-minute warm-up exercise. Warm-up number.................
2. Complete 4-minutes of Qi Gong exercise practice. Exercise number ....
3. Read your daily wisdom
4. Read a knowledge theory paragraph.
5. Write your affirmations.
6. Notes. Reflection and experience of your daily practice.

Wisdom. *Be thankful for every day and today because in one tiny moment, your entire life could change.*

Positive Affirmations.
Write in 'present tense' positive statements, use one emotion, add a goal, keep it brief and simple. Do not use 'doing' words.

I can.. I have...

I am... I let go of ....
Today I am grateful for..
....

Practice reflection notes.

DAILY PRACTICE & JOURNALING
6-minute morning practice is key to feel free and feel Qi
Date.................................
1. Complete a 1-minute warm-up exercise. Warm-up number.................
2. Complete 4-minutes of Qi Gong exercise practice. Exercise number ....
3. Read your daily wisdom
4. Read a knowledge theory paragraph.
5. Write your affirmations.
6. Notes. Reflection and experience of your daily practice.

Wisdom. *Fix your mind on truth, hold firm to virtue, rely on loving kindness, and find your recreation in the Arts.*

Positive Affirmations.
Write in 'present tense' positive statements, use one emotion, add a goal, keep it brief and simple. Do not use 'doing' words.

I can.. I have..

I am.. I let go of ....
Today I am grateful for...
....

Practice reflection notes.

DAILY PRACTICE & JOURNALING
6-minute morning practice is key to feel free and feel Qi
Date.................................
1. Complete a 1-minute warm-up exercise. Warm-up number.................
2. Complete 4-minutes of Qi Gong exercise practice. Exercise number ....
3. Read your daily wisdom
4. Read a knowledge theory paragraph.
5. Write your affirmations.
6. Notes. Reflection and experience of your daily practice.

Wisdom. *Learn to start each day by smiling inwardly to your vital organs and thank all of them for sustaining your life. Mantak Chia.*

Positive Affirmations.
Write in 'present tense' positive statements, use one emotion, add a goal, keep it brief and simple. Do not use 'doing' words.

I can.. I have..

I am.. I let go of ....
Today I am grateful for...
....

Practice reflection notes.

223

DAILY PRACTICE & JOURNALING
6-minute morning practice is key to feel free and feel Qi
Date..................................
1. Complete a 1-minute warm-up exercise. Warm-up number..................
2. Complete 4-minutes of Qi Gong exercise practice. Exercise number ....
3. Read your daily wisdom
4. Read a knowledge theory paragraph.
5. Write your affirmations.
6. Notes. Reflection and experience of your daily practice.

Wisdom. *The five virtues, order, trust, integrity, wisdom, compassion.*

Positive Affirmations.
Write in 'present tense' positive statements, use one emotion, add a goal, keep it brief and simple. Do not use 'doing' words.

I can.. I have..

I am.. I let go of ....
Today I am grateful for..
....

Practice reflection notes.

DAILY PRACTICE & JOURNALING
6-minute morning practice is key to feel free and feel Qi
Date..................................
1. Complete a 1-minute warm-up exercise. Warm-up number..................
2. Complete 4-minutes of Qi Gong exercise practice. Exercise number ....
3. Read your daily wisdom
4. Read a knowledge theory paragraph.
5. Write your affirmations.
6. Notes. Reflection and experience of your daily practice.

Wisdom. *The greatest glory in living lives is not in never falling, but in rising every time we fall. Nelson Mandela*

Positive Affirmations.
Write in 'present tense' positive statements, use one emotion, add a goal, keep it brief and simple. Do not use 'doing' words.

I can.. I have..

I am.. I let go of ....
Today I am grateful for..
....

Practice reflection notes.

DAILY PRACTICE & JOURNALING
6-minute morning practice is key to feel free and feel Qi
Date..................................
1. Complete a 1-minute warm-up exercise. Warm-up number..................
2. Complete 4-minutes of Qi Gong exercise practice. Exercise number ....
3. Read your daily wisdom
4. Read a knowledge theory paragraph.
5. Write your affirmations.
6. Notes. Reflection and experience of your daily practice.

Wisdom. *Not all of us can do great things, but we can all do small things with great love. Mother Teresa*

Positive Affirmations.
Write in 'present tense' positive statements, use one emotion, add a goal, keep it brief and simple. Do not use 'doing' words.

I can.. I have..

I am... I let go of ....
Today I am grateful for..
....

Practice reflection notes.

DAILY PRACTICE & JOURNALING
6-minute morning practice is key to feel free and feel Qi
Date..................................
1. Complete a 1-minute warm-up exercise. Warm-up number..................
2. Complete 4-minutes of Qi Gong exercise practice. Exercise number ....
3. Read your daily wisdom
4. Read a knowledge theory paragraph.
5. Write your affirmations.
6. Notes. Reflection and experience of your daily practice.

Wisdom. *Don't judge each day by the harvest you reap but by the seeds you plant. Robert Louis Stevenson.*

Positive Affirmations.
Write in 'present tense' positive statements, use one emotion, add a goal, keep it brief and simple. Do not use 'doing' words.

I can.. I have..

I am... I let go of ....
Today I am grateful for..
....

Practice reflection notes.

DAILY PRACTICE & JOURNALING
6-minute morning practice is key to feel free and feel Qi
Date.................................
1. Complete a 1-minute warm-up exercise. Warm-up number..................
2. Complete 4-minutes of Qi Gong exercise practice. Exercise number ....
3. Read your daily wisdom
4. Read a knowledge theory paragraph.
5. Write your affirmations.
6. Notes. Reflection and experience of your daily practice.

Wisdom. *To lead people, walk beside them. As for the best leaders, the people do not notice their existence. When the leader's work is done, the people say, we did it ourselves. Lao Tzu.*

Positive Affirmations.
Write in 'present tense' positive statements, use one emotion, add a goal, keep it brief and simple. Do not use 'doing' words.

I can.. I have...

I am.. I let go of ....
Today I am grateful for..
....

Practice reflection notes.

DAILY PRACTICE & JOURNALING
6-minute morning practice is key to feel free and feel Qi
Date.................................
1. Complete a 1-minute warm-up exercise. Warm-up number..................
2. Complete 4-minutes of Qi Gong exercise practice. Exercise number ....
3. Read your daily wisdom
4. Read a knowledge theory paragraph.
5. Write your affirmations.
6. Notes. Reflection and experience of your daily practice.

Wisdom. *Sharing your knowledge is the way to achieve immortality. Just be mindful of who you share it with.*

Positive Affirmations.
Write in 'present tense' positive statements, use one emotion, add a goal, keep it brief and simple. Do not use 'doing' words.

I can.. I have...

I am.. I let go of ....
Today I am grateful for..
....

Practice reflection notes.

DAILY PRACTICE & JOURNALING
6-minute morning practice is key to feel free and feel Qi
Date................................
1. Complete a 1-minute warm-up exercise. Warm-up number.................
2. Complete 4-minutes of Qi Gong exercise practice. Exercise number ....
3. Read your daily wisdom
4. Read a knowledge theory paragraph.
5. Write your affirmations.
6. Notes. Reflection and experience of your daily practice.

Wisdom. *The more you are motivated by Love, the more fearless and free your action will be. Dalai Lama.*

Positive Affirmations.
Write in 'present tense' positive statements, use one emotion, add a goal, keep it brief and simple. Do not use 'doing' words.

I can... I have...

I am.. I let go of ....
Today I am grateful for..
....

Practice reflection notes.

DAILY PRACTICE & JOURNALING
6-minute morning practice is key to feel free and feel Qi
Date................................
1. Complete a 1-minute warm-up exercise. Warm-up number.................
2. Complete 4-minutes of Qi Gong exercise practice. Exercise number ....
3. Read your daily wisdom
4. Read a knowledge theory paragraph.
5. Write your affirmations.
6. Notes. Reflection and experience of your daily practice.

Wisdom. *Be mindful of your ego dominating your communication, as ego results in vanity, pushing a person to boast with hypocrisy.*

Positive Affirmations.
Write in 'present tense' positive statements, use one emotion, add a goal, keep it brief and simple. Do not use 'doing' words.

I can... I have...

I am.. I let go of ....
Today I am grateful for..
....

Practice reflection notes.

DAILY PRACTICE & JOURNALING
6-minute morning practice is key to feel free and feel Qi
Date..................................
1. Complete a 1-minute warm-up exercise. Warm-up number..................
2. Complete 4-minutes of Qi Gong exercise practice. Exercise number ....
3. Read your daily wisdom
4. Read a knowledge theory paragraph.
5. Write your affirmations.
6. Notes. Reflection and experience of your daily practice.

Wisdom. *Embrace the Yin Yang symbol of harmony; it represents dualities, the up and downs joys and challenges, reminding us that life is a balancing act.*

Positive Affirmations.
Write in 'present tense' positive statements, use one emotion, add a goal, keep it brief and simple. Do not use 'doing' words.

I can.. I have..

I am.. I let go of ....
Today I am grateful for..
....

Practice reflection notes.

DAILY PRACTICE & JOURNALING
6-minute morning practice is key to feel free and feel Qi
Date..................................
1. Complete a 1-minute warm-up exercise. Warm-up number..................
2. Complete 4-minutes of Qi Gong exercise practice. Exercise number ....
3. Read your daily wisdom
4. Read a knowledge theory paragraph.
5. Write your affirmations.
6. Notes. Reflection and experience of your daily practice.

Wisdom. *The best and most beautiful thing in the world cannot be seen or even touched; it is felt with the heart. Helen Keller.*

Positive Affirmations.
Write in 'present tense' positive statements, use one emotion, add a goal, keep it brief and simple. Do not use 'doing' words.

I can.. I have..

I am.. I let go of ....
Today I am grateful for..
....

Practice reflection notes.

DAILY PRACTICE & JOURNALING
6-minute morning practice is key to feel free and feel Qi
Date.................................
1. Complete a 1-minute warm-up exercise. Warm-up number.................
2. Complete 4-minutes of Qi Gong exercise practice. Exercise number ....
3. Read your daily wisdom
4. Read a knowledge theory paragraph.
5. Write your affirmations.
6. Notes. Reflection and experience of your daily practice.

Wisdom. *It always seems impossible until it's done. Nelson Mandela.*

Positive Affirmations.
Write in 'present tense' positive statements, use one emotion, add a goal, keep it brief and simple. Do not use 'doing' words.

I can.. I have..

I am.. I let go of ....
Today I am grateful for..
....

Practice reflection notes.

DAILY PRACTICE & JOURNALING
6-minute morning practice is key to feel free and feel Qi
Date.................................
1. Complete a 1-minute warm-up exercise. Warm-up number.................
2. Complete 4-minutes of Qi Gong exercise practice. Exercise number ....
3. Read your daily wisdom
4. Read a knowledge theory paragraph.
5. Write your affirmations.
6. Notes. Reflection and experience of your daily practice.

Wisdom. *It's not happiness that brings us gratitude; it's gratitude that brings us happiness.*

Positive Affirmations.
Write in 'present tense' positive statements, use one emotion, add a goal, keep it brief and simple. Do not use 'doing' words.

I can.. I have..

I am.. I let go of ....
Today I am grateful for..
....

Practice reflection notes.

DAILY PRACTICE & JOURNALING
6-minute morning practice is key to feel free and feel Qi
Date...................................
1. Complete a 1-minute warm-up exercise. Warm-up number..................
2. Complete 4-minutes of Qi Gong exercise practice. Exercise number ....
3. Read your daily wisdom
4. Read a knowledge theory paragraph.
5. Write your affirmations.
6. Notes. Reflection and experience of your daily practice.

Wisdom. *You are far too smart to be the only thing standing in your way. Jennifer. J Freeman.*

Positive Affirmations.
Write in 'present tense' positive statements, use one emotion, add a goal, keep it brief and simple. Do not use 'doing' words.

I can... I have...

I am.. I let go of ....
Today I am grateful for...
....

Practice reflection notes.

DAILY PRACTICE & JOURNALING
6-minute morning practice is key to feel free and feel Qi
Date...................................
1. Complete a 1-minute warm-up exercise. Warm-up number..................
2. Complete 4-minutes of Qi Gong exercise practice. Exercise number ....
3. Read your daily wisdom
4. Read a knowledge theory paragraph.
5. Write your affirmations.
6. Notes. Reflection and experience of your daily practice.

Wisdom. *Be mindful not to let people who do so little for you occupy so much of your mind; let it go.*

Positive Affirmations.
Write in 'present tense' positive statements, use one emotion, add a goal, keep it brief and simple. Do not use 'doing' words.

I can.. I have..

I am.. I let go of ....
Today I am grateful for...
....

Practice reflection notes.

DAILY PRACTICE & JOURNALING
6-minute morning practice is key to feel free and feel Qi
Date.................................
1. Complete a 1-minute warm-up exercise. Warm-up number.................
2. Complete 4-minutes of Qi Gong exercise practice. Exercise number ....
3. Read your daily wisdom
4. Read a knowledge theory paragraph.
5. Write your affirmations.
6. Notes. Reflection and experience of your daily practice.

Wisdom. *Look for the bright side of things. If you cannot comprehend this, find an object that has become dull and polish it until it begins to shine.*

Positive Affirmations.
Write in 'present tense' positive statements, use one emotion, add a goal, keep it brief and simple. Do not use 'doing' words.

I can.. I have..

I am.. I let go of ....
Today I am grateful for...
....

Practice reflection notes.

DAILY PRACTICE & JOURNALING
6-minute morning practice is key to feel free and feel Qi
Date.................................
1. Complete a 1-minute warm-up exercise. Warm-up number.................
2. Complete 4-minutes of Qi Gong exercise practice. Exercise number ....
3. Read your daily wisdom
4. Read a knowledge theory paragraph.
5. Write your affirmations.
6. Notes. Reflection and experience of your daily practice.

Wisdom. *Honesty is the highest form of intimacy.*

Positive Affirmations.
Write in 'present tense' positive statements, use one emotion, add a goal, keep it brief and simple. Do not use 'doing' words.

I can.. I have..

I am.. I let go of ....
Today I am grateful for...
....

Practice reflection notes.

DAILY PRACTICE & JOURNALING

6-minute morning practice is key to feel free and feel Qi

Date..................................

1. Complete a 1-minute warm-up exercise. Warm-up number..................
2. Complete 4-minutes of Qi Gong exercise practice. Exercise number ....
3. Read your daily wisdom
4. Read a knowledge theory paragraph.
5. Write your affirmations.
6. Notes. Reflection and experience of your daily practice.

Wisdom. *If you light a lamp for someone, it will also brighten your path. Buddha.*

Positive Affirmations.

Write in 'present tense' positive statements, use one emotion, add a goal, keep it brief and simple. Do not use 'doing' words.

I can... I have...

I am... I let go of ....
Today I am grateful for...
....

Practice reflection notes.

DAILY PRACTICE & JOURNALING

6-minute morning practice is key to feel free and feel Qi

Date..................................

1. Complete a 1-minute warm-up exercise. Warm-up number..................
2. Complete 4-minutes of Qi Gong exercise practice. Exercise number ....
3. Read your daily wisdom
4. Read a knowledge theory paragraph.
5. Write your affirmations.
6. Notes. Reflection and experience of your daily practice.

Wisdom. *Where ignorance is our master, there is no possibility of real peace. Dalai Lama.*

Positive Affirmations.

Write in 'present tense' positive statements, use one emotion, add a goal, keep it brief and simple. Do not use 'doing' words.

I can... I have...
I am... I let go of ....
Today I am grateful for...
....

Practice reflection notes.

DAILY PRACTICE & JOURNALING

6-minute morning practice is key to feel free and feel Qi

Date.................................

1. Complete a 1-minute warm-up exercise. Warm-up number.................
2. Complete 4-minutes of Qi Gong exercise practice. Exercise number ....
3. Read your daily wisdom
4. Read a knowledge theory paragraph.
5. Write your affirmations.
6. Notes. Reflection and experience of your daily practice.

Wisdom. *New beginnings are often disguised as painful endings. Lao Tzu.*

Positive Affirmations.

Write in 'present tense' positive statements, use one emotion, add a goal, keep it brief and simple. Do not use 'doing' words.

I can.. I have..

I am.. I let go of ....
Today I am grateful for...
....

Practice reflection notes.

DAILY PRACTICE & JOURNALING

6-minute morning practice is key to feel free and feel Qi

Date.................................

1. Complete a 1-minute warm-up exercise. Warm-up number.................
2. Complete 4-minutes of Qi Gong exercise practice. Exercise number ....
3. Read your daily wisdom
4. Read a knowledge theory paragraph.
5. Write your affirmations.
6. Notes. Reflection and experience of your daily practice.

Wisdom. *The secret of change is to focus your energy not on fighting the old but on building the new. Socrates.*

Positive Affirmations.

Write in 'present tense' positive statements, use one emotion, add a goal, keep it brief and simple. Do not use 'doing' words.

I can.. I have..
I am.. I let go of ....
Today I am grateful for...
....

Practice reflection notes.

DAILY PRACTICE & JOURNALING
6-minute morning practice is key to feel free and feel Qi
Date.................................
1. Complete a 1-minute warm-up exercise. Warm-up number.................
2. Complete 4-minutes of Qi Gong exercise practice. Exercise number ....
3. Read your daily wisdom
4. Read a knowledge theory paragraph.
5. Write your affirmations.
6. Notes. Reflection and experience of your daily practice.

Wisdom. *At any given moment, we have two options: to step forward into growth or step back into safety.*
Abraham Maslow

Positive Affirmations.
Write in 'present tense' positive statements, use one emotion, add a goal, keep it brief and simple. Do not use 'doing' words.

I can.. I have..

I am.. I let go of ....
Today I am grateful for..
....

Practice reflection notes.

DAILY PRACTICE & JOURNALING
6-minute morning practice is key to feel free and feel Qi
Date.................................
1. Complete a 1-minute warm-up exercise. Warm-up number.................
2. Complete 4-minutes of Qi Gong exercise practice. Exercise number ....
3. Read your daily wisdom
4. Read a knowledge theory paragraph.
5. Write your affirmations.
6. Notes. Reflection and experience of your daily practice.

Wisdom. *Even if you cannot change all the people around you, you can change the people you choose to be around. Bennett*

Positive Affirmations.
Write in 'present tense' positive statements, use one emotion, add a goal, keep it brief and simple. Do not use 'doing' words.

I can.. I have..
I am.. I let go of ....
Today I am grateful for..
....

Practice reflection notes.

DAILY PRACTICE & JOURNALING
6-minute morning practice is key to feel free and feel Qi
Date..................................
1. Complete a 1-minute warm-up exercise. Warm-up number.................
2. Complete 4-minutes of Qi Gong exercise practice. Exercise number ....
3. Read your daily wisdom
4. Read a knowledge theory paragraph.
5. Write your affirmations.
6. Notes. Reflection and experience of your daily practice.

Wisdom. *We have to breathe anyway; we might as well be breathing efficiently and with power. Lee Holden.*

Positive Affirmations.
Write in 'present tense' positive statements, use one emotion, add a goal, keep it brief and simple. Do not use 'doing' words.

I can.. I have..

I am.. I let go of ....
Today I am grateful for..
....

Practice reflection notes.

DAILY PRACTICE & JOURNALING
6-minute morning practice is key to feel free and feel Qi
Date..................................
1. Complete a 1-minute warm-up exercise. Warm-up number.................
2. Complete 4-minutes of Qi Gong exercise practice. Exercise number ....
3. Read your daily wisdom
4. Read a knowledge theory paragraph.
5. Write your affirmations.
6. Notes. Reflection and experience of your daily practice.

Wisdom. *If the ocean can calm itself, so can you; we are both salt and water mixed with air. N Waheed.*

Positive Affirmations.
Write in 'present tense' positive statements, use one emotion, add a goal, keep it brief and simple. Do not use 'doing' words.

I can.. I have..
I am.. I let go of ....
Today I am grateful for..
....

Practice reflection notes.

DAILY PRACTICE & JOURNALING
6-minute morning practice is key to feel free and feel Qi
Date................................
1. Complete a 1-minute warm-up exercise. Warm-up number.................
2. Complete 4-minutes of Qi Gong exercise practice. Exercise number ....
3. Read your daily wisdom
4. Read a knowledge theory paragraph.
5. Write your affirmations.
6. Notes. Reflection and experience of your daily practice.

Wisdom. *Laughter is so healing, and it is the shortest distance between two people.*

Positive Affirmations.
Write in 'present tense' positive statements, use one emotion, add a goal, keep it brief and simple. Do not use 'doing' words.

I can... I have...

I am.. I let go of ....
Today I am grateful for...
....

Practice reflection notes.

DAILY PRACTICE & JOURNALING
6-minute morning practice is key to feel free and feel Qi
Date................................
1. Complete a 1-minute warm-up exercise. Warm-up number.................
2. Complete 4-minutes of Qi Gong exercise practice. Exercise number ....
3. Read your daily wisdom
4. Read a knowledge theory paragraph.
5. Write your affirmations.
6. Notes. Reflection and experience of your daily practice.

Wisdom. *Your body is precious; it is your vehicle for awakening, so treat it with care. Nourish rest love laughter.*

Positive Affirmations.
Write in 'present tense' positive statements, use one emotion, add a goal, keep it brief and simple. Do not use 'doing' words.

I can... I have...
I am.. I let go of ....
Today I am grateful for...
....

Practice reflection notes.

DAILY PRACTICE & JOURNALING
6-minute morning practice is key to feel free and feel Qi
Date................................
1. Complete a 1-minute warm-up exercise. Warm-up number.................
2. Complete 4-minutes of Qi Gong exercise practice. Exercise number ....
3. Read your daily wisdom
4. Read a knowledge theory paragraph.
5. Write your affirmations.
6. Notes. Reflection and experience of your daily practice.

Wisdom. *You don't have a soul; you are a soul; you have a body.*

Positive Affirmations.
Write in 'present tense' positive statements, use one emotion, add a goal, keep it brief and simple. Do not use 'doing' words.

I can.. I have..

I am.. I let go of ....
Today I am grateful for..
....

Practice reflection notes.

DAILY PRACTICE & JOURNALING
6-minute morning practice is key to feel free and feel Qi
Date................................
1. Complete a 1-minute warm-up exercise. Warm-up number.................
2. Complete 4-minutes of Qi Gong exercise practice. Exercise number ....
3. Read your daily wisdom
4. Read a knowledge theory paragraph.
5. Write your affirmations.
6. Notes. Reflection and experience of your daily practice.

Wisdom. *Peace comes from within. Do not seek it without.*

Positive Affirmations.
Write in 'present tense' positive statements, use one emotion, add a goal, keep it brief and simple. Do not use 'doing' words.

I can.. I have..

I am.. I let go of ....
Today I am grateful for..
....

Practice reflection notes.

DAILY PRACTICE & JOURNALING
6-minute morning practice is key to feel free and feel Qi
Date.................................
1. Complete a 1-minute warm-up exercise. Warm-up number.................
2. Complete 4-minutes of Qi Gong exercise practice. Exercise number ....
3. Read your daily wisdom
4. Read a knowledge theory paragraph.
5. Write your affirmations.
6. Notes. Reflection and experience of your daily practice.

Wisdom. *The higher we are placed, the more humbly we should walk.*

Positive Affirmations.
Write in 'present tense' positive statements, use one emotion, add a goal, keep it brief and simple. Do not use 'doing' words.

I can.. I have...

I am....................................... I let go of ....
Today I am grateful for...
....

Practice reflection notes.

DAILY PRACTICE & JOURNALING
6-minute morning practice is key to feel free and feel Qi
Date.................................
1. Complete a 1-minute warm-up exercise. Warm-up number.................
2. Complete 4-minutes of Qi Gong exercise practice. Exercise number ....
3. Read your daily wisdom
4. Read a knowledge theory paragraph.
5. Write your affirmations.
6. Notes. Reflection and experience of your daily practice.

Wisdom. *Embrace the messiness of life; there is beauty hidden in its layers. S. Ryan.*

Positive Affirmations.
Write in 'present tense' positive statements, use one emotion, add a goal, keep it brief and simple. Do not use 'doing' words.

I can.. I have...
I am....................................... I let go of ....
Today I am grateful for...
....

Practice reflection notes.

238

DAILY PRACTICE & JOURNALING
6-minute morning practice is key to feel free and feel Qi
Date................................
1. Complete a 1-minute warm-up exercise. Warm-up number.................
2. Complete 4-minutes of Qi Gong exercise practice. Exercise number ....
3. Read your daily wisdom
4. Read a knowledge theory paragraph.
5. Write your affirmations.
6. Notes. Reflection and experience of your daily practice.

Wisdom. *If you are always trying to be normal, you will never know how amazing you can be.*
Maya Angelou.

Positive Affirmations.
Write in 'present tense' positive statements, use one emotion, add a goal, keep it brief and simple. Do not use 'doing' words.

I can.. I have..

I am.. I let go of ....
Today I am grateful for...
....

Practice reflection notes.

DAILY PRACTICE & JOURNALING
6-minute morning practice is key to feel free and feel Qi
Date................................
1. Complete a 1-minute warm-up exercise. Warm-up number.................
2. Complete 4-minutes of Qi Gong exercise practice. Exercise number ....
3. Read your daily wisdom
4. Read a knowledge theory paragraph.
5. Write your affirmations.
6. Notes. Reflection and experience of your daily practice.

Wisdom. *I am no longer accepting the things I cannot change; I am changing the things I cannot accept.*
Dr Angela Davis.

Positive Affirmations.
Write in 'present tense' positive statements, use one emotion, add a goal, keep it brief and simple. Do not use 'doing' words.

I can.. I have..
I am.. I let go of ....
Today I am grateful for...
....

Practice reflection notes.

DAILY PRACTICE & JOURNALING
6-minute morning practice is key to feel free and feel Qi
Date...................................
1. Complete a 1-minute warm-up exercise. Warm-up number..................
2. Complete 4-minutes of Qi Gong exercise practice. Exercise number ....
3. Read your daily wisdom
4. Read a knowledge theory paragraph.
5. Write your affirmations.
6. Notes. Reflection and experience of your daily practice.

Wisdom. *If the problem can be solved, why worry?*
If the problem cannot be solved, worrying will do you no good. Look for another solution. Buddha.

Positive Affirmations.
Write in 'present tense' positive statements, use one emotion, add a goal, keep it brief and simple. Do not use 'doing' words.

I can... I have...

I am.. I let go of ....
Today I am grateful for..
....

Practice reflection notes.

DAILY PRACTICE & JOURNALING
6-minute morning practice is key to feel free and feel Qi
Date...................................
1. Complete a 1-minute warm-up exercise. Warm-up number..................
2. Complete 4-minutes of Qi Gong exercise practice. Exercise number ....
3. Read your daily wisdom
4. Read a knowledge theory paragraph.
5. Write your affirmations.
6. Notes. Reflection and experience of your daily practice.

Wisdom. *In the sky, there is no distinction between east and west; people create distinctions out of their own minds and then believe them to be true.*

Positive Affirmations.
Write in 'present tense' positive statements, use one emotion, add a goal, keep it brief and simple. Do not use 'doing' words.

I can... I have...
I am.. I let go of ....
Today I am grateful for..
....

Practice reflection notes.

DAILY PRACTICE & JOURNALING
6-minute morning practice is key to feel free and feel Qi
Date................................
1. Complete a 1-minute warm-up exercise. Warm-up number.................
2. Complete 4-minutes of Qi Gong exercise practice. Exercise number ....
3. Read your daily wisdom
4. Read a knowledge theory paragraph.
5. Write your affirmations.
6. Notes. Reflection and experience of your daily practice.

Wisdom. *Success is not about how much money you make; it's about the difference you make in people's lives. Michelle Obama*

Positive Affirmations.
Write in 'present tense' positive statements, use one emotion, add a goal, keep it brief and simple. Do not use 'doing' words.

I can... I have..

I am.. I let go of ....
Today I am grateful for...
....

Practice reflection notes.

DAILY PRACTICE & JOURNALING
6-minute morning practice is key to feel free and feel Qi
Date................................
1. Complete a 1-minute warm-up exercise. Warm-up number.................
2. Complete 4-minutes of Qi Gong exercise practice. Exercise number ....
3. Read your daily wisdom
4. Read a knowledge theory paragraph.
5. Write your affirmations.
6. Notes. Reflection and experience of your daily practice.

Wisdom. *If you always put limits on everything you do, physical or anything else, it will spread into your work and into your life. There are no limits. There are only plateaus, and you must not stay there; you must go beyond them. Bruce Lee.*

Positive Affirmations.
Write in 'present tense' positive statements, use one emotion, add a goal, keep it brief and simple. Do not use 'doing' words.

I can... I have..
I am.. I let go of ....
Today I am grateful for...
....

Practice reflection notes.

DAILY PRACTICE & JOURNALING
6-minute morning practice is key to feel free and feel Qi
Date.................................
1. Complete a 1-minute warm-up exercise. Warm-up number..................
2. Complete 4-minutes of Qi Gong exercise practice. Exercise number ....
3. Read your daily wisdom
4. Read a knowledge theory paragraph.
5. Write your affirmations.
6. Notes. Reflection and experience of your daily practice.

Wisdom. *It's not the mountains ahead to climb that wear you down. It's the pebbles in your shoes. Muhammad Ali.*

Positive Affirmations.
Write in 'present tense' positive statements, use one emotion, add a goal, keep it brief and simple. Do not use 'doing' words.

I can.. I have...

I am.. I let go of ....
Today I am grateful for..
....

Practice reflection notes.

DAILY PRACTICE & JOURNALING
6-minute morning practice is key to feel free and feel Qi
Date.................................
1. Complete a 1-minute warm-up exercise. Warm-up number..................
2. Complete 4-minutes of Qi Gong exercise practice. Exercise number ....
3. Read your daily wisdom
4. Read a knowledge theory paragraph.
5. Write your affirmations.
6. Notes. Reflection and experience of your daily practice.

Wisdom. *Qi Gong is a way of being soft yet strong. Qigong is a way of breathing deeply yet calm. Qigong is a way of standing alert yet relaxed. Nigel Mills.*

Positive Affirmations.
Write in 'present tense' positive statements, use one emotion, add a goal, keep it brief and simple. Do not use 'doing' words.

I can.. I have...
I am.. I let go of ....
Today I am grateful for..
....

Practice reflection notes.

DAILY PRACTICE & JOURNALING
6-minute morning practice is key to feel free and feel Qi
Date..................................
1. Complete a 1-minute warm-up exercise. Warm-up number.................
2. Complete 4-minutes of Qi Gong exercise practice. Exercise number ....
3. Read your daily wisdom
4. Read a knowledge theory paragraph.
5. Write your affirmations.
6. Notes. Reflection and experience of your daily practice.

Wisdom. *You will ruin a good day by thinking about a bad day; let yesterday go.*

Positive Affirmations.
Write in 'present tense' positive statements, use one emotion, add a goal, keep it brief and simple. Do not use 'doing' words.

I can... I have..

I am.. I let go of ....
Today I am grateful for..
....

Practice reflection notes.

DAILY PRACTICE & JOURNALING
6-minute morning practice is key to feel free and feel Qi
Date..................................
1. Complete a 1-minute warm-up exercise. Warm-up number.................
2. Complete 4-minutes of Qi Gong exercise practice. Exercise number ....
3. Read your daily wisdom
4. Read a knowledge theory paragraph.
5. Write your affirmations.
6. Notes. Reflection and experience of your daily practice.

Wisdom. *The heart of a human being is no different from the soul of heaven and earth. In your practice, always keep in your thoughts the interaction of heaven and earth, water and fire, yin and yang. Morihei Ueshiba*

Positive Affirmations.
Write in 'present tense' positive statements, use one emotion, add a goal, keep it brief and simple. Do not use 'doing' words.

I can.. I have...
I am.. I let go of ....
Today I am grateful for..
....

Practice reflection notes.

DAILY PRACTICE & JOURNALING

6-minute morning practice is key to feel free and feel Qi

Date.................................

1. Complete a 1-minute warm-up exercise. Warm-up number.................
2. Complete 4-minutes of Qi Gong exercise practice. Exercise number ....
3. Read your daily wisdom
4. Read a knowledge theory paragraph.
5. Write your affirmations.
6. Notes. Reflection and experience of your daily practice.

Wisdom. *Be like the bamboo; the higher you grow, the deeper you bow.*

Positive Affirmations.

Write in 'present tense' positive statements, use one emotion, add a goal, keep it brief and simple. Do not use 'doing' words.

I can.. I have..

I am.. I let go of ....
Today I am grateful for...
....

Practice reflection notes.

DAILY PRACTICE & JOURNALING

6-minute morning practice is key to feel free and feel Qi

Date.................................

1. Complete a 1-minute warm-up exercise. Warm-up number.................
2. Complete 4-minutes of Qi Gong exercise practice. Exercise number ....
3. Read your daily wisdom
4. Read a knowledge theory paragraph.
5. Write your affirmations.
6. Notes. Reflection and experience of your daily practice.

Wisdom. *You don't stop laughing because you grow older you grow older because you stop laughing. Maurice Chevalier.*

Positive Affirmations.

Write in 'present tense' positive statements, use one emotion, add a goal, keep it brief and simple. Do not use 'doing' words.

I can.. I have..
I am.. I let go of ....
Today I am grateful for...
....

Practice reflection notes.

DAILY PRACTICE & JOURNALING
6-minute morning practice is key to feel free and feel Qi
Date................................
1. Complete a 1-minute warm-up exercise. Warm-up number.................
2. Complete 4-minutes of Qi Gong exercise practice. Exercise number ....
3. Read your daily wisdom
4. Read a knowledge theory paragraph.
5. Write your affirmations.
6. Notes. Reflection and experience of your daily practice.

Wisdom. *Each person must live their life as a model for others. Rosa Parks.*

Positive Affirmations.
Write in 'present tense' positive statements, use one emotion, add a goal, keep it brief and simple. Do not use 'doing' words.

I can.. I have..

I am.. I let go of ....
Today I am grateful for..
....

Practice reflection notes.

DAILY PRACTICE & JOURNALING
6-minute morning practice is key to feel free and feel Qi
Date................................
1. Complete a 1-minute warm-up exercise. Warm-up number.................
2. Complete 4-minutes of Qi Gong exercise practice. Exercise number ....
3. Read your daily wisdom
4. Read a knowledge theory paragraph.
5. Write your affirmations.
6. Notes. Reflection and experience of your daily practice.

Wisdom. *In conversation, the fool talks about what they are going to do, the boaster talks about what they have done, and the wise one does and says nothing.*

Positive Affirmations.
Write in 'present tense' positive statements, use one emotion, add a goal, keep it brief and simple. Do not use 'doing' words.

I can.. I have..
I am.. I let go of ....
Today I am grateful for..
....

Practice reflection notes.

DAILY PRACTICE & JOURNALING
6-minute morning practice is key to feel free and feel Qi
Date................................
1. Complete a 1-minute warm-up exercise. Warm-up number.................
2. Complete 4-minutes of Qi Gong exercise practice. Exercise number ....
3. Read your daily wisdom
4. Read a knowledge theory paragraph.
5. Write your affirmations.
6. Notes. Reflection and experience of your daily practice.

Wisdom. *It is in the silence of the forest and true nature that one finds true bliss.*

Positive Affirmations.
Write in 'present tense' positive statements, use one emotion, add a goal, keep it brief and simple. Do not use 'doing' words.

I can.. I have..

I am.. I let go of ....
Today I am grateful for..
....

Practice reflection notes.

DAILY PRACTICE & JOURNALING
6-minute morning practice is key to feel free and feel Qi
Date................................
1. Complete a 1-minute warm-up exercise. Warm-up number.................
2. Complete 4-minutes of Qi Gong exercise practice. Exercise number ....
3. Read your daily wisdom
4. Read a knowledge theory paragraph.
5. Write your affirmations.
6. Notes. Reflection and experience of your daily practice.

Wisdom. *Bravado may stir the crowd, but courage needs no audience.*

Positive Affirmations.
Write in 'present tense' positive statements, use one emotion, add a goal, keep it brief and simple. Do not use 'doing' words.

I can.. I have..
I am.. I let go of ....
Today I am grateful for..
....

Practice reflection notes.

DAILY PRACTICE & JOURNALING

6-minute morning practice is key to feel free and feel Qi

Date................................

1. Complete a 1-minute warm-up exercise. Warm-up number.................

2. Complete 4-minutes of Qi Gong exercise practice. Exercise number ....

3. Read your daily wisdom

4. Read a knowledge theory paragraph.

5. Write your affirmations.

6. Notes. Reflection and experience of your daily practice.

Wisdom. *Simplicity, patience, compassion. These are your greatest treasures. Laozi.*

Positive Affirmations.

Write in 'present tense' positive statements, use one emotion, add a goal, keep it brief and simple. Do not use 'doing' words.

I can.. I have...

I am.. I let go of ....
Today I am grateful for...
....

Practice reflection notes.

DAILY PRACTICE & JOURNALING

6-minute morning practice is key to feel free and feel Qi

Date................................

1. Complete a 1-minute warm-up exercise. Warm-up number.................

2. Complete 4-minutes of Qi Gong exercise practice. Exercise number ....

3. Read your daily wisdom

4. Read a knowledge theory paragraph.

5. Write your affirmations.

6. Notes. Reflection and experience of your daily practice.

Wisdom. *Do not fear failure; it is the key to success. Each mistake teaches us something invaluable. Morihei Ueshiba.*

Positive Affirmations.

Write in 'present tense' positive statements, use one emotion, add a goal, keep it brief and simple. Do not use 'doing' words.

I can.. I have...
I am.. I let go of ....
Today I am grateful for...
....

Practice reflection notes.

DAILY PRACTICE & JOURNALING

6-minute morning practice is key to feel free and feel Qi

Date.................................

1. Complete a 1-minute warm-up exercise. Warm-up number.................

2. Complete 4-minutes of Qi Gong exercise practice. Exercise number ....

3. Read your daily wisdom

4. Read a knowledge theory paragraph.

5. Write your affirmations.

6. Notes. Reflection and experience of your daily practice.

Wisdom. *If you don't know what your passion is, realize that one reason for your existence on earth is to find it. Oprah Winfrey.*

Positive Affirmations.

Write in 'present tense' positive statements, use one emotion, add a goal, keep it brief and simple. Do not use 'doing' words.

I can... I have...

I am... I let go of ....

Today I am grateful for...

....

Practice reflection notes.

DAILY PRACTICE & JOURNALING

6-minute morning practice is key to feel free and feel Qi

Date.................................

1. Complete a 1-minute warm-up exercise. Warm-up number.................

2. Complete 4-minutes of Qi Gong exercise practice. Exercise number ....

3. Read your daily wisdom

4. Read a knowledge theory paragraph.

5. Write your affirmations.

6. Notes. Reflection and experience of your daily practice.

Wisdom. *Never be limited by other people's limitations. Mae Jemison.*

Positive Affirmations.

Write in 'present tense' positive statements, use one emotion, add a goal, keep it brief and simple. Do not use 'doing' words.

I can... I have...

I am... I let go of ....

Today I am grateful for...

....

Practice reflection notes.

DAILY PRACTICE & JOURNALING
6-minute morning practice is key to feel free and feel Qi
Date.................................
1. Complete a 1-minute warm-up exercise. Warm-up number..................
2. Complete 4-minutes of Qi Gong exercise practice. Exercise number ....
3. Read your daily wisdom
4. Read a knowledge theory paragraph.
5. Write your affirmations.
6. Notes. Reflection and experience of your daily practice.

Wisdom. *The path from dreams to success does exist. May you have the vision to find it, the courage to get on it, and the perseverance to follow it. Kalpana*

Positive Affirmations.
Write in 'present tense' positive statements, use one emotion, add a goal, keep it brief and simple. Do not use 'doing' words.

I can.. I have..

I am.. I let go of ....
Today I am grateful for..
....

Practice reflection notes.

DAILY PRACTICE & JOURNALING
6-minute morning practice is key to feel free and feel Qi
Date.................................
1. Complete a 1-minute warm-up exercise. Warm-up number..................
2. Complete 4-minutes of Qi Gong exercise practice. Exercise number ....
3. Read your daily wisdom
4. Read a knowledge theory paragraph.
5. Write your affirmations.
6. Notes. Reflection and experience of your daily practice.

Wisdom. *To bring about change, you must not be afraid to take the first step. We fail when we fail to try. Rosa Parks*

Positive Affirmations.
Write in 'present tense' positive statements, use one emotion, add a goal, keep it brief and simple. Do not use 'doing' words.

I can.. I have..
I am.. I let go of ....
Today I am grateful for..
....

Practice reflection notes.

DAILY PRACTICE & JOURNALING
6-minute morning practice is key to feel free and feel Qi
Date................................
1. Complete a 1-minute warm-up exercise. Warm-up number..................
2. Complete 4-minutes of Qi Gong exercise practice. Exercise number ....
3. Read your daily wisdom
4. Read a knowledge theory paragraph.
5. Write your affirmations.
6. Notes. Reflection and experience of your daily practice.

Wisdom. *Happiness does not depend on what you have or who you are. It solely relies on what you think and feel. Buddha.*

Positive Affirmations.
Write in 'present tense' positive statements, use one emotion, add a goal, keep it brief and simple. Do not use 'doing' words.

I can.. I have..

I am.. I let go of ....
Today I am grateful for..
....

Practice reflection notes.

DAILY PRACTICE & JOURNALING
6-minute morning practice is key to feel free and feel Qi
Date................................
1. Complete a 1-minute warm-up exercise. Warm-up number..................
2. Complete 4-minutes of Qi Gong exercise practice. Exercise number ....
3. Read your daily wisdom
4. Read a knowledge theory paragraph.
5. Write your affirmations.
6. Notes. Reflection and experience of your daily practice.

Wisdom. *Love is not persuasion; it's all appreciation—Chinese proverb.*

Positive Affirmations.
Write in 'present tense' positive statements, use one emotion, add a goal, keep it brief and simple. Do not use 'doing' words.

I can.. I have..
I am.. I let go of ....
Today I am grateful for..
....

Practice reflection notes.

DAILY PRACTICE & JOURNALING
6-minute morning practice is key to feel free and feel Qi
Date.................................
1. Complete a 1-minute warm-up exercise. Warm-up number.................
2. Complete 4-minutes of Qi Gong exercise practice. Exercise number ....
3. Read your daily wisdom
4. Read a knowledge theory paragraph.
5. Write your affirmations.
6. Notes. Reflection and experience of your daily practice.

Wisdom. *No problem can be solved by the same level of consciousness that created it. A, Einstein.*

Positive Affirmations.
Write in 'present tense' positive statements, use one emotion, add a goal, keep it brief and simple. Do not use 'doing' words.

I can... I have...

I am... I let go of ....
Today I am grateful for..
....

Practice reflection notes.

DAILY PRACTICE & JOURNALING
6-minute morning practice is key to feel free and feel Qi
Date.................................
1. Complete a 1-minute warm-up exercise. Warm-up number.................
2. Complete 4-minutes of Qi Gong exercise practice. Exercise number ....
3. Read your daily wisdom
4. Read a knowledge theory paragraph.
5. Write your affirmations.
6. Notes. Reflection and experience of your daily practice.

Wisdom. *Yin Yang. The light yearns for the peaceful balance of the darkness as much as darkness seeks the glory of the light. Solange Nicole*

Positive Affirmations.
Write in 'present tense' positive statements, use one emotion, add a goal, keep it brief and simple. Do not use 'doing' words.

I can... I have...
I am... I let go of ....
Today I am grateful for..
....

Practice reflection notes.
:

DAILY PRACTICE & JOURNALING
6-minute morning practice is key to feel free and feel Qi
Date.................................
1. Complete a 1-minute warm-up exercise. Warm-up number..................
2. Complete 4-minutes of Qi Gong exercise practice. Exercise number ....
3. Read your daily wisdom
4. Read a knowledge theory paragraph.
5. Write your affirmations.
6. Notes. Reflection and experience of your daily practice.

Wisdom. *I do not fix the problems; I fix my thinking. Then the problems fix themselves. Louise Hay.*

Positive Affirmations.
Write in 'present tense' positive statements, use one emotion, add a goal, keep it brief and simple. Do not use 'doing' words.

I can.. I have...

I am.. I let go of ....
Today I am grateful for...
....

Practice reflection notes.

DAILY PRACTICE & JOURNALING
6-minute morning practice is key to feel free and feel Qi
Date.................................
1. Complete a 1-minute warm-up exercise. Warm-up number..................
2. Complete 4-minutes of Qi Gong exercise practice. Exercise number ....
3. Read your daily wisdom
4. Read a knowledge theory paragraph.
5. Write your affirmations.
6. Notes. Reflection and experience of your daily practice.

Wisdom. *At any moment, you have a choice that either leads you closer to your spirit or further away from it. Thich V Hanh.*

Positive Affirmations.
Write in 'present tense' positive statements, use one emotion, add a goal, keep it brief and simple. Do not use 'doing' words.

I can.. I have..
I am.. I let go of ....
Today I am grateful for...
....

Practice reflection notes.

DAILY PRACTICE & JOURNALING
6-minute morning practice is key to feel free and feel Qi
Date.................................
1. Complete a 1-minute warm-up exercise. Warm-up number..................
2. Complete 4-minutes of Qi Gong exercise practice. Exercise number ....
3. Read your daily wisdom
4. Read a knowledge theory paragraph.
5. Write your affirmations.
6. Notes. Reflection and experience of your daily practice.

Wisdom. *The clearer I become about what I want, the more real what I want becomes.*

Positive Affirmations.
Write in 'present tense' positive statements, use one emotion, add a goal, keep it brief and simple. Do not use 'doing' words.

I can.. I have...

I am.. I let go of ....
Today I am grateful for..
....

Practice reflection notes.

DAILY PRACTICE & JOURNALING
6-minute morning practice is key to feel free and feel Qi
Date.................................
1. Complete a 1-minute warm-up exercise. Warm-up number..................
2. Complete 4-minutes of Qi Gong exercise practice. Exercise number ....
3. Read your daily wisdom
4. Read a knowledge theory paragraph.
5. Write your affirmations.
6. Notes. Reflection and experience of your daily practice.

Wisdom. *Fear leads to anger; anger leads to hate; hate leads to suffering. Be aware of characters who manipulative, deflect and project fear upon you. Their aim is to gain power by making you suffer.*

Positive Affirmations.
Write in 'present tense' positive statements, use one emotion, add a goal, keep it brief and simple. Do not use 'doing' words.

I can.. I have...
I am.. I let go of ....
Today I am grateful for..
....

Practice reflection notes.

DAILY PRACTICE & JOURNALING
6-minute morning practice is key to feel free and feel Qi
Date..................................
1. Complete a 1-minute warm-up exercise. Warm-up number..................
2. Complete 4-minutes of Qi Gong exercise practice. Exercise number ....
3. Read your daily wisdom
4. Read a knowledge theory paragraph.
5. Write your affirmations.
6. Notes. Reflection and experience of your daily practice.

Wisdom. *There is ceaseless charm to be found in the home of Mother Nature. As she dusts with snow, even cobwebs sparkle in her magic. Angie Crosby.*

Positive Affirmations.
Write in 'present tense' positive statements, use one emotion, add a goal, keep it brief and simple. Do not use 'doing' words.

I can.. I have...

I am... I let go of ....
Today I am grateful for...
....

Practice reflection notes.

DAILY PRACTICE & JOURNALING
6-minute morning practice is key to feel free and feel Qi
Date..................................
1. Complete a 1-minute warm-up exercise. Warm-up number..................
2. Complete 4-minutes of Qi Gong exercise practice. Exercise number ....
3. Read your daily wisdom
4. Read a knowledge theory paragraph.
5. Write your affirmations.
6. Notes. Reflection and experience of your daily practice.

Wisdom. *Your imagination is your preview of life's coming attractions. Albert Einstein*

Positive Affirmations.
Write in 'present tense' positive statements, use one emotion, add a goal, keep it brief and simple. Do not use 'doing' words.

I can.. I have...
I am... I let go of ....
Today I am grateful for...
....

Practice reflection notes.

DAILY PRACTICE & JOURNALING
6-minute morning practice is key to feel free and feel Qi
Date.................................
1. Complete a 1-minute warm-up exercise. Warm-up number.................
2. Complete 4-minutes of Qi Gong exercise practice. Exercise number ....
3. Read your daily wisdom
4. Read a knowledge theory paragraph.
5. Write your affirmations.
6. Notes. Reflection and experience of your daily practice.

Wisdom. *It is never too late to be what you might have been. George Elliot*

Positive Affirmations.
Write in 'present tense' positive statements, use one emotion, add a goal, keep it brief and simple. Do not use 'doing' words.

I can... I have...

I am... I let go of ....
Today I am grateful for...
....

Practice reflection notes.

DAILY PRACTICE & JOURNALING
6-minute morning practice is key to feel free and feel Qi
Date.................................
1. Complete a 1-minute warm-up exercise. Warm-up number.................
2. Complete 4-minutes of Qi Gong exercise practice. Exercise number ....
3. Read your daily wisdom
4. Read a knowledge theory paragraph.
5. Write your affirmations.
6. Notes. Reflection and experience of your daily practice.

Wisdom. *When thinking about life, remember this, no amount of guilt can change the past, and no amount of anxiety can change the future.*

Positive Affirmations.
Write in 'present tense' positive statements, use one emotion, add a goal, keep it brief and simple. Do not use 'doing' words.

I can... I have...
I am... I let go of ....
Today I am grateful for...
....

Practice reflection notes.

DAILY PRACTICE & JOURNALING
6-minute morning practice is key to feel free and feel Qi
Date.................................
1. Complete a 1-minute warm-up exercise. Warm-up number.................
2. Complete 4-minutes of Qi Gong exercise practice. Exercise number ....
3. Read your daily wisdom
4. Read a knowledge theory paragraph.
5. Write your affirmations.
6. Notes. Reflection and experience of your daily practice.

Wisdom. *Sometimes the wrong choices lead us unexpectedly to the right places.*

Positive Affirmations.
Write in 'present tense' positive statements, use one emotion, add a goal, keep it brief and simple. Do not use 'doing' words.

I can.. I have..

I am.. I let go of ....
Today I am grateful for...
....

Practice reflection notes.

DAILY PRACTICE & JOURNALING
6-minute morning practice is key to feel free and feel Qi
Date.................................
1. Complete a 1-minute warm-up exercise. Warm-up number.................
2. Complete 4-minutes of Qi Gong exercise practice. Exercise number ....
3. Read your daily wisdom
4. Read a knowledge theory paragraph.
5. Write your affirmations.
6. Notes. Reflection and experience of your daily practice.

Wisdom. *Thinking is difficult; that's why most people judge.*

Positive Affirmations.
Write in 'present tense' positive statements, use one emotion, add a goal, keep it brief and simple. Do not use 'doing' words.

I can.. I have..
I am.. I let go of ....
Today I am grateful for...
....

Practice reflection notes.

DAILY PRACTICE & JOURNALING

6-minute morning practice is key to feel free and feel Qi

Date.................................

1. Complete a 1-minute warm-up exercise. Warm-up number.................

2. Complete 4-minutes of Qi Gong exercise practice. Exercise number ....

3. Read your daily wisdom

4. Read a knowledge theory paragraph.

5. Write your affirmations.

6. Notes. Reflection and experience of your daily practice.

Wisdom. *When you plant a seed of love, it is you that blossoms. Ma Jaya Sati Bhagavati.*

Positive Affirmations.

Write in 'present tense' positive statements, use one emotion, add a goal, keep it brief and simple. Do not use 'doing' words.

I can.. I have..

I am.. I let go of ....

Today I am grateful for..

....

Practice reflection notes.

DAILY PRACTICE & JOURNALING

6-minute morning practice is key to feel free and feel Qi

Date.................................

1. Complete a 1-minute warm-up exercise. Warm-up number.................

2. Complete 4-minutes of Qi Gong exercise practice. Exercise number ....

3. Read your daily wisdom

4. Read a knowledge theory paragraph.

5. Write your affirmations.

6. Notes. Reflection and experience of your daily practice.

Wisdom. *You are the sky; everything else is the weather. Pema Chodron.*

Positive Affirmations.

Write in 'present tense' positive statements, use one emotion, add a goal, keep it brief and simple. Do not use 'doing' words.

I can.. I have..

I am.. I let go of ....

Today I am grateful for..

....

Practice reflection notes.

DAILY PRACTICE & JOURNALING
6-minute morning practice is key to feel free and feel Qi
Date..................................
1. Complete a 1-minute warm-up exercise. Warm-up number..................
2. Complete 4-minutes of Qi Gong exercise practice. Exercise number ....
3. Read your daily wisdom
4. Read a knowledge theory paragraph.
5. Write your affirmations.
6. Notes. Reflection and experience of your daily practice.

Wisdom. *In a controversy, the instant we feel anger, we have already ceased striving for the truth and have begun striving for only ourselves. Buddha.*

Positive Affirmations.
Write in 'present tense' positive statements, use one emotion, add a goal, keep it brief and simple. Do not use 'doing' words.

I can... I have..

I am.. I let go of ....
Today I am grateful for...
....

Practice reflection notes.

DAILY PRACTICE & JOURNALING
6-minute morning practice is key to feel free and feel Qi
Date..................................
1. Complete a 1-minute warm-up exercise. Warm-up number..................
2. Complete 4-minutes of Qi Gong exercise practice. Exercise number ....
3. Read your daily wisdom
4. Read a knowledge theory paragraph.
5. Write your affirmations.
6. Notes. Reflection and experience of your daily practice.

Wisdom. *Science is not only compatible with spirituality; it is a profound source of spirituality. Carl Sagan.*

Positive Affirmations.
Write in 'present tense' positive statements, use one emotion, add a goal, keep it brief and simple. Do not use 'doing' words.

I can... I have..
I am.. I let go of ....
Today I am grateful for...
....

Practice reflection notes.

DAILY PRACTICE & JOURNALING

6-minute morning practice is key to feel free and feel Qi

Date.................................

1. Complete a 1-minute warm-up exercise. Warm-up number.................

2. Complete 4-minutes of Qi Gong exercise practice. Exercise number ....

3. Read your daily wisdom

4. Read a knowledge theory paragraph.

5. Write your affirmations.

6. Notes. Reflection and experience of your daily practice.

Wisdom. *Use your smile to change the world; don't let the world change your smile.*

Positive Affirmations.

Write in 'present tense' positive statements, use one emotion, add a goal, keep it brief and simple. Do not use 'doing' words.

I can.. I have..

I am...................................... I let go of ....
Today I am grateful for..
....

Practice reflection notes.

DAILY PRACTICE & JOURNALING

6-minute morning practice is key to feel free and feel Qi

Date.................................

1. Complete a 1-minute warm-up exercise. Warm-up number.................

2. Complete 4-minutes of Qi Gong exercise practice. Exercise number ....

3. Read your daily wisdom

4. Read a knowledge theory paragraph.

5. Write your affirmations.

6. Notes. Reflection and experience of your daily practice.

Wisdom. *True strength is not how much you can lift. It is what you can let go of. Ralph Mat.*

Positive Affirmations.

Write in 'present tense' positive statements, use one emotion, add a goal, keep it brief and simple. Do not use 'doing' words.

I can.. I have...
I am...................................... I let go of ....
Today I am grateful for..
....

Practice reflection notes.

259

DAILY PRACTICE & JOURNALING
6-minute morning practice is key to feel free and feel Qi
Date.................................
1. Complete a 1-minute warm-up exercise. Warm-up number.................
2. Complete 4-minutes of Qi Gong exercise practice. Exercise number ....
3. Read your daily wisdom
4. Read a knowledge theory paragraph.
5. Write your affirmations.
6. Notes. Reflection and experience of your daily practice.

Wisdom. *You get in life what you have the courage to ask for.*

Positive Affirmations.
Write in 'present tense' positive statements, use one emotion, add a goal, keep it brief and simple. Do not use 'doing' words.

I can.. I have...

I am.. I let go of ....
Today I am grateful for..
....

Practice reflection notes.

DAILY PRACTICE & JOURNALING
6-minute morning practice is key to feel free and feel Qi
Date.................................
1. Complete a 1-minute warm-up exercise. Warm-up number.................
2. Complete 4-minutes of Qi Gong exercise practice. Exercise number ....
3. Read your daily wisdom
4. Read a knowledge theory paragraph.
5. Write your affirmations.
6. Notes. Reflection and experience of your daily practice.

Wisdom. *Nothing can dim the light that shines within. Maya Angelou.*

Positive Affirmations.
Write in 'present tense' positive statements, use one emotion, add a goal, keep it brief and simple. Do not use 'doing' words.

I can.. I have...
I am.. I let go of ....
Today I am grateful for..
....

Practice reflection notes.

DAILY PRACTICE & JOURNALING
6-minute morning practice is key to feel free and feel Qi
Date.................................
1. Complete a 1-minute warm-up exercise. Warm-up number..................
2. Complete 4-minutes of Qi Gong exercise practice. Exercise number ....
3. Read your daily wisdom
4. Read a knowledge theory paragraph.
5. Write your affirmations.
6. Notes. Reflection and experience of your daily practice.

Wisdom. *What you can't say owns you. What you hide controls you.*

Positive Affirmations.
Write in 'present tense' positive statements, use one emotion, add a goal, keep it brief and simple. Do not use 'doing' words.

I can.. I have..

I am.. I let go of ....
Today I am grateful for..
....

Practice reflection notes.

DAILY PRACTICE & JOURNALING
6-minute morning practice is key to feel free and feel Qi
Date.................................
1. Complete a 1-minute warm-up exercise. Warm-up number..................
2. Complete 4-minutes of Qi Gong exercise practice. Exercise number ....
3. Read your daily wisdom
4. Read a knowledge theory paragraph.
5. Write your affirmations.
6. Notes. Reflection and experience of your daily practice.

Wisdom. *The simple things are the ones that make us the happiest—Gal Ga dot.*

Positive Affirmations.
Write in 'present tense' positive statements, use one emotion, add a goal, keep it brief and simple. Do not use 'doing' words.

I can.. I have..
I am.. I let go of ....
Today I am grateful for..
....

Practice reflection notes.

DAILY PRACTICE & JOURNALING
6-minute morning practice is key to feel free and feel Qi
Date..................................
1. Complete a 1-minute warm-up exercise. Warm-up number..................
2. Complete 4-minutes of Qi Gong exercise practice. Exercise number ....
3. Read your daily wisdom
4. Read a knowledge theory paragraph.
5. Write your affirmations.
6. Notes. Reflection and experience of your daily practice.

Wisdom. *True humanity is not thinking less of yourself; it is thinking of yourself less. C.S.Lewis.*

Positive Affirmations.
Write in 'present tense' positive statements, use one emotion, add a goal, keep it brief and simple. Do not use 'doing' words.

I can.. I have...

I am.. I let go of ....
Today I am grateful for..
....

Practice reflection notes.

DAILY PRACTICE & JOURNALING
6-minute morning practice is key to feel free and feel Qi
Date..................................
1. Complete a 1-minute warm-up exercise. Warm-up number..................
2. Complete 4-minutes of Qi Gong exercise practice. Exercise number ....
3. Read your daily wisdom
4. Read a knowledge theory paragraph.
5. Write your affirmations.
6. Notes. Reflection and experience of your daily practice.

Wisdom. *New opportunities tend to come knocking on your door when we appreciate other people's contributions.*

Positive Affirmations.
Write in 'present tense' positive statements, use one emotion, add a goal, keep it brief and simple. Do not use 'doing' words.

I can.. I have...
I am.. I let go of ....
Today I am grateful for..
....

Practice reflection notes.

DAILY PRACTICE & JOURNALING

6-minute morning practice is key to feel free and feel Qi

Date.................................

1. Complete a 1-minute warm-up exercise. Warm-up number.................

2. Complete 4-minutes of Qi Gong exercise practice. Exercise number ....

3. Read your daily wisdom

4. Read a knowledge theory paragraph.

5. Write your affirmations.

6. Notes. Reflection and experience of your daily practice.

Wisdom. *We are stardust brought to life, then empowered by the universe to figure itself out. We have only just begun. Neil D Tyson.*

Positive Affirmations.

Write in 'present tense' positive statements, use one emotion, add a goal, keep it brief and simple. Do not use 'doing' words.

I can... I have..

I am... I let go of ....
Today I am grateful for...
....

Practice reflection notes.

DAILY PRACTICE & JOURNALING

6-minute morning practice is key to feel free and feel Qi

Date.................................

1. Complete a 1-minute warm-up exercise. Warm-up number.................

2. Complete 4-minutes of Qi Gong exercise practice. Exercise number ....

3. Read your daily wisdom

4. Read a knowledge theory paragraph.

5. Write your affirmations.

6. Notes. Reflection and experience of your daily practice.

Wisdom. *Remember, even if you don't feel creative, only you are the creator of your destiny, so be creative and be active.*

Positive Affirmations.

Write in 'present tense' positive statements, use one emotion, add a goal, keep it brief and simple. Do not use 'doing' words.

I can... I have..
I am... I let go of ....
Today I am grateful for...
....

Practice reflection notes.

DAILY PRACTICE & JOURNALING
6-minute morning practice is key to feel free and feel Qi
Date..................................
1. Complete a 1-minute warm-up exercise. Warm-up number..................
2. Complete 4-minutes of Qi Gong exercise practice. Exercise number ....
3. Read your daily wisdom
4. Read a knowledge theory paragraph.
5. Write your affirmations.
6. Notes. Reflection and experience of your daily practice.

Wisdom. *Your time is limited, so don't waste it living someone else's life.*

Positive Affirmations.
Write in 'present tense' positive statements, use one emotion, add a goal, keep it brief and simple. Do not use 'doing' words.

I can.. I have..

I am.. I let go of ....
Today I am grateful for...
....

Practice reflection notes.

DAILY PRACTICE & JOURNALING
6-minute morning practice is key to feel free and feel Qi
Date..................................
1. Complete a 1-minute warm-up exercise. Warm-up number..................
2. Complete 4-minutes of Qi Gong exercise practice. Exercise number ....
3. Read your daily wisdom
4. Read a knowledge theory paragraph.
5. Write your affirmations.
6. Notes. Reflection and experience of your daily practice.

Wisdom. *The comeback is always stronger than the setback.*

Positive Affirmations.
Write in 'present tense' positive statements, use one emotion, add a goal, keep it brief and simple. Do not use 'doing' words.

I can.. I have..
I am.. I let go of ....
Today I am grateful for...
....

Practice reflection notes.

264

DAILY PRACTICE & JOURNALING

6-minute morning practice is key to feel free and feel Qi

Date.................................

1. Complete a 1-minute warm-up exercise. Warm-up number.................
2. Complete 4-minutes of Qi Gong exercise practice. Exercise number ....
3. Read your daily wisdom
4. Read a knowledge theory paragraph.
5. Write your affirmations.
6. Notes. Reflection and experience of your daily practice.

Wisdom. *The most common way people give up their power is by thinking they don't have any. Alice Walker.*

Positive Affirmations.

Write in 'present tense' positive statements, use one emotion, add a goal, keep it brief and simple. Do not use 'doing' words.

I can.. I have..

I am.................................... I let go of ....
Today I am grateful for..
....

Practice reflection notes.

DAILY PRACTICE & JOURNALING

6-minute morning practice is key to feel free and feel Qi

Date.................................

1. Complete a 1-minute warm-up exercise. Warm-up number.................
2. Complete 4-minutes of Qi Gong exercise practice. Exercise number ....
3. Read your daily wisdom
4. Read a knowledge theory paragraph.
5. Write your affirmations.
6. Notes. Reflection and experience of your daily practice.

Wisdom. *Life is like a camera. Just focus on what's important. Capture the good times, develop from the negatives and if things don't turn out right, take another shot.*

Positive Affirmations.

Write in 'present tense' positive statements, use one emotion, add a goal, keep it brief and simple. Do not use 'doing' words.

I can.. I have..
I am.................................... I let go of ....
Today I am grateful for..
....

Practice reflection notes.

DAILY PRACTICE & JOURNALING
6-minute morning practice is key to feel free and feel Qi
Date..................................
1. Complete a 1-minute warm-up exercise. Warm-up number..................
2. Complete 4-minutes of Qi Gong exercise practice. Exercise number ....
3. Read your daily wisdom
4. Read a knowledge theory paragraph.
5. Write your affirmations.
6. Notes. Reflection and experience of your daily practice.

Wisdom. *Try not to let the shadows of your past darken the doorstep of your future.*

Positive Affirmations.
Write in 'present tense' positive statements, use one emotion, add a goal, keep it brief and simple. Do not use 'doing' words.

I can.. I have...

I am.. I let go of ....
Today I am grateful for..
....

Practice reflection notes.

DAILY PRACTICE & JOURNALING
6-minute morning practice is key to feel free and feel Qi
Date..................................
1. Complete a 1-minute warm-up exercise. Warm-up number..................
2. Complete 4-minutes of Qi Gong exercise practice. Exercise number ....
3. Read your daily wisdom
4. Read a knowledge theory paragraph.
5. Write your affirmations.
6. Notes. Reflection and experience of your daily practice.

Wisdom. *Keep peace in the mind, strength in the body, and love in the heart.*

Positive Affirmations.
Write in 'present tense' positive statements, use one emotion, add a goal, keep it brief and simple. Do not use 'doing' words.

I can.. I have...
I am.. I let go of ....
Today I am grateful for..
....

Practice reflection notes.

DAILY PRACTICE & JOURNALING
6-minute morning practice is key to feel free and feel Qi
Date.................................
1. Complete a 1-minute warm-up exercise. Warm-up number.................
2. Complete 4-minutes of Qi Gong exercise practice. Exercise number ....
3. Read your daily wisdom
4. Read a knowledge theory paragraph.
5. Write your affirmations.
6. Notes. Reflection and experience of your daily practice.

Wisdom. *If you survive a storm, you will not be bothered by the rain—Chinese proverb.*

Positive Affirmations.
Write in 'present tense' positive statements, use one emotion, add a goal, keep it brief and simple. Do not use 'doing' words.

I can... I have...

I am... I let go of ....
Today I am grateful for...
....

Practice reflection notes.

DAILY PRACTICE & JOURNALING
6-minute morning practice is key to feel free and feel Qi
Date.................................
1. Complete a 1-minute warm-up exercise. Warm-up number.................
2. Complete 4-minutes of Qi Gong exercise practice. Exercise number ....
3. Read your daily wisdom
4. Read a knowledge theory paragraph.
5. Write your affirmations.
6. Notes. Reflection and experience of your daily practice.

Wisdom. *A wise person makes their own decisions; an ignorant man follows public opinion—Chinese proverb.*

Positive Affirmations.
Write in 'present tense' positive statements, use one emotion, add a goal, keep it brief and simple. Do not use 'doing' words.

I can... I have...
I am... I let go of ....
Today I am grateful for...
....

Practice reflection notes.

DAILY PRACTICE & JOURNALING
6-minute morning practice is key to feel free and feel Qi
Date..................................
1. Complete a 1-minute warm-up exercise. Warm-up number..................
2. Complete 4-minutes of Qi Gong exercise practice. Exercise number ....
3. Read your daily wisdom
4. Read a knowledge theory paragraph.
5. Write your affirmations.
6. Notes. Reflection and experience of your daily practice.

Wisdom. *Happiness is the absence of striving for happiness in Chiang Tzu.*

Positive Affirmations.
Write in 'present tense' positive statements, use one emotion, add a goal, keep it brief and simple. Do not use 'doing' words.

I can... I have...

I am.. I let go of ....
Today I am grateful for..
....

Practice reflection notes.

DAILY PRACTICE & JOURNALING
6-minute morning practice is key to feel free and feel Qi
Date..................................
1. Complete a 1-minute warm-up exercise. Warm-up number..................
2. Complete 4-minutes of Qi Gong exercise practice. Exercise number ....
3. Read your daily wisdom
4. Read a knowledge theory paragraph.
5. Write your affirmations.
6. Notes. Reflection and experience of your daily practice.

Wisdom. *We don't meet people by accident; they are meant to cross our path for a reason. Look for the lessons.*

Positive Affirmations.
Write in 'present tense' positive statements, use one emotion, add a goal, keep it brief and simple. Do not use 'doing' words.

I can... I have...
I am.. I let go of ....
Today I am grateful for..
....

Practice reflection notes.

DAILY PRACTICE & JOURNALING
6-minute morning practice is key to feel free and feel Qi
Date.................................
1. Complete a 1-minute warm-up exercise. Warm-up number.................
2. Complete 4-minutes of Qi Gong exercise practice. Exercise number ....
3. Read your daily wisdom
4. Read a knowledge theory paragraph.
5. Write your affirmations.
6. Notes. Reflection and experience of your daily practice.

Wisdom. *Don't follow the crowd if you know in your heart it's the wrong thing to do. Be strong, be silent, be true, be free, be you. Jenna Robins.*

Positive Affirmations.
Write in 'present tense' positive statements, use one emotion, add a goal, keep it brief and simple. Do not use 'doing' words.

I can.. I have...

I am.. I let go of ....
Today I am grateful for..
....

Practice reflection notes.

DAILY PRACTICE & JOURNALING
6-minute morning practice is key to feel free and feel Qi
Date.................................
1. Complete a 1-minute warm-up exercise. Warm-up number.................
2. Complete 4-minutes of Qi Gong exercise practice. Exercise number ....
3. Read your daily wisdom
4. Read a knowledge theory paragraph.
5. Write your affirmations.
6. Notes. Reflection and experience of your daily practice.

Wisdom. *Life is a challenge; the challenge is to turn your wounds into wisdom. Jenna Robins.*

Positive Affirmations.
Write in 'present tense' positive statements, use one emotion, add a goal, keep it brief and simple. Do not use 'doing' words.

I can.. I have...
I am.. I let go of ....
Today I am grateful for..
....

Practice reflection notes.

DAILY PRACTICE & JOURNALING
6-minute morning practice is key to feel free and feel Qi
Date.................................
1. Complete a 1-minute warm-up exercise. Warm-up number..................
2. Complete 4-minutes of Qi Gong exercise practice. Exercise number ....
3. Read your daily wisdom
4. Read a knowledge theory paragraph.
5. Write your affirmations.
6. Notes. Reflection and experience of your daily practice.

Wisdom. *From infinity space through your practice, you can visualise the completion of your healing. Bring your healing to form and existence; this is healing and wisdom.*

Positive Affirmations.
Write in 'present tense' positive statements, use one emotion, add a goal, keep it brief and simple. Do not use 'doing' words.

I can.. I have...

I am.................................... I let go of ....
Today I am grateful for...
....

Practice reflection notes.

DAILY PRACTICE & JOURNALING
6-minute morning practice is key to feel free and feel Qi
Date.................................
1. Complete a 1-minute warm-up exercise. Warm-up number..................
2. Complete 4-minutes of Qi Gong exercise practice. Exercise number ....
3. Read your daily wisdom
4. Read a knowledge theory paragraph.
5. Write your affirmations.
6. Notes. Reflection and experience of your daily practice.

Wisdom. *The wise one knows that it is better to sit on the banks of a remote mountain stream than to be emperor of the whole world. Tzu.*

Positive Affirmations.
Write in 'present tense' positive statements, use one emotion, add a goal, keep it brief and simple. Do not use 'doing' words.

I can.. I have...
I am.................................... I let go of ....
Today I am grateful for...
....

Practice reflection notes.

DAILY PRACTICE & JOURNALING
6-minute morning practice is key to feel free and feel Qi

Date................................

1. Complete a 1-minute warm-up exercise. Warm-up number................
2. Complete 4-minutes of Qi Gong exercise practice. Exercise number ....
3. Read your daily wisdom
4. Read a knowledge theory paragraph.
5. Write your affirmations.
6. Notes. Reflection and experience of your daily practice.

Wisdom. *The more you can let go of the material, the more you will feel free.*

Positive Affirmations.
Write in 'present tense' positive statements, use one emotion, add a goal, keep it brief and simple. Do not use 'doing' words.

I can.. I have...

I am.. I let go of ....
Today I am grateful for..
....

Practice reflection notes.

DAILY PRACTICE & JOURNALING
6-minute morning practice is key to feel free and feel Qi

Date................................

1. Complete a 1-minute warm-up exercise. Warm-up number................
2. Complete 4-minutes of Qi Gong exercise practice. Exercise number ....
3. Read your daily wisdom
4. Read a knowledge theory paragraph.
5. Write your affirmations.
6. Notes. Reflection and experience of your daily practice.

Wisdom. *Remember, you can't reach what's in front of you until you let go of what's behind you.*

Positive Affirmations.
Write in 'present tense' positive statements, use one emotion, add a goal, keep it brief and simple. Do not use 'doing' words.

I can.. I have...
I am.. I let go of ....
Today I am grateful for..
....

Practice reflection notes.

271

DAILY PRACTICE & JOURNALING
6-minute morning practice is key to feel free and feel Qi
Date.................................
1. Complete a 1-minute warm-up exercise. Warm-up number.................
2. Complete 4-minutes of Qi Gong exercise practice. Exercise number ....
3. Read your daily wisdom
4. Read a knowledge theory paragraph.
5. Write your affirmations.
6. Notes. Reflection and experience of your daily practice.

Wisdom. *Try to be still like a mountain and flow like a great river. Lao Tse Tung.*

Positive Affirmations.
Write in 'present tense' positive statements, use one emotion, add a goal, keep it brief and simple. Do not use 'doing' words.

I can.. I have...

I am.. I let go of ....
Today I am grateful for...
....

Practice reflection notes.

DAILY PRACTICE & JOURNALING
6-minute morning practice is key to feel free and feel Qi
Date.................................
1. Complete a 1-minute warm-up exercise. Warm-up number.................
2. Complete 4-minutes of Qi Gong exercise practice. Exercise number ....
3. Read your daily wisdom
4. Read a knowledge theory paragraph.
5. Write your affirmations.
6. Notes. Reflection and experience of your daily practice.

Wisdom. *If the spirit is strong, one will appear like a deep-flowing river, calm on the surface but with tremendous power hidden in the depths. H Onuma.*

Positive Affirmations.
Write in 'present tense' positive statements, use one emotion, add a goal, keep it brief and simple. Do not use 'doing' words.

I can.. I have...
I am.. I let go of ....
Today I am grateful for...
....

Practice reflection notes.

DAILY PRACTICE & JOURNALING
6-minute morning practice is key to feel free and feel Qi
Date.................................
1. Complete a 1-minute warm-up exercise. Warm-up number.................
2. Complete 4-minutes of Qi Gong exercise practice. Exercise number ....
3. Read your daily wisdom
4. Read a knowledge theory paragraph.
5. Write your affirmations.
6. Notes. Reflection and experience of your daily practice.

Wisdom. *It's not who you are that holds you back; it's who you think you're not. Think about all that you are instead of all that you are not.*

Positive Affirmations.
Write in 'present tense' positive statements, use one emotion, add a goal, keep it brief and simple. Do not use 'doing' words.

I can.. I have...

I am.. I let go of ....
Today I am grateful for..
....

Practice reflection notes.

DAILY PRACTICE & JOURNALING
6-minute morning practice is key to feel free and feel Qi
Date.................................
1. Complete a 1-minute warm-up exercise. Warm-up number.................
2. Complete 4-minutes of Qi Gong exercise practice. Exercise number ....
3. Read your daily wisdom
4. Read a knowledge theory paragraph.
5. Write your affirmations.
6. Notes. Reflection and experience of your daily practice.

Wisdom. *Energy like you has no beginning and no end. It can never be destroyed; it is only ever shifting states. Panache Desai.*

Positive Affirmations.
Write in 'present tense' positive statements, use one emotion, add a goal, keep it brief and simple. Do not use 'doing' words.

I can.. I have...
I am.. I let go of ....
Today I am grateful for..
....

Practice reflection notes.

DAILY PRACTICE & JOURNALING
6-minute morning practice is key to feel free and feel Qi
Date..................................
1. Complete a 1-minute warm-up exercise. Warm-up number..................
2. Complete 4-minutes of Qi Gong exercise practice. Exercise number ....
3. Read your daily wisdom
4. Read a knowledge theory paragraph.
5. Write your affirmations.
6. Notes. Reflection and experience of your daily practice.

Wisdom. *You may be feeling emotional pain because you are about to transform.*

Positive Affirmations.
Write in 'present tense' positive statements, use one emotion, add a goal, keep it brief and simple. Do not use 'doing' words.

I can.. I have..

I am.. I let go of ....
Today I am grateful for...
....

Practice reflection notes.

DAILY PRACTICE & JOURNALING
6-minute morning practice is key to feel free and feel Qi
Date..................................
1. Complete a 1-minute warm-up exercise. Warm-up number..................
2. Complete 4-minutes of Qi Gong exercise practice. Exercise number ....
3. Read your daily wisdom
4. Read a knowledge theory paragraph.
5. Write your affirmations.
6. Notes. Reflection and experience of your daily practice.

Wisdom. *Write in 'present tense' positive statements, use one emotion, add a goal, keep it brief and simple. Do not use 'doing' words*

Positive Affirmations.
Write in 'present tense' positive statements, use one emotion, add a goal, keep it brief and simple. Do not use 'doing' words.

I can.. I have..
I am.. I let go of ....
Today I am grateful for...
....

Practice reflection notes.

DAILY PRACTICE & JOURNALING
6-minute morning practice is key to feel free and feel Qi
Date.................................
1. Complete a 1-minute warm-up exercise. Warm-up number.................
2. Complete 4-minutes of Qi Gong exercise practice. Exercise number ....
3. Read your daily wisdom
4. Read a knowledge theory paragraph.
5. Write your affirmations.
6. Notes. Reflection and experience of your daily practice.

Wisdom. *In the modern world, people are materially rich but spiritually poor. It is pointless to have a large home when having little space in hearts and minds. Qi revolution*

Positive Affirmations.
Write in 'present tense' positive statements, use one emotion, add a goal, keep it brief and simple. Do not use 'doing' words.

I can.. I have...

I am.. I let go of ....
Today I am grateful for..
....

Practice reflection notes.

DAILY PRACTICE & JOURNALING
6-minute morning practice is key to feel free and feel Qi
Date.................................
1. Complete a 1-minute warm-up exercise. Warm-up number.................
2. Complete 4-minutes of Qi Gong exercise practice. Exercise number ....
3. Read your daily wisdom
4. Read a knowledge theory paragraph.
5. Write your affirmations.
6. Notes. Reflection and experience of your daily practice.

Wisdom. *It can be said that whatever energies you experience, you will sooner or later also experience their opposites. Master B Frantzis.*

Positive Affirmations.
Write in 'present tense' positive statements, use one emotion, add a goal, keep it brief and simple. Do not use 'doing' words.

I can.. I have...
I am.. I let go of ....
Today I am grateful for..
....

Practice reflection notes.

DAILY PRACTICE & JOURNALING
6-minute morning practice is key to feel free and feel Qi
Date..................................
1. Complete a 1-minute warm-up exercise. Warm-up number.................
2. Complete 4-minutes of Qi Gong exercise practice. Exercise number ....
3. Read your daily wisdom
4. Read a knowledge theory paragraph.
5. Write your affirmations.
6. Notes. Reflection and experience of your daily practice.

Wisdom. *The heart is like a garden. It can grow compassion or fear, resentment, or love. What seeds will you plant there? Buddha.*

Positive Affirmations.
Write in 'present tense' positive statements, use one emotion, add a goal, keep it brief and simple. Do not use 'doing' words.

I can.. I have..

I am.. I let go of ....
Today I am grateful for..
....

Practice reflection notes.

DAILY PRACTICE & JOURNALING
6-minute morning practice is key to feel free and feel Qi
Date..................................
1. Complete a 1-minute warm-up exercise. Warm-up number.................
2. Complete 4-minutes of Qi Gong exercise practice. Exercise number ....
3. Read your daily wisdom
4. Read a knowledge theory paragraph.
5. Write your affirmations.
6. Notes. Reflection and experience of your daily practice.

Wisdom. *It took a hundred times to remember the moves, a thousand times to make them beautiful, and ten thousand times to grasp essence. Tao.*

Positive Affirmations.
Write in 'present tense' positive statements, use one emotion, add a goal, keep it brief and simple. Do not use 'doing' words.

I can.. I have..
I am.. I let go of ....
Today I am grateful for..
....

Practice reflection notes.

DAILY PRACTICE & JOURNALING

6-minute morning practice is key to feel free and feel Qi

Date.................................

1. Complete a 1-minute warm-up exercise. Warm-up number.................
2. Complete 4-minutes of Qi Gong exercise practice. Exercise number ....
3. Read your daily wisdom
4. Read a knowledge theory paragraph.
5. Write your affirmations.
6. Notes. Reflection and experience of your daily practice.

Wisdom. *When the pools of perception are clear, everything appears as it is. Zen Proverb.*

Positive Affirmations.

Write in 'present tense' positive statements, use one emotion, add a goal, keep it brief and simple. Do not use 'doing' words.

I can... I have...

I am.. I let go of ....
Today I am grateful for...
....

Practice reflection notes.

DAILY PRACTICE.

6-minute morning practice is key to feel free and feel Qi

Date.................................

1. Complete a 1-minute warm-up exercise. Warm-up number.................
2. Complete 4-minutes of Qi Gong exercise practice. Exercise number ....
3. Read your daily wisdom
4. Read a knowledge theory paragraph.
5. Write your affirmations.
6. Notes. Reflection and experience of your daily practice.

Wisdom. *If people are doubting how far you can climb, climb so far that you can't hear them anymore.*

Positive Affirmations.

Write in 'present tense' positive statements, use one emotion, add a goal, keep it brief and simple. Do not use 'doing' words

I can...I have...
I am .... I let go of ....
Today I am grateful for...

....

Practice reflection notes

DAILY PRACTICE.
6-minute morning practice is key to feel free and feel Qi
Date.................................
1. Complete a 1-minute warm-up exercise. Warm-up number.................
2. Complete 4-minutes of Qi Gong exercise practice. Exercise number ....
3. Read your daily wisdom
4. Read a knowledge theory paragraph.
5. Write your affirmations.
6. Notes. Reflection and experience of your daily practice.

Wisdom. *True success is liking yourself, liking what you do, and liking how you do it. Maya Angelou.*

Positive Affirmations.
Write in 'present tense' positive statements, use one emotion, add a goal, keep it brief and simple. Do not use 'doing' words

I can..I have..

I am .... I let go of ....

Today I am grateful for...

....

Practice reflection notes

DAILY PRACTICE.
6-minute morning practice is key to feel free and feel Qi
Date.................................
1. Complete a 1-minute warm-up exercise. Warm-up number.................
2. Complete 4-minutes of Qi Gong exercise practice. Exercise number ....
3. Read your daily wisdom
4. Read a knowledge theory paragraph.
5. Write your affirmations.
6. Notes. Reflection and experience of your daily practice.

Wisdom. *When writing affirmations, you will accidentally stumble upon something wonderful, something you have been writing about. You have created an energy shift manifesting a new reality.*

Positive Affirmations.
Write in 'present tense' positive statements, use one emotion, add a goal, keep it brief and simple. Do not use 'doing' words
I can..I have..
I am .... I let go of ....
Today I am grateful for...
....
Practice reflection notes

278

DAILY PRACTICE.
6-minute morning practice is key to feel free and feel Qi
Date....................................
1. Complete a 1-minute warm-up exercise. Warm-up number.................
2. Complete 4-minutes of Qi Gong exercise practice. Exercise number ....
3. Read your daily wisdom
4. Read a knowledge theory paragraph.
5. Write your affirmations.
6. Notes. Reflection and experience of your daily practice.

Wisdom. *Respect your elders, and the world will respect you.*

Positive Affirmations.
Write in 'present tense' positive statements, use one emotion, add a goal, keep it brief and simple. Do not use 'doing' words

I can..I have...

I am .... I let go of ....

Today I am grateful for..

....

Practice reflection notes

DAILY PRACTICE.
6-minute morning practice is key to feel free and feel Qi
Date....................................
1. Complete a 1-minute warm-up exercise. Warm-up number.................
2. Complete 4-minutes of Qi Gong exercise practice. Exercise number ....
3. Read your daily wisdom
4. Read a knowledge theory paragraph.
5. Write your affirmations.
6. Notes. Reflection and experience of your daily practice.

Wisdom. *Joy comes from appreciation; appreciation comes from paying attention. Paying attention is practice, and practice is cultivation.*

Positive Affirmations.
Write in 'present tense' positive statements, use one emotion, add a goal, keep it brief and simple. Do not use 'doing' words

I can..I have...
I am .... I let go of ....
Today I am grateful for..
....

Practice reflection notes

DAILY PRACTICE.
6-minute morning practice is key to feel free and feel Qi
Date.................................
1. Complete a 1-minute warm-up exercise. Warm-up number..................
2. Complete 4-minutes of Qi Gong exercise practice. Exercise number ....
3. Read your daily wisdom
4. Read a knowledge theory paragraph.
5. Write your affirmations.
6. Notes. Reflection and experience of your daily practice.

Wisdom. *Life is a combination of opposites, a combination of balance; it is not one or the other; it's both yin yang. Jet Li.*

Positive Affirmations.
Write in 'present tense' positive statements, use one emotion, add a goal, keep it brief and simple. Do not use 'doing' words

I can...I have...

I am .... I let go of ....

Today I am grateful for..

....

Practice reflection notes

DAILY PRACTICE.
6-minute morning practice is key to feel free and feel Qi
Date.................................
1. Complete a 1-minute warm-up exercise. Warm-up number..................
2. Complete 4-minutes of Qi Gong exercise practice. Exercise number ....
3. Read your daily wisdom
4. Read a knowledge theory paragraph.
5. Write your affirmations.
6. Notes. Reflection and experience of your daily practice.

Wisdom. *Knowing is not enough; we must apply. Willing is not enough; we must do. Bruce Lee.*

Positive Affirmations.
Write in 'present tense' positive statements, use one emotion, add a goal, keep it brief and simple. Do not use 'doing' words

I can...I have...
I am .... I let go of ....
Today I am grateful for..

....

Practice reflection notes

DAILY PRACTICE.
6-minute morning practice is key to feel free and feel Qi
Date.................................
1. Complete a 1-minute warm-up exercise. Warm-up number.................
2. Complete 4-minutes of Qi Gong exercise practice. Exercise number ....
3. Read your daily wisdom
4. Read a knowledge theory paragraph.
5. Write your affirmations.
6. Notes. Reflection and experience of your daily practice.

Wisdom. *The 'Tao' is the infinite common source eternally present within you, no beginning, no end. The essence of this wisdom to be.*

Positive Affirmations.
Write in 'present tense' positive statements, use one emotion, add a goal, keep it brief and simple. Do not use 'doing' words

I can..I have...

I am .... I let go of ....

Today I am grateful for..

....

Practice reflection notes

DAILY PRACTICE.
6-minute morning practice is key to feel free and feel Qi
Date.................................
1. Complete a 1-minute warm-up exercise. Warm-up number.................
2. Complete 4-minutes of Qi Gong exercise practice. Exercise number ....
3. Read your daily wisdom
4. Read a knowledge theory paragraph.
5. Write your affirmations.
6. Notes. Reflection and experience of your daily practice.

Wisdom *The secret of change is to focus all your energy not on fighting the old but on building the new. Socrates.*

Positive Affirmations.
Write in 'present tense' positive statements, use one emotion, add a goal, keep it brief and simple. Do not use 'doing' words

I can..I have...
I am .... I let go of ....
Today I am grateful for..
....

Practice reflection notes

DAILY PRACTICE.
6-minute morning practice is key to feel free and feel Qi
Date..................................
1. Complete a 1-minute warm-up exercise. Warm-up number..................
2. Complete 4-minutes of Qi Gong exercise practice. Exercise number ....
3. Read your daily wisdom
4. Read a knowledge theory paragraph.
5. Write your affirmations.
6. Notes. Reflection and experience of your daily practice.

Wisdom. *Embrace solitude and trust to see your oneness with the whole universe in your practice. Go deep with the breath movement, and the mind don't live on the surface vision.*

Positive Affirmations.
Write in 'present tense' positive statements, use one emotion, add a goal, keep it brief and simple. Do not use 'doing' words

I can...I have...

I am .... I let go of ....

Today I am grateful for...

....

Practice reflection notes

DAILY PRACTICE.
6-minute morning practice is key to feel free and feel Qi
Date..................................
1. Complete a 1-minute warm-up exercise. Warm-up number..................
2. Complete 4-minutes of Qi Gong exercise practice. Exercise number ....
3. Read your daily wisdom
4. Read a knowledge theory paragraph.
5. Write your affirmations.
6. Notes. Reflection and experience of your daily practice.

Wisdom. Practice tolerance. *"One of the greatest problems in the world today is intolerance of each other."*

Positive Affirmations.
Write in 'present tense' positive statements, use one emotion, add a goal, keep it brief and simple. Do not use 'doing' words

I can...I have...
I am .... I let go of ....
Today I am grateful for...
....

Practice reflection notes

DAILY PRACTICE.
6-minute morning practice is key to feel free and feel Qi
Date..................................
1. Complete a 1-minute warm-up exercise. Warm-up number.................
2. Complete 4-minutes of Qi Gong exercise practice. Exercise number ....
3. Read your daily wisdom
4. Read a knowledge theory paragraph.
5. Write your affirmations.
6. Notes. Reflection and experience of your daily practice.

Wisdom. *Don't be too quick to judge; think bigger, walk in the other person's shoes first, then try to make a balanced decision.*

Positive Affirmations.
Write in 'present tense' positive statements, use one emotion, add a goal, keep it brief and simple. Do not use 'doing' words

I can...I have..

I am .... I let go of ....

Today I am grateful for...

....

Practice reflection notes

DAILY PRACTICE.
6-minute morning practice is key to feel free and feel Qi
Date..................................
1. Complete a 1-minute warm-up exercise. Warm-up number.................
2. Complete 4-minutes of Qi Gong exercise practice. Exercise number ....
3. Read your daily wisdom
4. Read a knowledge theory paragraph.
5. Write your affirmations.
6. Notes. Reflection and experience of your daily practice.

Wisdom. *Stillness and action are relative, not absolute principles. It's important to find balance of Yin Yang, not just in Qi Gong but in everyday life. In movement, seek stillness. In rest, be mindful and attentive. Ken Cohen.*

Positive Affirmations.
Write in 'present tense' positive statements, use one emotion, add a goal, keep it brief and simple. Do not use 'doing' words

I can...I have..
I am .... I let go of ....
Today I am grateful for...
....
Practice reflection notes

DAILY PRACTICE.
6-minute morning practice is key to feel free and feel Qi
Date.................................
1. Complete a 1-minute warm-up exercise. Warm-up number.................
2. Complete 4-minutes of Qi Gong exercise practice. Exercise number ....
3. Read your daily wisdom
4. Read a knowledge theory paragraph.
5. Write your affirmations.
6. Notes. Reflection and experience of your daily practice.

Wisdom. *Small daily improvements are the key to staggering long-term results. Bruce Lee.*

Positive Affirmations.
Write in 'present tense' positive statements, use one emotion, add a goal, keep it brief and simple. Do not use 'doing' words

I can..I have...

I am .... I let go of ....

Today I am grateful for...

....

Practice reflection notes

DAILY PRACTICE.
6-minute morning practice is key to feel free and feel Qi
Date.................................
1. Complete a 1-minute warm-up exercise. Warm-up number.................
2. Complete 4-minutes of Qi Gong exercise practice. Exercise number ....
3. Read your daily wisdom
4. Read a knowledge theory paragraph.
5. Write your affirmations.
6. Notes. Reflection and experience of your daily practice.

Wisdom. *The stronger you become, the gentler you can be. Martial Masters.*

Positive Affirmations.
Write in 'present tense' positive statements, use one emotion, add a goal, keep it brief and simple. Do not use 'doing' words

I can..I have...
I am .... I let go of ....
Today I am grateful for...
....

Practice reflection notes

DAILY PRACTICE.
6-minute morning practice is key to feel free and feel Qi
Date....................................
1. Complete a 1-minute warm-up exercise. Warm-up number..................
2. Complete 4-minutes of Qi Gong exercise practice. Exercise number ....
3. Read your daily wisdom
4. Read a knowledge theory paragraph.
5. Write your affirmations.
6. Notes. Reflection and experience of your daily practice.

Wisdom. *Outside is form. Inside is thought. Deepest is the soul. Deng M Dao.*

Positive Affirmations.
Write in 'present tense' positive statements, use one emotion, add a goal, keep it brief and simple. Do not use 'doing' words

I can..I have...

I am .... I let go of ....

Today I am grateful for...

....

Practice reflection notes

DAILY PRACTICE.
6-minute morning practice is key to feel free and feel Qi
Date....................................
1. Complete a 1-minute warm-up exercise. Warm-up number..................
2. Complete 4-minutes of Qi Gong exercise practice. Exercise number ....
3. Read your daily wisdom
4. Read a knowledge theory paragraph.
5. Write your affirmations.
6. Notes. Reflection and experience of your daily practice.

Wisdom. *The paradox is 'the way.' When the Tao is forgotten, humanity goes off course. The world is sacred as is. Trust in the Tao. (The way) Study the Tao.*

Positive Affirmations.
Write in 'present tense' positive statements, use one emotion, add a goal, keep it brief and simple. Do not use 'doing' words

I can...I have...
I am .... I let go of ....
Today I am grateful for...
....

Practice reflection notes

DAILY PRACTICE.
6-minute morning practice is key to feel free and feel Qi
Date.................................
1. Complete a 1-minute warm-up exercise. Warm-up number..................
2. Complete 4-minutes of Qi Gong exercise practice. Exercise number ....
3. Read your daily wisdom
4. Read a knowledge theory paragraph.
5. Write your affirmations.
6. Notes. Reflection and experience of your daily practice.

Wisdom. *Strong because I've been weak, fearless because I've been afraid, wise because I've been foolish.*

Positive Affirmations.
Write in 'present tense' positive statements, use one emotion, add a goal, keep it brief and simple. Do not use 'doing' words

I can..I have..

I am .... I let go of ....

Today I am grateful for...

....

Practice reflection notes

DAILY PRACTICE.
6-minute morning practice is key to feel free and feel Qi
Date.................................
1. Complete a 1-minute warm-up exercise. Warm-up number..................
2. Complete 4-minutes of Qi Gong exercise practice. Exercise number ....
3. Read your daily wisdom
4. Read a knowledge theory paragraph.
5. Write your affirmations.
6. Notes. Reflection and experience of your daily practice.

Wisdom. *Remember, don't take yourself too seriously. Laugh at yourself and be lighter; a day without laughter is lost.*

Positive Affirmations.
Write in 'present tense' positive statements, use one emotion, add a goal, keep it brief and simple. Do not use 'doing' words

I can..I have..
I am .... I let go of ....
Today I am grateful for...
....

Practice reflection notes

DAILY PRACTICE.
6-minute morning practice is key to feel free and feel Qi
Date.................................
1. Complete a 1-minute warm-up exercise. Warm-up number.................
2. Complete 4-minutes of Qi Gong exercise practice. Exercise number ....
3. Read your daily wisdom
4. Read a knowledge theory paragraph.
5. Write your affirmations.
6. Notes. Reflection and experience of your daily practice.

Wisdom. *For things to reveal themselves to us, we need to be ready to abandon our views about them. Thich Nhat Hanh.*

Positive Affirmations.
Write in 'present tense' positive statements, use one emotion, add a goal, keep it brief and simple. Do not use 'doing' words

I can...I have..

I am .... I let go of ....

Today I am grateful for...

....

Practice reflection notes

DAILY PRACTICE.
6-minute morning practice is key to feel free and feel Qi
Date.................................
1. Complete a 1-minute warm-up exercise. Warm-up number.................
2. Complete 4-minutes of Qi Gong exercise practice. Exercise number ....
3. Read your daily wisdom
4. Read a knowledge theory paragraph.
5. Write your affirmations.
6. Notes. Reflection and experience of your daily practice.

Wisdom. *The body achieves that which the mind believes.*

Positive Affirmations.
Write in 'present tense' positive statements, use one emotion, add a goal, keep it brief and simple. Do not use 'doing' words

I can...I have..
I am .... I let go of ....
Today I am grateful for...
....

Practice reflection notes

DAILY PRACTICE.
6-minute morning practice is key to feel free and feel Qi
Date................................
1. Complete a 1-minute warm-up exercise. Warm-up number..................
2. Complete 4-minutes of Qi Gong exercise practice. Exercise number ....
3. Read your daily wisdom
4. Read a knowledge theory paragraph.
5. Write your affirmations.
6. Notes. Reflection and experience of your daily practice.

Wisdom. *Dare to be different today; commit to something exciting that will nourish your spirit.*

Positive Affirmations.
Write in 'present tense' positive statements, use one emotion, add a goal, keep it brief and simple. Do not use 'doing' words

I can...I have...

I am .... I let go of ....

Today I am grateful for..

....

Practice reflection notes

DAILY PRACTICE.
6-minute morning practice is key to feel free and feel Qi
Date................................
1. Complete a 1-minute warm-up exercise. Warm-up number..................
2. Complete 4-minutes of Qi Gong exercise practice. Exercise number ....
3. Read your daily wisdom
4. Read a knowledge theory paragraph.
5. Write your affirmations.
6. Notes. Reflection and experience of your daily practice.

Wisdom. *It may seem difficult at first, but everything is difficult at first. Musashi.*

Positive Affirmations.
Write in 'present tense' positive statements, use one emotion, add a goal, keep it brief and simple. Do not use 'doing' words

I can...I have...
I am .... I let go of ....
Today I am grateful for..
....

Practice reflection notes

DAILY PRACTICE.
6-minute morning practice is key to feel free and feel Qi
Date.................................
1. Complete a 1-minute warm-up exercise. Warm-up number.................
2. Complete 4-minutes of Qi Gong exercise practice. Exercise number ....
3. Read your daily wisdom
4. Read a knowledge theory paragraph.
5. Write your affirmations.
6. Notes. Reflection and experience of your daily practice.

Wisdom. *Follow not in the wise one's footsteps but rather seek what they sought first.*

Positive Affirmations.
Write in 'present tense' positive statements, use one emotion, add a goal, keep it brief and simple. Do not use 'doing' words

I can...I have...

I am .... I let go of ....

Today I am grateful for...

....

Practice reflection notes

DAILY PRACTICE.
6-minute morning practice is key to feel free and feel Qi
Date.................................
1. Complete a 1-minute warm-up exercise. Warm-up number.................
2. Complete 4-minutes of Qi Gong exercise practice. Exercise number ....
3. Read your daily wisdom
4. Read a knowledge theory paragraph.
5. Write your affirmations.
6. Notes. Reflection and experience of your daily practice.

Wisdom. *The first half of life is devoted to forming a healthy ego. The second half is going inward and letting go of it. C G Jung.*

Positive Affirmations.
Write in 'present tense' positive statements, use one emotion, add a goal, keep it brief and simple. Do not use 'doing' words

I can...I have...
I am .... I let go of ....
Today I am grateful for..
....

Practice reflection notes

DAILY PRACTICE.
6-minute morning practice is key to feel free and feel Qi
Date....................................
1. Complete a 1-minute warm-up exercise. Warm-up number..................
2. Complete 4-minutes of Qi Gong exercise practice. Exercise number ....
3. Read your daily wisdom
4. Read a knowledge theory paragraph.
5. Write your affirmations.
6. Notes. Reflection and experience of your daily practice.

Wisdom. *On the other side of the resistance is the flow of Qi.*

Positive Affirmations.
Write in 'present tense' positive statements, use one emotion, add a goal, keep it brief and simple. Do not use 'doing' words

I can..I have...

I am .... I let go of ....

Today I am grateful for...

....

Practice reflection notes

DAILY PRACTICE.
6-minute morning practice is key to feel free and feel Qi
Date....................................
1. Complete a 1-minute warm-up exercise. Warm-up number..................
2. Complete 4-minutes of Qi Gong exercise practice. Exercise number ....
3. Read your daily wisdom
4. Read a knowledge theory paragraph.
5. Write your affirmations.
6. Notes. Reflection and experience of your daily practice.

Wisdom. *Yin Yang. Happiness and unhappiness from one state to another. On the toughest of days, remind yourself, if you have felt ultimate despair, you can feel ultimate bliss.*

Positive Affirmations.
Write in 'present tense' positive statements, use one emotion, add a goal, keep it brief and simple. Do not use 'doing' words

I can..I have...
I am .... I let go of ....
Today I am grateful for...
....

Practice reflection notes

DAILY PRACTICE.
6-minute morning practice is key to feel free and feel Qi
Date.................................
1. Complete a 1-minute warm-up exercise. Warm-up number.................
2. Complete 4-minutes of Qi Gong exercise practice. Exercise number ....
3. Read your daily wisdom
4. Read a knowledge theory paragraph.
5. Write your affirmations.
6. Notes. Reflection and experience of your daily practice.

Wisdom. *Each new moment is a place you've never been to.*

Positive Affirmations.
Write in 'present tense' positive statements, use one emotion, add a goal, keep it brief and simple. Do not use 'doing' words

I can...I have...

I am .... I let go of ....

Today I am grateful for...

....

Practice reflection notes

DAILY PRACTICE.
6-minute morning practice is key to feel free and feel Qi
Date.................................
1. Complete a 1-minute warm-up exercise. Warm-up number.................
2. Complete 4-minutes of Qi Gong exercise practice. Exercise number ....
3. Read your daily wisdom
4. Read a knowledge theory paragraph.
5. Write your affirmations.
6. Notes. Reflection and experience of your daily practice.

Wisdom. *Time will decide who you meet in life; your heart decides who you want in your life and your behaviour decides who stays in your life.*

Positive Affirmations.
Write in 'present tense' positive statements, use one emotion, add a goal, keep it brief and simple. Do not use 'doing' words

I can...I have..
I am .... I let go of ....
Today I am grateful for..
....

Practice reflection notes

DAILY PRACTICE.
6-minute morning practice is key to feel free and feel Qi
Date....................................
1. Complete a 1-minute warm-up exercise. Warm-up number..................
2. Complete 4-minutes of Qi Gong exercise practice. Exercise number ....
3. Read your daily wisdom
4. Read a knowledge theory paragraph.
5. Write your affirmations.
6. Notes. Reflection and experience of your daily practice.

Wisdom. *Start by doing what's necessary, then do what's possible, and suddenly you are doing the impossible.*

Positive Affirmations.
Write in 'present tense' positive statements, use one emotion, add a goal, keep it brief and simple. Do not use 'doing' words

I can...I have...

I am .... I let go of ....

Today I am grateful for..

....

Practice reflection notes

DAILY PRACTICE.
6-minute morning practice is key to feel free and feel Qi
Date....................................
1. Complete a 1-minute warm-up exercise. Warm-up number..................
2. Complete 4-minutes of Qi Gong exercise practice. Exercise number ....
3. Read your daily wisdom
4. Read a knowledge theory paragraph.
5. Write your affirmations.
6. Notes. Reflection and experience of your daily practice.

Wisdom. *A common mistake is losing yourself in the process of valuing someone else so much that you forget to value yourself. Jenna Robins.*

Positive Affirmations.
Write in 'present tense' positive statements, use one emotion, add a goal, keep it brief and simple. Do not use 'doing' words

I can...I have...
I am .... I let go of ....
Today I am grateful for..
....

Practice reflection notes

DAILY PRACTICE.
6-minute morning practice is key to feel free and feel Qi
Date.................................
1. Complete a 1-minute warm-up exercise. Warm-up number.................
2. Complete 4-minutes of Qi Gong exercise practice. Exercise number ....
3. Read your daily wisdom
4. Read a knowledge theory paragraph.
5. Write your affirmations.
6. Notes. Reflection and experience of your daily practice.

Wisdom. *If you want to achieve greatness, stop asking for permission. Jessica Ennis.*

Positive Affirmations.
Write in 'present tense' positive statements, use one emotion, add a goal, keep it brief and simple. Do not use 'doing' words

I can..I have...

I am .... I let go of ....

Today I am grateful for...

....

Practice reflection notes

DAILY PRACTICE.
6-minute morning practice is key to feel free and feel Qi
Date.................................
1. Complete a 1-minute warm-up exercise. Warm-up number.................
2. Complete 4-minutes of Qi Gong exercise practice. Exercise number ....
3. Read your daily wisdom
4. Read a knowledge theory paragraph.
5. Write your affirmations.
6. Notes. Reflection and experience of your daily practice.

Wisdom. *Is it not better to regret the risks that didn't work out than the chances you didn't take at all?*

Positive Affirmations.
Write in 'present tense' positive statements, use one emotion, add a goal, keep it brief and simple. Do not use 'doing' words

I can..I have...
I am .... I let go of ....
Today I am grateful for...
....

Practice reflection notes

DAILY PRACTICE.
6-minute morning practice is key to feel free and feel Qi
Date..................................
1. Complete a 1-minute warm-up exercise. Warm-up number..................
2. Complete 4-minutes of Qi Gong exercise practice. Exercise number ....
3. Read your daily wisdom
4. Read a knowledge theory paragraph.
5. Write your affirmations.
6. Notes. Reflection and experience of your daily practice.

Wisdom. *Those who know that enough is enough will always have enough.*

Positive Affirmations.
Write in 'present tense' positive statements, use one emotion, add a goal, keep it brief and simple. Do not use 'doing' words

I can...I have...…......................

I am .... I let go of ....

Today I am grateful for...

....

Practice reflection notes

DAILY PRACTICE.
6-minute morning practice is key to feel free and feel Qi
Date..................................
1. Complete a 1-minute warm-up exercise. Warm-up number..................
2. Complete 4-minutes of Qi Gong exercise practice. Exercise number ....
3. Read your daily wisdom
4. Read a knowledge theory paragraph.
5. Write your affirmations.
6. Notes. Reflection and experience of your daily practice.

Wisdom. *Qi Ging practice is not a matter of months and years; it's lifetime helping hand to self-love, growth, and self-cultivation. Jenna Robins*

Positive Affirmations.
Write in 'present tense' positive statements, use one emotion, add a goal, keep it brief and simple. Do not use 'doing' words

I can...I have...…......................
I am .... I let go of ....
Today I am grateful for...
....

Practice reflection notes

DAILY PRACTICE.
6-minute morning practice is key to feel free and feel Qi
Date.................................
1. Complete a 1-minute warm-up exercise. Warm-up number.................
2. Complete 4-minutes of Qi Gong exercise practice. Exercise number ....
3. Read your daily wisdom
4. Read a knowledge theory paragraph.
5. Write your affirmations.
6. Notes. Reflection and experience of your daily practice.

Wisdom. *In practice, where there is silence, one finds the anchor the to the universe. Tao Te Ching.*

Positive Affirmations.
Write in 'present tense' positive statements, use one emotion, add a goal, keep it brief and simple. Do not use 'doing' words

I can...I have...

I am .... I let go of ....

Today I am grateful for...

....

Practice reflection notes

DAILY PRACTICE.
6-minute morning practice is key to feel free and feel Qi
Date.................................
1. Complete a 1-minute warm-up exercise. Warm-up number.................
2. Complete 4-minutes of Qi Gong exercise practice. Exercise number ....
3. Read your daily wisdom
4. Read a knowledge theory paragraph.
5. Write your affirmations.
6. Notes. Reflection and experience of your daily practice.

Wisdom. *Dance when your broken; dance if you have torn the bandage off. Dance in the middle of the fighting. Dance in your blood. Dance when you are perfectly free. Rumi*

Positive Affirmations.
Write in 'present tense' positive statements, use one emotion, add a goal, keep it brief and simple. Do not use 'doing' words

I can...I have...
I am .... I let go of ....
Today I am grateful for...
....

Practice reflection notes

DAILY PRACTICE.
6-minute morning practice is key to feel free and feel Qi
Date................................
1. Complete a 1-minute warm-up exercise. Warm-up number.................
2. Complete 4-minutes of Qi Gong exercise practice. Exercise number ....
3. Read your daily wisdom
4. Read a knowledge theory paragraph.
5. Write your affirmations.
6. Notes. Reflection and experience of your daily practice.

Wisdom. *If you want to fly, give up what is weighing you down.*

Positive Affirmations.
Write in 'present tense' positive statements, use one emotion, add a goal, keep it brief and simple. Do not use 'doing' words

I can..I have...

I am .... I let go of ....

Today I am grateful for...

....

Practice reflection notes

DAILY PRACTICE.
6-minute morning practice is key to feel free and feel Qi
Date................................
1. Complete a 1-minute warm-up exercise. Warm-up number.................
2. Complete 4-minutes of Qi Gong exercise practice. Exercise number ....
3. Read your daily wisdom
4. Read a knowledge theory paragraph.
5. Write your affirmations.
6. Notes. Reflection and experience of your daily practice.

Wisdom. *Our entire biological system, the brain and the earth itself, work on the same frequencies. Nikola Tesla.*

Positive Affirmations.
Write in 'present tense' positive statements, use one emotion, add a goal, keep it brief and simple. Do not use 'doing' words

I can..I have...
I am .... I let go of ....
Today I am grateful for...
....
Practice reflection notes

296

DAILY PRACTICE.
6-minute morning practice is key to feel free and feel Qi
Date...................................
1. Complete a 1-minute warm-up exercise. Warm-up number.................
2. Complete 4-minutes of Qi Gong exercise practice. Exercise number ....
3. Read your daily wisdom
4. Read a knowledge theory paragraph.
5. Write your affirmations.
6. Notes. Reflection and experience of your daily practice.

Wisdom. *Sometimes we expect too much from others because we would be willing to do too much for them.*

Positive Affirmations.
Write in 'present tense' positive statements, use one emotion, add a goal, keep it brief and simple. Do not use 'doing' words

I can..I have...

I am .... I let go of ....

Today I am grateful for..

....

Practice reflection notes

DAILY PRACTICE.
6-minute morning practice is key to feel free and feel Qi
Date...................................
1. Complete a 1-minute warm-up exercise. Warm-up number.................
2. Complete 4-minutes of Qi Gong exercise practice. Exercise number ....
3. Read your daily wisdom
4. Read a knowledge theory paragraph.
5. Write your affirmations.
6. Notes. Reflection and experience of your daily practice.

Wisdom. *Qi Ging practice is not a matter of months and years; it's lifetime helping hand to self-love, growth, and self-cultivation. Jenna Robins*

Positive Affirmations.
Write in 'present tense' positive statements, use one emotion, add a goal, keep it brief and simple. Do not use 'doing' words

I can..I have...
I am .... I let go of ....
Today I am grateful for..
....
Practice reflection notes

DAILY PRACTICE.
6-minute morning practice is key to feel free and feel Qi
Date.................................
1. Complete a 1-minute warm-up exercise. Warm-up number..................
2. Complete 4-minutes of Qi Gong exercise practice. Exercise number ....
3. Read your daily wisdom
4. Read a knowledge theory paragraph.
5. Write your affirmations.
6. Notes. Reflection and experience of your daily practice.

Wisdom *In whatever form it takes, life sings because it has a song. The meaning is in the lyrics. Robert Lanza.*

Positive Affirmations.
Write in 'present tense' positive statements, use one emotion, add a goal, keep it brief and simple. Do not use 'doing' words

I can...I have..

I am .... I let go of ....

Today I am grateful for...

....

Practice reflection notes

DAILY PRACTICE.
6-minute morning practice is key to feel free and feel Qi
Date.................................
1. Complete a 1-minute warm-up exercise. Warm-up number..................
2. Complete 4-minutes of Qi Gong exercise practice. Exercise number ....
3. Read your daily wisdom
4. Read a knowledge theory paragraph.
5. Write your affirmations.
6. Notes. Reflection and experience of your daily practice.

Wisdom. *When the power of love overcomes the love of power, the world will know peace.*

Positive Affirmations.
Write in 'present tense' positive statements, use one emotion, add a goal, keep it brief and simple. Do not use 'doing' words

I can...I have..
I am .... I let go of ....
Today I am grateful for...
....

Practice reflection notes

DAILY PRACTICE.
6-minute morning practice is key to feel free and feel Qi
Date.................................
1. Complete a 1-minute warm-up exercise. Warm-up number.................
2. Complete 4-minutes of Qi Gong exercise practice. Exercise number ....
3. Read your daily wisdom
4. Read a knowledge theory paragraph.
5. Write your affirmations.
6. Notes. Reflection and experience of your daily practice.

Wisdom. *Listen, observe and learn. A wise person never knows all. Only the fools know everything.*

Positive Affirmations.
Write in 'present tense' positive statements, use one emotion, add a goal, keep it brief and simple. Do not use 'doing' words

I can..I have..

I am .... I let go of ....

Today I am grateful for...

....

Practice reflection notes

DAILY PRACTICE.
6-minute morning practice is key to feel free and feel Qi
Date.................................
1. Complete a 1-minute warm-up exercise. Warm-up number.................
2. Complete 4-minutes of Qi Gong exercise practice. Exercise number ....
3. Read your daily wisdom
4. Read a knowledge theory paragraph.
5. Write your affirmations.
6. Notes. Reflection and experience of your daily practice.

Wisdom. *Allow your feet to take you where your heart, mind and spirit wants to go.*

Positive Affirmations.
Write in 'present tense' positive statements, use one emotion, add a goal, keep it brief and simple. Do not use 'doing' words

I can..I have..
I am .... I let go of ....
Today I am grateful for...
....

Practice reflection notes

DAILY PRACTICE.
6-minute morning practice is key to feel free and feel Qi
Date.................................
1. Complete a 1-minute warm-up exercise. Warm-up number..................
2. Complete 4-minutes of Qi Gong exercise practice. Exercise number ....
3. Read your daily wisdom
4. Read a knowledge theory paragraph.
5. Write your affirmations.
6. Notes. Reflection and experience of your daily practice.

Wisdom. *A man's errors are his portals of discovery. James Joyce.*

Positive Affirmations.
Write in 'present tense' positive statements, use one emotion, add a goal, keep it brief and simple. Do not use 'doing' words

I can...I have...

I am .... I let go of ....

Today I am grateful for...

....

Practice reflection notes

DAILY PRACTICE.
6-minute morning practice is key to feel free and feel Qi
Date.................................
1. Complete a 1-minute warm-up exercise. Warm-up number..................
2. Complete 4-minutes of Qi Gong exercise practice. Exercise number ....
3. Read your daily wisdom
4. Read a knowledge theory paragraph.
5. Write your affirmations.
6. Notes. Reflection and experience of your daily practice.

Wisdom. *Without frustration, you will not discover that you might be able to do something on your own. We grow through conflict. Bruce. Lee.*

Positive Affirmations.
Write in 'present tense' positive statements, use one emotion, add a goal, keep it brief and simple. Do not use 'doing' words

I can...I have...
I am .... I let go of ....
Today I am grateful for...
....

Practice reflection notes

DAILY PRACTICE.
6-minute morning practice is key to feel free and feel Qi
Date.................................
1. Complete a 1-minute warm-up exercise. Warm-up number..................
2. Complete 4-minutes of Qi Gong exercise practice. Exercise number ....
3. Read your daily wisdom
4. Read a knowledge theory paragraph.
5. Write your affirmations.
6. Notes. Reflection and experience of your daily practice.

Wisdom. *It is important for you to find a way. If not, you will find an excuse.*

Positive Affirmations.
Write in 'present tense' positive statements, use one emotion, add a goal, keep it brief and simple. Do not use 'doing' words

I can...I have..

I am .... I let go of ....

Today I am grateful for...

....

Practice reflection notes

DAILY PRACTICE.
6-minute morning practice is key to feel free and feel Qi
Date.................................
1. Complete a 1-minute warm-up exercise. Warm-up number..................
2. Complete 4-minutes of Qi Gong exercise practice. Exercise number ....
3. Read your daily wisdom
4. Read a knowledge theory paragraph.
5. Write your affirmations.
6. Notes. Reflection and experience of your daily practice.

Wisdom. *Laughter and irony are at the heart reminders that we are not prisoners in this world but voyagers through it. Eben Alexander.*

Positive Affirmations.
Write in 'present tense' positive statements, use one emotion, add a goal, keep it brief and simple. Do not use 'doing' words

I can...I have...
I am .... I let go of ....
Today I am grateful for...
....

Practice reflection notes

DAILY PRACTICE.
6-minute morning practice is key to feel free and feel Qi
Date.................................
1. Complete a 1-minute warm-up exercise. Warm-up number.................
2. Complete 4-minutes of Qi Gong exercise practice. Exercise number ....
3. Read your daily wisdom
4. Read a knowledge theory paragraph.
5. Write your affirmations.
6. Notes. Reflection and experience of your daily practice.

Wisdom. *When eating the fruit, think of the person who planted the tree—Chinese Proverb.*

Positive Affirmations.
Write in 'present tense' positive statements, use one emotion, add a goal, keep it brief and simple. Do not use 'doing' words

I can..I have...

I am .... I let go of ....

Today I am grateful for...

....

Practice reflection notes

DAILY PRACTICE.
6-minute morning practice is key to feel free and feel Qi
Date.................................
1. Complete a 1-minute warm-up exercise. Warm-up number.................
2. Complete 4-minutes of Qi Gong exercise practice. Exercise number ....
3. Read your daily wisdom
4. Read a knowledge theory paragraph.
5. Write your affirmations.
6. Notes. Reflection and experience of your daily practice.

Wisdom. *Without consciousness, space and time are nothing. Robert Lanza*

Positive Affirmations.
Write in 'present tense' positive statements, use one emotion, add a goal, keep it brief and simple. Do not use 'doing' words

I can..I have...
I am .... I let go of ....
Today I am grateful for...
....

Practice reflection notes

DAILY PRACTICE.
6-minute morning practice is key to feel free and feel Qi
Date..................................
1. Complete a 1-minute warm-up exercise. Warm-up number.................
2. Complete 4-minutes of Qi Gong exercise practice. Exercise number ....
3. Read your daily wisdom
4. Read a knowledge theory paragraph.
5. Write your affirmations.
6. Notes. Reflection and experience of your daily practice.

Wisdom. *A world of algorithms, platforms, and hashtags is no replacement for soulful human contact and connection.*

Positive Affirmations.
Write in 'present tense' positive statements, use one emotion, add a goal, keep it brief and simple. Do not use 'doing' words

I can..I have...

I am .... I let go of ....

Today I am grateful for...

....

Practice reflection notes

DAILY PRACTICE.
6-minute morning practice is key to feel free and feel Qi
Date..................................
1. Complete a 1-minute warm-up exercise. Warm-up number.................
2. Complete 4-minutes of Qi Gong exercise practice. Exercise number ....
3. Read your daily wisdom
4. Read a knowledge theory paragraph.
5. Write your affirmations.
6. Notes. Reflection and experience of your daily practice.

Wisdom. *It isn't what we say to others; it's what we do. Ego seeks outward recognition; soul seeks inner authenticity.*

Positive Affirmations.
Write in 'present tense' positive statements, use one emotion, add a goal, keep it brief and simple. Do not use 'doing' words

I can..I have...
I am .... I let go of ....
Today I am grateful for...
....
Practice reflection notes

DAILY PRACTICE.
6-minute morning practice is key to feel free and feel Qi
Date.................................
1. Complete a 1-minute warm-up exercise. Warm-up number.................
2. Complete 4-minutes of Qi Gong exercise practice. Exercise number ....
3. Read your daily wisdom
4. Read a knowledge theory paragraph.
5. Write your affirmations.
6. Notes. Reflection and experience of your daily practice.

Wisdom. *Though no one can go back and make a brand-new start, anyone can start from now and make a brand-new ending. Carl Bard.*

Positive Affirmations.
Write in 'present tense' positive statements, use one emotion, add a goal, keep it brief and simple. Do not use 'doing' words

I can...I have..

I am .... I let go of ....

Today I am grateful for...

....

Practice reflection notes

DAILY PRACTICE.
6-minute morning practice is key to feel free and feel Qi
Date.................................
1. Complete a 1-minute warm-up exercise. Warm-up number.................
2. Complete 4-minutes of Qi Gong exercise practice. Exercise number ....
3. Read your daily wisdom
4. Read a knowledge theory paragraph.
5. Write your affirmations.
6. Notes. Reflection and experience of your daily practice.

Wisdom. *What lies behind us and what lies before us are tiny matters compared to what lies within us.*

Positive Affirmations.
Write in 'present tense' positive statements, use one emotion, add a goal, keep it brief and simple. Do not use 'doing' words

I can...I have..
I am .... I let go of ....
Today I am grateful for...
....

Practice reflection notes

DAILY PRACTICE.
6-minute morning practice is key to feel free and feel Qi
Date..................................
1. Complete a 1-minute warm-up exercise. Warm-up number.................
2. Complete 4-minutes of Qi Gong exercise practice. Exercise number ....
3. Read your daily wisdom
4. Read a knowledge theory paragraph.
5. Write your affirmations.
6. Notes. Reflection and experience of your daily practice.

Wisdom. *It's easy to stand in the crowd, but it takes courage to stand alone. Mahatma Gandhi.*

Positive Affirmations.
Write in 'present tense' positive statements, use one emotion, add a goal, keep it brief and simple. Do not use 'doing' words

I can..I have..

I am .... I let go of ....

Today I am grateful for..

....

Practice reflection notes

DAILY PRACTICE.
6-minute morning practice is key to feel free and feel Qi
Date..................................
1. Complete a 1-minute warm-up exercise. Warm-up number.................
2. Complete 4-minutes of Qi Gong exercise practice. Exercise number ....
3. Read your daily wisdom
4. Read a knowledge theory paragraph.
5. Write your affirmations.
6. Notes. Reflection and experience of your daily practice.

Wisdom. *Those who try to control, who use force to protect their power, go against the direction of the Tao. They take from those who do not have enough and give to those who have far too much. Tao*

Positive Affirmations.
Write in 'present tense' positive statements, use one emotion, add a goal, keep it brief and simple. Do not use 'doing' words

I can..I have..
I am .... I let go of ....
Today I am grateful for..
....

Practice reflection notes

DAILY PRACTICE.
6-minute morning practice is key to feel free and feel Qi
Date....................................
1. Complete a 1-minute warm-up exercise. Warm-up number..................
2. Complete 4-minutes of Qi Gong exercise practice. Exercise number ....
3. Read your daily wisdom
4. Read a knowledge theory paragraph.
5. Write your affirmations.
6. Notes. Reflection and experience of your daily practice.

Wisdom. *Only the free-minded can truly discover. That is obvious, is it not? You cannot discover the truth of anything by merely being told what it is because then the discovery is not yours. If you're merely told what is happiness, is that happiness?*

Positive Affirmations.
Write in 'present tense' positive statements, use one emotion, add a goal, keep it brief and simple. Do not use 'doing' words

I can..I have...

I am .... I let go of ....

Today I am grateful for...

....

Practice reflection notes

DAILY PRACTICE.
6-minute morning practice is key to feel free and feel Qi
Date....................................
1. Complete a 1-minute warm-up exercise. Warm-up number..................
2. Complete 4-minutes of Qi Gong exercise practice. Exercise number ....
3. Read your daily wisdom
4. Read a knowledge theory paragraph.
5. Write your affirmations.
6. Notes. Reflection and experience of your daily practice.

Wisdom. *An invisible red thread connects those who are destined to meet, regardless of time, place, or circumstance. The thread may stretch or tangle but will never break—Chinese proverb.*

Positive Affirmations.
Write in 'present tense' positive statements, use one emotion, add a goal, keep it brief and simple. Do not use 'doing' words

I can..I have...
I am .... I let go of ....
Today I am grateful for...
....
Practice reflection notes

DAILY PRACTICE.
6-minute morning practice is key to feel free and feel Qi
Date.................................
1. Complete a 1-minute warm-up exercise. Warm-up number.................
2. Complete 4-minutes of Qi Gong exercise practice. Exercise number ....
3. Read your daily wisdom
4. Read a knowledge theory paragraph.
5. Write your affirmations.
6. Notes. Reflection and experience of your daily practice.

Wisdom. *Magic is to believe magical things can happen. If you believe and put magical thoughts into your written affirmations, get excited by them, change the energy, and see what you manifest. Jenna Robins*

Positive Affirmations.
Write in 'present tense' positive statements, use one emotion, add a goal, keep it brief and simple. Do not use 'doing' words

I can...I have...

I am .... I let go of ....

Today I am grateful for..

....

Practice reflection notes

DAILY PRACTICE.
6-minute morning practice is key to feel free and feel Qi
Date.................................
1. Complete a 1-minute warm-up exercise. Warm-up number.................
2. Complete 4-minutes of Qi Gong exercise practice. Exercise number ....
3. Read your daily wisdom
4. Read a knowledge theory paragraph.
5. Write your affirmations.
6. Notes. Reflection and experience of your daily practice.

Wisdom. *Sometimes our lives must be completely shaken up, changed, and rearranged to relocate us to the place we are meant to be.*

Positive Affirmations.
Write in 'present tense' positive statements, use one emotion, add a goal, keep it brief and simple. Do not use 'doing' words

I can...I have...
I am .... I let go of ....
Today I am grateful for..
....
Practice reflection notes

DAILY PRACTICE.
6-minute morning practice is key to feel free and feel Qi
Date.................................
1. Complete a 1-minute warm-up exercise. Warm-up number.................
2. Complete 4-minutes of Qi Gong exercise practice. Exercise number ....
3. Read your daily wisdom
4. Read a knowledge theory paragraph.
5. Write your affirmations.
6. Notes. Reflection and experience of your daily practice.

Wisdom. *Be brave enough to start a conversation that matters. Dau Voire*

Positive Affirmations.
Write in 'present tense' positive statements, use one emotion, add a goal, keep it brief and simple. Do not use 'doing' words

I can...I have..

I am .... I let go of ....

Today I am grateful for..

....

Practice reflection notes

DAILY PRACTICE.
6-minute morning practice is key to feel free and feel Qi
Date.................................
1. Complete a 1-minute warm-up exercise. Warm-up number.................
2. Complete 4-minutes of Qi Gong exercise practice. Exercise number ....
3. Read your daily wisdom
4. Read a knowledge theory paragraph.
5. Write your affirmations.
6. Notes. Reflection and experience of your daily practice.

Wisdom. *If we have no peace, it is because we have forgotten that we belong to each other. Mother Teresa.*

Positive Affirmations.
Write in 'present tense' positive statements, use one emotion, add a goal, keep it brief and simple. Do not use 'doing' words

I can...I have..
I am .... I let go of ....
Today I am grateful for..
....

Practice reflection notes

DAILY PRACTICE.
6-minute morning practice is key to feel free and feel Qi
Date...................................
1. Complete a 1-minute warm-up exercise. Warm-up number.................
2. Complete 4-minutes of Qi Gong exercise practice. Exercise number ....
3. Read your daily wisdom
4. Read a knowledge theory paragraph.
5. Write your affirmations.
6. Notes. Reflection and experience of your daily practice.

Wisdom. *You are not the drop in the ocean; you are the entire drop. Rumi.*

Positive Affirmations.
Write in 'present tense' positive statements, use one emotion, add a goal, keep it brief and simple. Do not use 'doing' words

I can...I have...

I am .... I let go of ....

Today I am grateful for...

....

Practice reflection notes

DAILY PRACTICE.
6-minute morning practice is key to feel free and feel Qi
Date...................................
1. Complete a 1-minute warm-up exercise. Warm-up number.................
2. Complete 4-minutes of Qi Gong exercise practice. Exercise number ....
3. Read your daily wisdom
4. Read a knowledge theory paragraph.
5. Write your affirmations.
6. Notes. Reflection and experience of your daily practice.

Wisdom. *Never be afraid to start over how little or great the problem. You are not starting from scratch your starting from experience.*

Positive Affirmations.
Write in 'present tense' positive statements, use one emotion, add a goal, keep it brief and simple. Do not use 'doing' words

I can...I have...
I am .... I let go of ....
Today I am grateful for...
....

Practice reflection notes

DAILY PRACTICE.
6-minute morning practice is key to feel free and feel Qi
Date..................................
1. Complete a 1-minute warm-up exercise. Warm-up number.................
2. Complete 4-minutes of Qi Gong exercise practice. Exercise number ....
3. Read your daily wisdom
4. Read a knowledge theory paragraph.
5. Write your affirmations.
6. Notes. Reflection and experience of your daily practice.

Wisdom. *Pleasure and pain are equal in a clear heat. No mountain hides the moon.*

Positive Affirmations.
Write in 'present tense' positive statements, use one emotion, add a goal, keep it brief and simple. Do not use 'doing' words

I can...I have...

I am .... I let go of ....

Today I am grateful for...

....

Practice reflection notes

DAILY PRACTICE.
6-minute morning practice is key to feel free and feel Qi
Date..................................
1. Complete a 1-minute warm-up exercise. Warm-up number.................
2. Complete 4-minutes of Qi Gong exercise practice. Exercise number ....
3. Read your daily wisdom
4. Read a knowledge theory paragraph.
5. Write your affirmations.
6. Notes. Reflection and experience of your daily practice.

Wisdom. *To lead people, walk behind them.*

Positive Affirmations.
Write in 'present tense' positive statements, use one emotion, add a goal, keep it brief and simple. Do not use 'doing' words

I can...I have...
I am .... I let go of ....
Today I am grateful for...
....

Practice reflection notes

DAILY PRACTICE.
6-minute morning practice is key to feel free and feel Qi
Date.................................
1. Complete a 1-minute warm-up exercise. Warm-up number.................
2. Complete 4-minutes of Qi Gong exercise practice. Exercise number ....
3. Read your daily wisdom
4. Read a knowledge theory paragraph.
5. Write your affirmations.
6. Notes. Reflection and experience of your daily practice.

Wisdom. *Have no fear of perfection; you will never reach it. Nothing in life is to be feared; it is only to be understood. Marie Sktodowska Curie.*

Positive Affirmations.
Write in 'present tense' positive statements, use one emotion, add a goal, keep it brief and simple. Do not use 'doing' words

I can..I have..

I am .... I let go of ....

Today I am grateful for...

....

Practice reflection notes

DAILY PRACTICE.
6-minute morning practice is key to feel free and feel Qi
Date.................................
1. Complete a 1-minute warm-up exercise. Warm-up number.................
2. Complete 4-minutes of Qi Gong exercise practice. Exercise number ....
3. Read your daily wisdom
4. Read a knowledge theory paragraph.
5. Write your affirmations.
6. Notes. Reflection and experience of your daily practice.

Wisdom. *Health is the greatest gift. Contentment is the greatest wealth. Buddha.*

Positive Affirmations.
Write in 'present tense' positive statements, use one emotion, add a goal, keep it brief and simple. Do not use 'doing' words

I can..I have..
I am .... I let go of ....
Today I am grateful for...
....

Practice reflection notes

DAILY PRACTICE.
6-minute morning practice is key to feel free and feel Qi
Date.................................
1. Complete a 1-minute warm-up exercise. Warm-up number.................
2. Complete 4-minutes of Qi Gong exercise practice. Exercise number ....
3. Read your daily wisdom
4. Read a knowledge theory paragraph.
5. Write your affirmations.
6. Notes. Reflection and experience of your daily practice.

Wisdom. *Your mind is like the water, my friend. It becomes difficult to see. But if you allow it to settle, the answer becomes clear. Master Oogway.*

Positive Affirmations.
Write in 'present tense' positive statements, use one emotion, add a goal, keep it brief and simple. Do not use 'doing' words

I can...I have..

I am .... I let go of ....

Today I am grateful for..

....

Practice reflection notes

DAILY PRACTICE.
6-minute morning practice is key to feel free and feel Qi
Date.................................
1. Complete a 1-minute warm-up exercise. Warm-up number.................
2. Complete 4-minutes of Qi Gong exercise practice. Exercise number ....
3. Read your daily wisdom
4. Read a knowledge theory paragraph.
5. Write your affirmations.
6. Notes. Reflection and experience of your daily practice.

Wisdom. *When you find peace within yourself, you become the kind of person who can find peace within others.*

Positive Affirmations.
Write in 'present tense' positive statements, use one emotion, add a goal, keep it brief and simple. Do not use 'doing' words

I can...I have..
I am .... I let go of ....
Today I am grateful for..
....
Practice reflection notes

DAILY PRACTICE.
6-minute morning practice is key to feel free and feel Qi
Date...................................
1. Complete a 1-minute warm-up exercise. Warm-up number.................
2. Complete 4-minutes of Qi Gong exercise practice. Exercise number ....
3. Read your daily wisdom
4. Read a knowledge theory paragraph.
5. Write your affirmations.
6. Notes. Reflection and experience of your daily practice.

Wisdom. *There is force in the universe, which, if we permit it, will flow through us and produce miraculous results. Mahatma Gandhi.*

Positive Affirmations.
Write in 'present tense' positive statements, use one emotion, add a goal, keep it brief and simple. Do not use 'doing' words

I can..I have...

I am .... I let go of ....

Today I am grateful for...

....

Practice reflection notes

DAILY PRACTICE.
6-minute morning practice is key to feel free and feel Qi
Date...................................
1. Complete a 1-minute warm-up exercise. Warm-up number.................
2. Complete 4-minutes of Qi Gong exercise practice. Exercise number ....
3. Read your daily wisdom
4. Read a knowledge theory paragraph.
5. Write your affirmations.
6. Notes. Reflection and experience of your daily practice.

Wisdom. *Never give up no matter what is going on around you; never give in; your life means too much. Dalai Lama.*

Positive Affirmations.
Write in 'present tense' positive statements, use one emotion, add a goal, keep it brief and simple. Do not use 'doing' words

I can..I have...
I am .... I let go of ....
Today I am grateful for...
....
Practice reflection notes

313

DAILY PRACTICE.
6-minute morning practice is key to feel free and feel Qi
Date....................................
1. Complete a 1-minute warm-up exercise. Warm-up number..................
2. Complete 4-minutes of Qi Gong exercise practice. Exercise number ....
3. Read your daily wisdom
4. Read a knowledge theory paragraph.
5. Write your affirmations.
6. Notes. Reflection and experience of your daily practice.

Wisdom. *True emptiness is without form. Mistakenly we create something to grasp.*

Positive Affirmations.
Write in 'present tense' positive statements, use one emotion, add a goal, keep it brief and simple. Do not use 'doing' words

I can...I have..

I am .... I let go of ....

Today I am grateful for..

....

Practice reflection notes

DAILY PRACTICE.
6-minute morning practice is key to feel free and feel Qi
Date....................................
1. Complete a 1-minute warm-up exercise. Warm-up number..................
2. Complete 4-minutes of Qi Gong exercise practice. Exercise number ....
3. Read your daily wisdom
4. Read a knowledge theory paragraph.
5. Write your affirmations.
6. Notes. Reflection and experience of your daily practice.

Wisdom. *Qi Gong is the art and science of cultivating your mindfulness, consciousness, breath and experiencing your internal Yin energies. Sometimes the only way out is in. Jenna Robins.*

Positive Affirmations.
Write in 'present tense' positive statements, use one emotion, add a goal, keep it brief and simple. Do not use 'doing' words

I can...I have..
I am .... I let go of ....
Today I am grateful for..
....

Practice reflection notes

DAILY PRACTICE.
6-minute morning practice is key to feel free and feel Qi
Date...................................
1. Complete a 1-minute warm-up exercise. Warm-up number.................
2. Complete 4-minutes of Qi Gong exercise practice. Exercise number ....
3. Read your daily wisdom
4. Read a knowledge theory paragraph.
5. Write your affirmations.
6. Notes. Reflection and experience of your daily practice.

Wisdom. *Try to do something beyond what you have already mastered, or you will never grow.*

Positive Affirmations.
Write in 'present tense' positive statements, use one emotion, add a goal, keep it brief and simple. Do not use 'doing' words

I can..I have...

I am .... I let go of ....

Today I am grateful for..

....

Practice reflection notes

DAILY PRACTICE.
6-minute morning practice is key to feel free and feel Qi
Date...................................
1. Complete a 1-minute warm-up exercise. Warm-up number.................
2. Complete 4-minutes of Qi Gong exercise practice. Exercise number ....
3. Read your daily wisdom
4. Read a knowledge theory paragraph.
5. Write your affirmations.
6. Notes. Reflection and experience of your daily practice.

Wisdom. *Seven social sins. Wealth without work. Pleasure without conscience. Knowledge without character. Commerce without morality. Science without humanity. Worship without sacrifice—politics without principle.*

Positive Affirmations.
Write in 'present tense' positive statements, use one emotion, add a goal, keep it brief and simple. Do not use 'doing' words

I can..I have...
I am .... I let go of ....
Today I am grateful for..
....
Practice reflection notes

DAILY PRACTICE.
6-minute morning practice is key to feel free and feel Qi
Date.................................
1. Complete a 1-minute warm-up exercise. Warm-up number.................
2. Complete 4-minutes of Qi Gong exercise practice. Exercise number ....
3. Read your daily wisdom
4. Read a knowledge theory paragraph.
5. Write your affirmations.
6. Notes. Reflection and experience of your daily practice.

Wisdom. *There is as much internal space inside you as there is in the whole external universe.*

Positive Affirmations.
Write in 'present tense' positive statements, use one emotion, add a goal, keep it brief and simple. Do not use 'doing' words

I can...I have...

I am .... I let go of ....

Today I am grateful for...

....

Practice reflection notes

DAILY PRACTICE.
6-minute morning practice is key to feel free and feel Qi
Date.................................
1. Complete a 1-minute warm-up exercise. Warm-up number.................
2. Complete 4-minutes of Qi Gong exercise practice. Exercise number ....
3. Read your daily wisdom
4. Read a knowledge theory paragraph.
5. Write your affirmations.
6. Notes. Reflection and experience of your daily practice.

Wisdom. *Be open and subjective and help others to be the same. We simply can't hate what we don't understand.*

Positive Affirmations.
Write in 'present tense' positive statements, use one emotion, add a goal, keep it brief and simple. Do not use 'doing' words

I can...I have...
I am .... I let go of ....
Today I am grateful for...
....

Practice reflection notes

DAILY PRACTICE.
6-minute morning practice is key to feel free and feel Qi
Date...............................
1. Complete a 1-minute warm-up exercise. Warm-up number.................
2. Complete 4-minutes of Qi Gong exercise practice. Exercise number ....
3. Read your daily wisdom
4. Read a knowledge theory paragraph.
5. Write your affirmations.
6. Notes. Reflection and experience of your daily practice.

Wisdom. *It's a journey. No one is ahead of you or behind you. You are not more advanced or less enlightened. We are all teachers, and we are all students.*

Positive Affirmations.
Write in 'present tense' positive statements, use one emotion, add a goal, keep it brief and simple. Do not use 'doing' words

I can...I have..

I am .... I let go of ....

Today I am grateful for...

....

Practice reflection notes

DAILY PRACTICE.
6-minute morning practice is key to feel free and feel Qi
Date...............................
1. Complete a 1-minute warm-up exercise. Warm-up number.................
2. Complete 4-minutes of Qi Gong exercise practice. Exercise number ....
3. Read your daily wisdom
4. Read a knowledge theory paragraph.
5. Write your affirmations.
6. Notes. Reflection and experience of your daily practice.

Wisdom. *We cannot see our reflection in running water; it is only in the still water we can clearly see.*

Positive Affirmations.
Write in 'present tense' positive statements, use one emotion, add a goal, keep it brief and simple. Do not use 'doing' words

I can...I have..
I am .... I let go of ....
Today I am grateful for..
....

Practice reflection notes

317

DAILY PRACTICE.
6-minute morning practice is key to feel free and feel Qi
Date.................................
1. Complete a 1-minute warm-up exercise. Warm-up number..................
2. Complete 4-minutes of Qi Gong exercise practice. Exercise number ....
3. Read your daily wisdom
4. Read a knowledge theory paragraph.
5. Write your affirmations.
6. Notes. Reflection and experience of your daily practice.

Wisdom. *The more you know, the less you understand. Lao Tzu.*

Positive Affirmations.
Write in 'present tense' positive statements, use one emotion, add a goal, keep it brief and simple. Do not use 'doing' words

I can...I have..

I am .... I let go of ....

Today I am grateful for...

....

Practice reflection notes

DAILY PRACTICE.
6-minute morning practice is key to feel free and feel Qi
Date.................................
1. Complete a 1-minute warm-up exercise. Warm-up number..................
2. Complete 4-minutes of Qi Gong exercise practice. Exercise number ....
3. Read your daily wisdom
4. Read a knowledge theory paragraph.
5. Write your affirmations.
6. Notes. Reflection and experience of your daily practice.

Wisdom. *Remember, what is too deeply rooted cannot be pulled out.*

Positive Affirmations.
Write in 'present tense' positive statements, use one emotion, add a goal, keep it brief and simple. Do not use 'doing' words

I can...I have..
I am .... I let go of ....
Today I am grateful for...
....

Practice reflection notes

318

DAILY PRACTICE.
6-minute morning practice is key to feel free and feel Qi
Date..................................
1. Complete a 1-minute warm-up exercise. Warm-up number.................
2. Complete 4-minutes of Qi Gong exercise practice. Exercise number ....
3. Read your daily wisdom
4. Read a knowledge theory paragraph.
5. Write your affirmations.
6. Notes. Reflection and experience of your daily practice.

Wisdom. *The smallest, good deed is better than the grandest good intention.*

Positive Affirmations.
Write in 'present tense' positive statements, use one emotion, add a goal, keep it brief and simple. Do not use 'doing' words

I can...I have..

I am .... I let go of ....

Today I am grateful for..

....

Practice reflection notes

DAILY PRACTICE.
6-minute morning practice is key to feel free and feel Qi
Date..................................
1. Complete a 1-minute warm-up exercise. Warm-up number.................
2. Complete 4-minutes of Qi Gong exercise practice. Exercise number ....
3. Read your daily wisdom
4. Read a knowledge theory paragraph.
5. Write your affirmations.
6. Notes. Reflection and experience of your daily practice.

Wisdom. *The more a thing tends to be permeant, the more it tends to be lifeless. Alan Watts.*

Positive Affirmations.
Write in 'present tense' positive statements, use one emotion, add a goal, keep it brief and simple. Do not use 'doing' words

I can...I have..
I am .... I let go of ....
Today I am grateful for..
....

Practice reflection notes

DAILY PRACTICE.
6-minute morning practice is key to feel free and feel Qi
Date..................................
1. Complete a 1-minute warm-up exercise. Warm-up number.................
2. Complete 4-minutes of Qi Gong exercise practice. Exercise number ....
3. Read your daily wisdom
4. Read a knowledge theory paragraph.
5. Write your affirmations.
6. Notes. Reflection and experience of your daily practice.

Wisdom. *If just one Qi Gong movement flows completely with the breath and mind as one, this one flowing meditation experience is more profound than 100 movements with no Qi flow. Jenna Robins.*

Positive Affirmations.
Write in 'present tense' positive statements, use one emotion, add a goal, keep it brief and simple. Do not use 'doing' words

I can..I have...

I am .... I let go of ....

Today I am grateful for...

....

Practice reflection notes

DAILY PRACTICE.
6-minute morning practice is key to feel free and feel Qi
Date..................................
1. Complete a 1-minute warm-up exercise. Warm-up number.................
2. Complete 4-minutes of Qi Gong exercise practice. Exercise number ....
3. Read your daily wisdom
4. Read a knowledge theory paragraph.
5. Write your affirmations.
6. Notes. Reflection and experience of your daily practice.

Wisdom. *A wise person can learn more from a foolish question than a fool can learn from a wise answer. Bruce Lee.*

Positive Affirmations.
Write in 'present tense' positive statements, use one emotion, add a goal, keep it brief and simple. Do not use 'doing' words

I can..I have...
I am .... I let go of ....
Today I am grateful for...
....
Practice reflection notes

DAILY PRACTICE.
6-minute morning practice is key to feel free and feel Qi
Date...................................
1. Complete a 1-minute warm-up exercise. Warm-up number.................
2. Complete 4-minutes of Qi Gong exercise practice. Exercise number ....
3. Read your daily wisdom
4. Read a knowledge theory paragraph.
5. Write your affirmations.
6. Notes. Reflection and experience of your daily practice.

Wisdom. *Success depends on where intention is. Gita Bellin.*

Positive Affirmations.
Write in 'present tense' positive statements, use one emotion, add a goal, keep it brief and simple. Do not use 'doing' words

I can...I have...

I am .... I let go of ....

Today I am grateful for...

....

Practice reflection notes

DAILY PRACTICE.
6-minute morning practice is key to feel free and feel Qi
Date...................................
1. Complete a 1-minute warm-up exercise. Warm-up number.................
2. Complete 4-minutes of Qi Gong exercise practice. Exercise number ....
3. Read your daily wisdom
4. Read a knowledge theory paragraph.
5. Write your affirmations.
6. Notes. Reflection and experience of your daily practice.

Wisdom. *What one chooses to believe in and what one is compelled to believe in, there is a difference.*

Positive Affirmations.
Write in 'present tense' positive statements, use one emotion, add a goal, keep it brief and simple. Do not use 'doing' words

I can...I have...
I am .... I let go of ....
Today I am grateful for...
....
Practice reflection notes

DAILY PRACTICE.
6-minute morning practice is key to feel free and feel Qi
Date..................................
1. Complete a 1-minute warm-up exercise. Warm-up number..................
2. Complete 4-minutes of Qi Gong exercise practice. Exercise number ....
3. Read your daily wisdom
4. Read a knowledge theory paragraph.
5. Write your affirmations.
6. Notes. Reflection and experience of your daily practice.

Wisdom. *Patience is a flower which does not grow in everybody's garden.*

Positive Affirmations.
Write in 'present tense' positive statements, use one emotion, add a goal, keep it brief and simple. Do not use 'doing' words

I can...I have..

I am .... I let go of ....

Today I am grateful for...

....

Practice reflection notes

DAILY PRACTICE.
6-minute morning practice is key to feel free and feel Qi
Date..................................
1. Complete a 1-minute warm-up exercise. Warm-up number..................
2. Complete 4-minutes of Qi Gong exercise practice. Exercise number ....
3. Read your daily wisdom
4. Read a knowledge theory paragraph.
5. Write your affirmations.
6. Notes. Reflection and experience of your daily practice.

Wisdom. *Everything and everyone are your teachers unless you are a poor student.*

Positive Affirmations.
Write in 'present tense' positive statements, use one emotion, add a goal, keep it brief and simple. Do not use 'doing' words

I can...I have..
I am .... I let go of ....
Today I am grateful for...
....
Practice reflection notes

DAILY PRACTICE.
6-minute morning practice is key to feel free and feel Qi
Date...................................
1. Complete a 1-minute warm-up exercise. Warm-up number..................
2. Complete 4-minutes of Qi Gong exercise practice. Exercise number ....
3. Read your daily wisdom
4. Read a knowledge theory paragraph.
5. Write your affirmations.
6. Notes. Reflection and experience of your daily practice.

Wisdom. *Longevity is the cultivation of harnessing the internal-external power of Chi. Cultivating life by guiding the Chi. Grandmaster Lu Zijjian.*

Positive Affirmations.
Write in 'present tense' positive statements, use one emotion, add a goal, keep it brief and simple. Do not use 'doing' words

I can...I have..

I am .... I let go of ....

Today I am grateful for..

....

Practice reflection notes

DAILY PRACTICE.
6-minute morning practice is key to feel free and feel Qi
Date...................................
1. Complete a 1-minute warm-up exercise. Warm-up number..................
2. Complete 4-minutes of Qi Gong exercise practice. Exercise number ....
3. Read your daily wisdom
4. Read a knowledge theory paragraph.
5. Write your affirmations.
6. Notes. Reflection and experience of your daily practice.

Wisdom. *In the end, these things matter most. How well did you love? How fully did you live? How deeply did you let go? Buddha.*

Positive Affirmations.
Write in 'present tense' positive statements, use one emotion, add a goal, keep it brief and simple. Do not use 'doing' words

I can...I have..
I am .... I let go of ....
Today I am grateful for..
....
Practice reflection notes

DAILY PRACTICE.
6-minute morning practice is key to feel free and feel Qi
Date.................................
1. Complete a 1-minute warm-up exercise. Warm-up number.................
2. Complete 4-minutes of Qi Gong exercise practice. Exercise number ....
3. Read your daily wisdom
4. Read a knowledge theory paragraph.
5. Write your affirmations.
6. Notes. Reflection and experience of your daily practice.

Wisdom. *Challenges and changes can be painful, but nothing is as painful as staying stuck where you don't belong.*

Positive Affirmations.
Write in 'present tense' positive statements, use one emotion, add a goal, keep it brief and simple. Do not use 'doing' words

I can..I have...…....................

I am .... I let go of ....

Today I am grateful for...

....

Practice reflection notes

DAILY PRACTICE.
6-minute morning practice is key to feel free and feel Qi
Date.................................
1. Complete a 1-minute warm-up exercise. Warm-up number.................
2. Complete 4-minutes of Qi Gong exercise practice. Exercise number ....
3. Read your daily wisdom
4. Read a knowledge theory paragraph.
5. Write your affirmations.
6. Notes. Reflection and experience of your daily practice.

Wisdom. *If you wait until you're ready, you'll be waiting for the rest of your life.*

Positive Affirmations.
Write in 'present tense' positive statements, use one emotion, add a goal, keep it brief and simple. Do not use 'doing' words

I can..I have...…....................
I am .... I let go of ....
Today I am grateful for...
....

Practice reflection notes

DAILY PRACTICE.
6-minute morning practice is key to feel free and feel Qi
Date.................................
1. Complete a 1-minute warm-up exercise. Warm-up number.................
2. Complete 4-minutes of Qi Gong exercise practice. Exercise number ....
3. Read your daily wisdom
4. Read a knowledge theory paragraph.
5. Write your affirmations.
6. Notes. Reflection and experience of your daily practice.

Wisdom. *Simply experience your Qi Gong practice day to day and moment to moment. Yesterday was yesterday; today is today. Every day is different. Jenna Robins.*

Positive Affirmations.
Write in 'present tense' positive statements, use one emotion, add a goal, keep it brief and simple. Do not use 'doing' words

I can...I have..

I am .... I let go of ....

Today I am grateful for..

....

Practice reflection notes

DAILY PRACTICE.
6-minute morning practice is key to feel free and feel Qi
Date.................................
1. Complete a 1-minute warm-up exercise. Warm-up number.................
2. Complete 4-minutes of Qi Gong exercise practice. Exercise number ....
3. Read your daily wisdom
4. Read a knowledge theory paragraph.
5. Write your affirmations.
6. Notes. Reflection and experience of your daily practice.

Wisdom. *Every day with a smooth deep breath, 'let go' of any negativity, send it down to the earth. This is the way. Jenna Robins.*

Positive Affirmations.
Write in 'present tense' positive statements, use one emotion, add a goal, keep it brief and simple. Do not use 'doing' words

I can...I have..
I am .... I let go of ....
Today I am grateful for..
....
Practice reflection notes

DAILY PRACTICE.
6-minute morning practice is key to feel free and feel Qi
Date.................................
1. Complete a 1-minute warm-up exercise. Warm-up number.................
2. Complete 4-minutes of Qi Gong exercise practice. Exercise number ....
3. Read your daily wisdom
4. Read a knowledge theory paragraph.
5. Write your affirmations.
6. Notes. Reflection and experience of your daily practice.

Wisdom. *The soul would have no rainbow if the eyes had no tears.*

Positive Affirmations.
Write in 'present tense' positive statements, use one emotion, add a goal, keep it brief and simple. Do not use 'doing' words

I can...I have..

I am .... I let go of ....

Today I am grateful for...

....

Practice reflection notes

DAILY PRACTICE.
6-minute morning practice is key to feel free and feel Qi
Date.................................
1. Complete a 1-minute warm-up exercise. Warm-up number.................
2. Complete 4-minutes of Qi Gong exercise practice. Exercise number ....
3. Read your daily wisdom
4. Read a knowledge theory paragraph.
5. Write your affirmations.
6. Notes. Reflection and experience of your daily practice.

Wisdom. *Qi Gong helps us feel strong but with softness, rooted but with branches, silent with all senses. In moving medication, we access a shift in space and time, the void beyond, where we see everything. Jenna Robins.*

Positive Affirmations.
Write in 'present tense' positive statements, use one emotion, add a goal, keep it brief and simple. Do not use 'doing' words

I can...I have..
I am .... I let go of ....
Today I am grateful for...
....
Practice reflection notes

DAILY PRACTICE.
6-minute morning practice is key to feel free and feel Qi
Date..................................
1. Complete a 1-minute warm-up exercise. Warm-up number..................
2. Complete 4-minutes of Qi Gong exercise practice. Exercise number ....
3. Read your daily wisdom
4. Read a knowledge theory paragraph.
5. Write your affirmations.
6. Notes. Reflection and experience of your daily practice.

Wisdom. *Growth can be uncomfortable because you have never been there.*

Positive Affirmations.
Write in 'present tense' positive statements, use one emotion, add a goal, keep it brief and simple. Do not use 'doing' words

I can..I have..

I am .... I let go of ....

Today I am grateful for...

....

Practice reflection notes

DAILY PRACTICE.
6-minute morning practice is key to feel free and feel Qi
Date..................................
1. Complete a 1-minute warm-up exercise. Warm-up number..................
2. Complete 4-minutes of Qi Gong exercise practice. Exercise number ....
3. Read your daily wisdom
4. Read a knowledge theory paragraph.
5. Write your affirmations.
6. Notes. Reflection and experience of your daily practice.

Wisdom. *To influence and change human behaviour, do not manipulate it but inspire it.*

Positive Affirmations.
Write in 'present tense' positive statements, use one emotion, add a goal, keep it brief and simple. Do not use 'doing' words

I can..I have..
I am .... I let go of ....
Today I am grateful for...
....
Practice reflection notes

DAILY PRACTICE.
6-minute morning practice is key to feel free and feel Qi
Date....................................
1. Complete a 1-minute warm-up exercise. Warm-up number..................
2. Complete 4-minutes of Qi Gong exercise practice. Exercise number ....
3. Read your daily wisdom
4. Read a knowledge theory paragraph.
5. Write your affirmations.
6. Notes. Reflection and experience of your daily practice.

Wisdom. *It is better to conquer yourself than win a thousand battles.*

Positive Affirmations.
Write in 'present tense' positive statements, use one emotion, add a goal, keep it brief and simple. Do not use 'doing' words

I can...I have...….....................

I am .... I let go of ....

Today I am grateful for..

....

Practice reflection notes

DAILY PRACTICE.
6-minute morning practice is key to feel free and feel Qi
Date....................................
1. Complete a 1-minute warm-up exercise. Warm-up number..................
2. Complete 4-minutes of Qi Gong exercise practice. Exercise number ....
3. Read your daily wisdom
4. Read a knowledge theory paragraph.
5. Write your affirmations.
6. Notes. Reflection and experience of your daily practice.

Wisdom. *Begin your morning writing with optimism; end each day with forgiveness. Peace and positivity begin and ends with your spirit. Jenna Robins.*

Positive Affirmations.
Write in 'present tense' positive statements, use one emotion, add a goal, keep it brief and simple. Do not use 'doing' words

I can...I have...….....................
I am .... I let go of ....
Today I am grateful for..
....
Practice reflection notes

DAILY PRACTICE.
6-minute morning practice is key to feel free and feel Qi
Date.................................
1. Complete a 1-minute warm-up exercise. Warm-up number.................
2. Complete 4-minutes of Qi Gong exercise practice. Exercise number ....
3. Read your daily wisdom
4. Read a knowledge theory paragraph.
5. Write your affirmations.
6. Notes. Reflection and experience of your daily practice.

Wisdom. *Around us, life bursts with miracles. If we live in this awareness, It's easy to see miracles everywhere. T Nhat Hanh.*

Positive Affirmations.
Write in 'present tense' positive statements, use one emotion, add a goal, keep it brief and simple. Do not use 'doing' words

I can...I have..

I am .... I let go of ....

Today I am grateful for..

....

Practice reflection notes

DAILY PRACTICE.
6-minute morning practice is key to feel free and feel Qi
Date.................................
1. Complete a 1-minute warm-up exercise. Warm-up number.................
2. Complete 4-minutes of Qi Gong exercise practice. Exercise number ....
3. Read your daily wisdom
4. Read a knowledge theory paragraph.
5. Write your affirmations.
6. Notes. Reflection and experience of your daily practice.

Wisdom. *One's destination is never a place but a new way of seeing things.*

Positive Affirmations.
Write in 'present tense' positive statements, use one emotion, add a goal, keep it brief and simple. Do not use 'doing' words

I can...I have..
I am .... I let go of ....
Today I am grateful for..
....

Practice reflection notes

329

DAILY PRACTICE.
6-minute morning practice is key to feel free and feel Qi
Date.................................
1. Complete a 1-minute warm-up exercise. Warm-up number.................
2. Complete 4-minutes of Qi Gong exercise practice. Exercise number ....
3. Read your daily wisdom
4. Read a knowledge theory paragraph.
5. Write your affirmations.
6. Notes. Reflection and experience of your daily practice.

Wisdom. *Amplifying what is great within you will accelerate your life faster than fixing what you think limits you. Brendan Burchard.*

Positive Affirmations.
Write in 'present tense' positive statements, use one emotion, add a goal, keep it brief and simple. Do not use 'doing' words

I can...I have...…....................

I am .... I let go of ....

Today I am grateful for...

....

Practice reflection notes

DAILY PRACTICE.
6-minute morning practice is key to feel free and feel Qi
Date.................................
1. Complete a 1-minute warm-up exercise. Warm-up number.................
2. Complete 4-minutes of Qi Gong exercise practice. Exercise number ....
3. Read your daily wisdom
4. Read a knowledge theory paragraph.
5. Write your affirmations.
6. Notes. Reflection and experience of your daily practice.

Wisdom. *. Know when to replenish; don't burn out all your fuel. The body and mind need maintenance just like a car. You would not fill half a tank and leave the engine running all night. Jenna Robins.*

Positive Affirmations.
Write in 'present tense' positive statements, use one emotion, add a goal, keep it brief and simple. Do not use 'doing' words

I can...I have...…....................
I am .... I let go of ....
Today I am grateful for...
....
Practice reflection notes

330

DAILY PRACTICE.
6-minute morning practice is key to feel free and feel Qi
Date.................................
1. Complete a 1-minute warm-up exercise. Warm-up number.................
2. Complete 4-minutes of Qi Gong exercise practice. Exercise number ....
3. Read your daily wisdom
4. Read a knowledge theory paragraph.
5. Write your affirmations.
6. Notes. Reflection and experience of your daily practice.

Wisdom. *Everything in the physical world is made of atoms. Atoms are made of energy; energy is Qi and Qi is everywhere. Jenna Robins.*

Positive Affirmations.
Write in 'present tense' positive statements, use one emotion, add a goal, keep it brief and simple. Do not use 'doing' words

I can...I have..

I am .... I let go of ....

Today I am grateful for...

....

Practice reflection notes

DAILY PRACTICE.
6-minute morning practice is key to feel free and feel Qi
Date.................................
1. Complete a 1-minute warm-up exercise. Warm-up number.................
2. Complete 4-minutes of Qi Gong exercise practice. Exercise number ....
3. Read your daily wisdom
4. Read a knowledge theory paragraph.
5. Write your affirmations.
6. Notes. Reflection and experience of your daily practice.

Wisdom. *Quantum physics tells us that nothing that is observed is unaffected by the observer. That statement from science holds an enormous and powerful Insight. It means that everyone sees a different truth; everyone is creating what they see. Neal Donald Walsh.*

Positive Affirmations.
Write in 'present tense' positive statements, use one emotion, add a goal, keep it brief and simple. Do not use 'doing' words

I can...I have..
I am .... I let go of ....
Today I am grateful for...
....

Practice reflection notes

DAILY PRACTICE.
6-minute morning practice is key to feel free and feel Qi
Date..................................
1. Complete a 1-minute warm-up exercise. Warm-up number..................
2. Complete 4-minutes of Qi Gong exercise practice. Exercise number ....
3. Read your daily wisdom
4. Read a knowledge theory paragraph.
5. Write your affirmations.
6. Notes. Reflection and experience of your daily practice.

Wisdom. *Qi is energy. The breath is the bridge to the higher conscious energy; motion is the force of energy, the mind intention drives the energy direction. The meridians are the highways, and the gateways are the acupuncture points. Jenna Robins.*

Positive Affirmations.
Write in 'present tense' positive statements, use one emotion, add a goal, keep it brief and simple. Do not use 'doing' words

I can...I have...

I am .... I let go of ....

Today I am grateful for..

....

Practice reflection notes

DAILY PRACTICE.
6-minute morning practice is key to feel free and feel Qi
Date..................................
1. Complete a 1-minute warm-up exercise. Warm-up number..................
2. Complete 4-minutes of Qi Gong exercise practice. Exercise number ....
3. Read your daily wisdom
4. Read a knowledge theory paragraph.
5. Write your affirmations.
6. Notes. Reflection and experience of your daily practice.

Wisdom. *The great Sage acts without reacting.*

Positive Affirmations.
Write in 'present tense' positive statements, use one emotion, add a goal, keep it brief and simple. Do not use 'doing' words

I can...I have...
I am .... I let go of ....
Today I am grateful for..
....
Practice reflection notes

332

DAILY PRACTICE.
6-minute morning practice is key to feel free and feel Qi
Date..................................
1. Complete a 1-minute warm-up exercise. Warm-up number.................
2. Complete 4-minutes of Qi Gong exercise practice. Exercise number ....
3. Read your daily wisdom
4. Read a knowledge theory paragraph.
5. Write your affirmations.
6. Notes. Reflection and experience of your daily practice.

Wisdom. *If the mind becomes scattered, close your eyes, focus only on the breath. You now have the breath and movement and 'skill' to anchor your mind intention. You can do this.*

Positive Affirmations.
Write in 'present tense' positive statements, use one emotion, add a goal, keep it brief and simple. Do not use 'doing' words

I can...I have...

I am .... I let go of ....

Today I am grateful for..

....

Practice reflection notes

DAILY PRACTICE.
6-minute morning practice is key to feel free and feel Qi
Date..................................
1. Complete a 1-minute warm-up exercise. Warm-up number.................
2. Complete 4-minutes of Qi Gong exercise practice. Exercise number ....
3. Read your daily wisdom
4. Read a knowledge theory paragraph.
5. Write your affirmations.
6. Notes. Reflection and experience of your daily practice.

Wisdom. *We are not walking in a circle; we are ascending; the circle is a spiral, and we have already climbed many of its steps. H. Hesse.*

Positive Affirmations.
Write in 'present tense' positive statements, use one emotion, add a goal, keep it brief and simple. Do not use 'doing' words

I can...I have...
I am .... I let go of ....
Today I am grateful for..
....
Practice reflection notes

DAILY PRACTICE.
6-minute morning practice is key to feel free and feel Qi
Date.................................
1. Complete a 1-minute warm-up exercise. Warm-up number.................
2. Complete 4-minutes of Qi Gong exercise practice. Exercise number ....
3. Read your daily wisdom
4. Read a knowledge theory paragraph.
5. Write your affirmations.
6. Notes. Reflection and experience of your daily practice.

Wisdom. *No violence is the highest form of humanity; it is supreme courage. Daisaku Ikeda.*

Positive Affirmations.
Write in 'present tense' positive statements, use one emotion, add a goal, keep it brief and simple. Do not use 'doing' words

I can...I have...

I am .... I let go of ....

Today I am grateful for..

....

Practice reflection notes

DAILY PRACTICE.
6-minute morning practice is key to feel free and feel Qi
Date.................................
1. Complete a 1-minute warm-up exercise. Warm-up number.................
2. Complete 4-minutes of Qi Gong exercise practice. Exercise number ....
3. Read your daily wisdom
4. Read a knowledge theory paragraph.
5. Write your affirmations.
6. Notes. Reflection and experience of your daily practice.

Wisdom. *Life is quite simple, but our wants, need, and desires make it more complicated.*

Positive Affirmations.
Write in 'present tense' positive statements, use one emotion, add a goal, keep it brief and simple. Do not use 'doing' words

I can...I have...
I am .... I let go of ....
Today I am grateful for..
....
Practice reflection notes

334

DAILY PRACTICE.
6-minute morning practice is key to feel free and feel Qi
Date.................................
1. Complete a 1-minute warm-up exercise. Warm-up number.................
2. Complete 4-minutes of Qi Gong exercise practice. Exercise number ....
3. Read your daily wisdom
4. Read a knowledge theory paragraph.
5. Write your affirmations.
6. Notes. Reflection and experience of your daily practice.

Wisdom. *Real knowledge is to know the extent of one's own ignorance. Confucius.*

Positive Affirmations.
Write in 'present tense' positive statements, use one emotion, add a goal, keep it brief and simple. Do not use 'doing' words

I can...I have...

I am .... I let go of ....

Today I am grateful for...

....

Practice reflection notes

DAILY PRACTICE.
6-minute morning practice is key to feel free and feel Qi
Date.................................
1. Complete a 1-minute warm-up exercise. Warm-up number.................
2. Complete 4-minutes of Qi Gong exercise practice. Exercise number ....
3. Read your daily wisdom
4. Read a knowledge theory paragraph.
5. Write your affirmations.
6. Notes. Reflection and experience of your daily practice.

Wisdom. *Positivity generates more positive energies and attracts more positive experiences. In the face of negativity and adversity, keep searching for the positives. Jenna Robins.*

Positive Affirmations.
Write in 'present tense' positive statements, use one emotion, add a goal, keep it brief and simple. Do not use 'doing' words

I can...I have...
I am .... I let go of ....
Today I am grateful for...
....

Practice reflection notes

DAILY PRACTICE.
6-minute morning practice is key to feel free and feel Qi
Date....................................
1. Complete a 1-minute warm-up exercise. Warm-up number..................
2. Complete 4-minutes of Qi Gong exercise practice. Exercise number ....
3. Read your daily wisdom
4. Read a knowledge theory paragraph.
5. Write your affirmations.
6. Notes. Reflection and experience of your daily practice.

Wisdom. *Yin yang. In each difficult loss, there is a gain, and in each difficult gain, there is a loss.*

Positive Affirmations.
Write in 'present tense' positive statements, use one emotion, add a goal, keep it brief and simple. Do not use 'doing' words

I can..I have...

I am .... I let go of ....

Today I am grateful for...

....

Practice reflection notes

DAILY PRACTICE.
6-minute morning practice is key to feel free and feel Qi
Date....................................
1. Complete a 1-minute warm-up exercise. Warm-up number..................
2. Complete 4-minutes of Qi Gong exercise practice. Exercise number ....
3. Read your daily wisdom
4. Read a knowledge theory paragraph.
5. Write your affirmations.
6. Notes. Reflection and experience of your daily practice.

Wisdom. *The person who masters self-control and discipline is truly undefeatable. Gautama Buddha.*

Positive Affirmations.
Write in 'present tense' positive statements, use one emotion, add a goal, keep it brief and simple. Do not use 'doing' words

I can..I have...
I am .... I let go of ....
Today I am grateful for...
....

Practice reflection notes

DAILY PRACTICE.
6-minute morning practice is key to feel free and feel Qi
Date.................................
1. Complete a 1-minute warm-up exercise. Warm-up number.................
2. Complete 4-minutes of Qi Gong exercise practice. Exercise number ....
3. Read your daily wisdom
4. Read a knowledge theory paragraph.
5. Write your affirmations.
6. Notes. Reflection and experience of your daily practice.

Wisdom. Affliction is such as craving, anger, doubt, fear, and forgetfulness, are feelings that block the light; life practice is to remove these five hindrances. T Nhat Hana.

Positive Affirmations.
Write in 'present tense' positive statements, use one emotion, add a goal, keep it brief and simple. Do not use 'doing' words

I can..I have...

I am .... I let go of ....

Today I am grateful for...

....

Practice reflection notes

DAILY PRACTICE.
6-minute morning practice is key to feel free and feel Qi
Date.................................
1. Complete a 1-minute warm-up exercise. Warm-up number.................
2. Complete 4-minutes of Qi Gong exercise practice. Exercise number ....
3. Read your daily wisdom
4. Read a knowledge theory paragraph.
5. Write your affirmations.
6. Notes. Reflection and experience of your daily practice.

Wisdom. *Be careful that you're not so involved in the process that you lose yourself.*

Positive Affirmations.
Write in 'present tense' positive statements, use one emotion, add a goal, keep it brief and simple. Do not use 'doing' words

I can...I have...
I am .... I let go of ....
Today I am grateful for...
....

Practice reflection notes

DAILY PRACTICE.
6-minute morning practice is key to feel free and feel Qi
Date..................................
1. Complete a 1-minute warm-up exercise. Warm-up number..................
2. Complete 4-minutes of Qi Gong exercise practice. Exercise number ....
3. Read your daily wisdom
4. Read a knowledge theory paragraph.
5. Write your affirmations.
6. Notes. Reflection and experience of your daily practice.

Wisdom. *It is essential to understand the seeker before you try to find out what it is he is seeking. Jim Rohn.*

Positive Affirmations.
Write in 'present tense' positive statements, use one emotion, add a goal, keep it brief and simple. Do not use 'doing' words

I can...I have...

I am .... I let go of ....

Today I am grateful for..

....

Practice reflection notes

DAILY PRACTICE.
6-minute morning practice is key to feel free and feel Qi
Date..................................
1. Complete a 1-minute warm-up exercise. Warm-up number..................
2. Complete 4-minutes of Qi Gong exercise practice. Exercise number ....
3. Read your daily wisdom
4. Read a knowledge theory paragraph.
5. Write your affirmations.
6. Notes. Reflection and experience of your daily practice.

Wisdom. *We work hard on ourselves to help others, but we help others to work on ourselves. Pema Chodron.*

Positive Affirmations.
Write in 'present tense' positive statements, use one emotion, add a goal, keep it brief and simple. Do not use 'doing' words

I can...I have...
I am .... I let go of ....
Today I am grateful for..
....
Practice reflection notes

DAILY PRACTICE.
6-minute morning practice is key to feel free and feel Qi
Date..................................
1. Complete a 1-minute warm-up exercise. Warm-up number..................
2. Complete 4-minutes of Qi Gong exercise practice. Exercise number ....
3. Read your daily wisdom
4. Read a knowledge theory paragraph.
5. Write your affirmations.
6. Notes. Reflection and experience of your daily practice.

Wisdom. *The only position from which you can never fall is the awakened state.*

Positive Affirmations.
Write in 'present tense' positive statements, use one emotion, add a goal, keep it brief and simple. Do not use 'doing' words

I can...I have...

I am .... I let go of ....

Today I am grateful for...

....

Practice reflection notes

DAILY PRACTICE.
6-minute morning practice is key to feel free and feel Qi
Date..................................
1. Complete a 1-minute warm-up exercise. Warm-up number..................
2. Complete 4-minutes of Qi Gong exercise practice. Exercise number ....
3. Read your daily wisdom
4. Read a knowledge theory paragraph.
5. Write your affirmations.
6. Notes. Reflection and experience of your daily practice.

Wisdom. *Life is the most difficult exam. Many people fail because they try to copy others, not realising that everyone has a different question paper.*

Positive Affirmations.
Write in 'present tense' positive statements, use one emotion, add a goal, keep it brief and simple. Do not use 'doing' words

I can...I have...
I am .... I let go of ....
Today I am grateful for...
....

Practice reflection notes

DAILY PRACTICE.
6-minute morning practice is key to feel free and feel Qi
Date.................................
1. Complete a 1-minute warm-up exercise. Warm-up number.................
2. Complete 4-minutes of Qi Gong exercise practice. Exercise number ....
3. Read your daily wisdom
4. Read a knowledge theory paragraph.
5. Write your affirmations.
6. Notes. Reflection and experience of your daily practice.

Wisdom. *Daily practice will cultivate our inner and outer world. Cultivate your mind, body and spirit like you would nourish and cultivate a garden.*

Positive Affirmations.
Write in 'present tense' positive statements, use one emotion, add a goal, keep it brief and simple. Do not use 'doing' words

I can...I have..

I am .... I let go of ....

Today I am grateful for...

....

Practice reflection notes

DAILY PRACTICE.
6-minute morning practice is key to feel free and feel Qi
Date.................................
1. Complete a 1-minute warm-up exercise. Warm-up number.................
2. Complete 4-minutes of Qi Gong exercise practice. Exercise number ....
3. Read your daily wisdom
4. Read a knowledge theory paragraph.
5. Write your affirmations.
6. Notes. Reflection and experience of your daily practice.

Wisdom. *Without aligning Qi energy flow, daily life clogs. Terri Guillements.*

Positive Affirmations.
Write in 'present tense' positive statements, use one emotion, add a goal, keep it brief and simple. Do not use 'doing' words

I can...I have..
I am .... I let go of ....
Today I am grateful for...
....

Practice reflection notes

DAILY PRACTICE.
6-minute morning practice is key to feel free and feel Qi
Date.................................
1. Complete a 1-minute warm-up exercise. Warm-up number.................
2. Complete 4-minutes of Qi Gong exercise practice. Exercise number ....
3. Read your daily wisdom
4. Read a knowledge theory paragraph.
5. Write your affirmations.
6. Notes. Reflection and experience of your daily practice.

Wisdom. *Little and often is effective and powerful; only you can master the healing force of your Qi and higher intuition. Remember, the power is within you in daily practice. It is key to feel free. Jenna Robins.*

Positive Affirmations.
Write in 'present tense' positive statements, use one emotion, add a goal, keep it brief and simple. Do not use 'doing' words

I can..I have...

I am .... I let go of ....

Today I am grateful for..

....

Practice reflection notes

To my 6-minute practice students.

Congratulations, you did it! You have completed a year of daily Qi Gong meditation practice and affirmations. You truly are a committed student, and I am so immensely proud of you. No matter if it took you longer, you have still committed to self-cultivation practice and wellbeing. You are on your way to mastering emotional freedom, mental, spiritual, and physical wellbeing.

Reflections. How do you feel every day compared to when you started your journal? Can you feel the Qi energy flow? Are you more aware? Do you have more intuition? What changes do you feel? Are you more positive and peaceful? Can you let go of negatives more easily? What have you manifested? Have you experienced more serendipity? Have you manifested more positive experiences? Look back to the start of this journal and your reflective notes. This Journal is for your life journey. Simply move on to your next journal as I do.

Continue to self-cultivate and grow, connect to your higher self as we continue through our positive daily practice. Remember, every day is different in practice. Practice gives us the peace, clarity, energy, and awareness to manifest positive change and simply 'Let Go' of negative energy.

I would really love to hear about your 12-month practice Journal experience. www.jennarobins.co.uk.

2nd Journal. You can now continue your journey of self-cultivation with your follow up journal book available on amazon as you have your Qi Gong instructions and knowledge book. All you now need is your journal pages to continue your 6-minute self-mastery morning practice.

Come and join in on my live stream classes or take a private one to one personnel session. Find me @ Qi for life with Jenna on Instagram, Facebook, and YouTube.

Enjoy the benefits of daily practice, feeling Qi energy flow, feel peace, positivity, and wellness in your mind-body, and soul and happy Qi Gong Journaling to all students. Blessings, love Jenna.

Bibliography.

Journals.

Ahmed Haroun et al. (2016) Journal of Diabetes and Cholesterol Metabolism (DCM) Investigation of Kinetic Energy Harvesting from Human Body Motion Activities using Free/Impact Based Micro Electromagnetic Generator. Research article. 1-5.

Zou L, et al . (2017). A Systematic Review and Meta-Analysis of Baduanjin Qi Gong for Health Benefits Randomized Controlled Trials. *Evidence-Based Complementary and Alternative Medicine Journal.* 2017 (10), 10-1115

Rodgers, C E et al . (2008). A Review of Clinical Trials of Tai Chi and QIGONG in older adults. *Western Journal of Nursing Research.* 10 (10), 1177.

Williams. H et al. (1995) Meditation, T-cells, Anxiety, Depression and HIV Infection. Journal of Experimental Subtle Energies Vol 6 1-93

Peng, J et al . (2020). The effect of qigong for pulmonary function and quality of life in patients with Covid-19. *Medicine Baltimore.* 99 (38), 22041.

Chow YW, Tsang HW. (2007). 25. Biopsychosocial effects of qigong as a mindful exercise for people with anxiety disorders: A speculative review. *25. J Altern Complement Med.* 13 (1), 831-839.

Johansson M, Hassmèn P. Acute psychological responses to qigong exercise of varying durations. Am J Chin Med 2008;36:449–458. 26. Jouper J, Hassèman P. Intrinsically motivated qigong exercisers are more concentrated and less stressful. Am J Chinese Med 2008;36:1051–1060.

Tsang HW, Fung KM. A review of neurobiological and psychological mechanisms underlying the anti-depressive effects of qigong exercise. J Health Psychol 2008;13:857–863. 30. Griffith JM, Hasley JP, Liu H, et al. Qigong stress reduction in hospital staff. J Altern Complement Med 2008;14:939–945.

Grodin MA, Piwowarczyk, L Fulker D, et al. Treating survivors of torture and refugee trauma: A preliminary case series using qigong and tai chi. J Altern Complement Med 2008;14:801–806. 32. Yang Y, Verkuilen J, Rosengren KS, et al. Effects of a traditional taiji/ qigong curriculum on older adults' immune response to influenza vaccine. Med Sport Sci 2008;52:64–76.

Tsang HW. Psychophysiological outcomes of health qigong for chronic conditions: A systematic review. Psychophysiology 2009;46: 257–269.

Craske NJ, Turner W, Zammit-Maempe J, Lee MS. Qigong ameliorates symptoms of chronic fatigue. Evid-Based Complement Alternat Med 2008;6:265–270.

Manzaneque JM, Vera FM, Rodriquez FM, et al. Serum cytokines, mood, and sleep after a qigong program: Is qigong an effective psychobiological tool? J Health Psychol 2009;14:60–67. 36. Li M, Chen K, Mo Z. Use of qigong therapy in the detoxification of heroin addicts. Altern Ther Health Med 2002;8:50–54,56–59.

Bayat-Movahed S, Shayesteh Y, Mehrizi H, et al. Effects of qigong exercises on 3 different parameters of human saliva. Clin J Integr Med 2008; 14:262–266. 38. Siu JY, Sung HC, Lee WL. Qigong practice among chronically ill patients during the SARS outbreak. J Clin Nurs 2007;16:769–776.

Rogers CE, Larkey LK, Keller C. A review of clinical trials of Tai Qi and qigong in older adults. West J Nurs Res 2009;31:245–279.

Tsai YK, Chen HH, Lin IH, Yeh ML. Qigong improving physical status in middle-aged women. West J Nurs Res 2008;30:915–927.

Qin Z, Jin Y, Lin S, Hermanowicz NS. A forty-five-year follow-up EEG study of qigong practice. Int J Neurosci 2009;119:538–552.

Stephens S, Feldman BM, Bradley N, et al. Feasibility and effectiveness of an aerobic exercise program in children with fibromyalgia: Results of a randomized controlled pilot trial. Arthritis Rheum 2008;59:1399–140Silva LM, Ayres R, Schalock M. Outcomes of a pilot training program in a qigong massage intervention for young children with autism. Am J Occup Ther 2008;62:538–546.

Witt C, Becker M, Bandelin K, et al. Qigong for schoolchildren: A pilot study. J Altern Complement Med 2005;11:41–47. To order reprints of this article, e-mail

Lee MS, Chen KW, Sancier KM, Ernst E.. (2007). Qigong for cancer treatment: A systematic review of controlled clinical trials.Acta Oncol. 46 (46), 717-722.

Chow YW, Tsang HW. . (2007). 25. Biopsychosocial effects of qigong as a mindful exercise for people with anxiety disorders: A speculative review. 25. J Altern Complement Med. 13 (1), 831-839.

Johansson M, Hassmèn P. Acute psychological responses to qigong exercise of varying durations. Am J Chin Med 2008;36:449–458. 26. Jouper J, Hassèman P. Intrinsically motivated qigong exercisers are more concentrated and less stressful. Am J Chinese Med 2008;36:1051–1060.

Epton. t., Harris, P.R. (2008) self-affirmation promotes health behaviour change Health Psychology, 27(6) 746-752.

Bach, D Groesbeck, G Stapleton, P . (2019 Feb 19). Clinical EFT9Emotional Freedom Techniques) improve Multiple Physiological Markers of Health. .J Evid Based Integrated Med. 24 (1), 7-44.

Kemp, C A . (2004). Qigong as a therapeutic intervention with older adults. Journal of Holistic Nursing. . 10 (4), 351-73

Geronilla L, Minewiser L, Mollon P, McWilliams M, Clond M. (2016). (Emotional Freedom Techniques) remediates PTSD and psychological symptoms in veterans: a randomized controlled replication trial. J Evid Based Integrated Med. 8 (10), 29-41.

Kathleen K.S. (2010). Acupuncture, the Limbic System, and the Anti correlated Networks of the Brain.Auton Neurosci.. 21 (157), 81-90.

D'Ambrogio, K (2019). Everything, including the human body, is made of energy. Available: www.massagemag.com/energy-field-120110. Last accessed 16th October 2021.

Ahani,A et al . (2014). Change in physiological signals during mindfulness meditation. . *HHS Author manuscript IEEE Neural Engineering (NER)* . 10 (1), 1109.

Self-awareness blog . (2020). *Why you should you hold onto ego according to Buddhist scholars.*. Available: https://selfawareness.blog/dont-let-go-of-your-ego/. Last accessed 16th October 2021.

Russo, M et al . (2017). The physiological effects of slow breathing in the healthy human. . *Breathe practice-focused education for respiratory professionals.* 13 (10), 298-309.

Lazar, S. W., Kerr, C., Wasserman, R. H., Gray, J. R., Greve, D., Treadway, M. T., ... Fischl, B. (2005). Meditation experience is associated with increased cortical thickness. Neuro report, 16, 1893–1897.

Davidson, R. J., Kabat-Zinn, J., Schumacher, J., Rosenkranz, M., Muller, D., Santorelli, S. F., ... Sheridan, J. F. (2003). Alterations in brain and immune function produced by mindfulness meditation. Psychosomatic Medicine, 65, 564–570.

Fulda, S et al . (2010). Cellular Stress Responses: Cell Survival and Cell Death . *International Journal of Cell Biology.* 2010 (10), 1155.

McLeod, S. (2010). *Stress illness and the immune system* . Available: https://www.simplypsychology.org/stress-immune.html. Last accessed 16th October 2021.

Books.

Chia, M and Holden L (2005). *Cosmic orbit: Connect to the universe from within.* Thailand: Universal Tao. 108-118.

Chia, Mantak (2008). *The Inner Smile* . United Kingdom: Majestic Books. 5-80.

Kenneth Cohen (1997).*The Way of Qigong: The Art and Science of Chinese Energy Healing.* New York: Ballantine Books. 1-409.

Chia, M (1985).*Taoist Ways to Transform Stress into vitality.* Huntington NY: Healing tao books. 7-37.

Women's Qigong for Health and Longevity: A Practical Guide for Women Forty and Older by Deborah Davis, L.Ac., M.A.O.M. Boston: Shambhala, 2008

Heal Yourself with Qigong by Suzanne Friedman, L.Ac., D.M.Q.
Chinese doctorate in medical qigong therapy] Oakland, CA: New Harbinger Books, 2009

Deadman P (2016). *Live well Live Long: Teaching from the Chinese Nourishment of Life Tradition and Modern Research.* London: The journal of Chinese medicine. 1-440.

TZU L (1963).*Tao Te Ching.* Suffolk England: Penguin classics.131

J R (1994).*Tao Te Ching, The Book of The Way and its Power.* Berkley CA: The Apocryphile Press. 1-

Micheal Talbot (1991). *The Holographic Universe*. London: Haper Collins publishers. 1-305.
Maoshing, Ni PhD (1995).*The Yellow Emperors Classic of medicine of the Neijing Suwen with Commentary*. Boulder CO: Shambhala publication. 5-290.

Maoshing, Ni PhD (1995).*The Yellow Emperors Classic of medicine of the Neijing Suwen with Commentary*. Boulder CO: Shambhala publication. 5-290.

Ursula, K. (2011). chapter 1. In Ursula, k L. Guin, L *Lao Tzu Tao teaching a book about the way and the power of the way*. United Kingdom: Shambhala publication. 62.

Websites:

Masaki Kobayashi. Daisuke Kikuchi, Hitoshi Okamura Published: July 16, 2009, https://doi.org/10.1371/journal.pone.0006256 Imaging of Ultraweak Spontaneous Photon Emission from Human Body Displaying Diurnal Rhythm.

Moore, C MBA. (2020).*Positive Daily Affirmations: Is There Science Behind It?*. Available: https://positive psychology.com/daily-affirmations/. Last accessed 13th Sept 2020.

Epton. t., Harris, P.R. (2008) self-affirmation promotes health behaviour change Health Psychology, 27(6) 746-

Acupuncture, the Limbic System, and the Anticorrelated Networks of theBrain
Kathleen K.S. Hui, Ovidiu Marina, Jing Liu, Bruce R. Rosen, Kenneth K. Kwong
Auton Neurosci. Author manuscript; available in PMC 2013 Aug 27.
Published in final edited form as:Auton Neurosci. 2010 Oct 28; 157(0): 81–90. Published online 2010 May 21.doi:10.1016/j.autneu.2010.03.022
PMCID:PMC3754836 ArticlePubReaderPDF–3.1MCitation

Acupuncture or posttraumatic stress disorder: Conceptual, Clinical, and Biological Data Support Further Research Michael Hollifield
CNS Neuroscience Ther.2011 Dec;17(6): 769–779.Published online 2011 Feb 26.doi:10.1111/j.1755-5949.2011.00241.x PMCID: PMC6493831
ArticlePubReaderPDF–1.9MCitation

Acupuncture in stroke rehabilitation: Literature retrieval based on international databases
Feng Sun, Jinchun Wang, Xia Wen
Neural Regen Res. 2012 May 25; 7(15): 1192–1199. doi: 10.3969/j.issn.1673-5374.2012.15.011
PMCID: PMC4340038 ArticlePubReaderCitation

EA at PC6 Promo Self-affirmation. APA psyc Net Epton. t., Harris, P.R. (2008) self-affirmation promotes health behaviour change Health Psychology, 27(6) 746-752. https://doi.org/10.1037/0278-6133.276.746
The Impact of Self-Affirmation on Health Cognition, Health Behaviour, and Other Health-Related Responses: A Narrative Revie Peter R. Harris Tracy Epton First published:27 November 2009 https://doi.org/10.1111/j.1751-9004.2009.00233.x Citations:92

Neural Mechanisms of Self-Affirmation's Stress Buffering Effects. Janine M Dutcher, Naomi I Eisenberger, William M P Klein, Peter R Harris, John M Levine, J David Creswell *Social Cognitive and Affective Neuroscience*, nsaa042,https://doi.org/10.1093/scan/nsaa042 Published: 04 April

2020

Gastric Motility: Role of Brainstem Vagovagal Neurocircuits
Mengjiang Lu, Chien-Chih Chen, Wen Li, Zhi Yu, Bin Xu
Evid Based Complement Alternat Med.2019;2019: 7457485.Published online 2019 Jul 15.doi:10.1155/2019/7457485PMCID: PMC6662446 ArticlePubReaderPDF–1.7MCitation
Treating Depression with Transcutaneous Auricular Vagus Nerve Stimulation: State of the Art and Future Perspectives Jian Kong, Jiliang Fang, Joel Park, Shaoyuan Li, Peijing Rong
Front Psychiatry.2018;9: 20.Published online 2018 Feb 5.doi:10.3389/fpsyt.2018.00020
PMCID: PMC5807379 ArticlePubReaderPDF–540KCitation

The Involvement of Descending Pain Inhibitory System in Electroacupuncture-Induced Analgesia
Qiuyi Lv, Fengzhi Wu, Xiulun Gan, Xueqin Yang, Ling Zhou, Jie Chen, Yinjia He, Rong Zhang, Bixiu Zhu, Lanying Liu Front Integr Neurosci.2019;13: 38. Published online 2019 Aug 21.doi:10.3389/fnint.2019.00038
PMCID: PMC6712431ArticlePubReaderPDF–791KCitation

Self-affirmation. APA psyc Net Epton. t., Harris, P.R. (2008) self-affirmation promotes health behaviour change Health Psychology, 27(6) 746-752. https://doi.org/10.1037/0278-6133.276.746
The Impact of Self-Affirmation on Health Cognition, Health Behaviour, and Other Health-Related Responses: A Narrative Revie Peter R. Harris Tracy Epton First published:27 November 2009 https://doi.org/10.1111/j.1751-9004.2009.00233.x Citations:92

One More Thing Before You Go…

If you enjoyed reading this book or found it useful, I'd be very grateful if you'd post a short review on Amazon.

Your support really does make a difference, and I read all the reviews personally, so I can get your feedback and make this book even better.

If you would like to leave a review, then all you need to do is click the review link on Amazon here:
xxxxxxxxxx
And if you live in the UK, you can leave it here:
xxxxxxxxxx

Thanks again for your support!